S0-ADV-318

977.311 D549b
Blakely, Robert J.
Earl B. Dickerson

Circs/Date/t set use

SEP 2 7 2006

EARL B. DICKERSON

HISTORY & TRAVEL

CENTRAL LIBRARY OF ROCHESTER
AND MONROE COUNTY
115 SOUTH AVE
ROCHESTER NY 14604-1896

EARL B.
DICKERSON

A VOICE FOR FREEDOM AND EQUALITY

ROBERT J. BLAKELY
WITH MARCUS SHEPARD

*Forewords by John Hope Franklin
and Alta M. Blakely*

NORTHWESTERN UNIVERSITY PRESS
EVANSTON, ILLINOIS

Northwestern University Press
www.nupress.northwestern.edu

Copyright © 2006 by Alta M. Blakely.
Published 2006 by Northwestern University Press.
All rights reserved.

Printed in the United States of America

10 9 8 7 6 5 4 3 2 1

ISBN 0-8101-2335-5

Endpapers photograph of Earl B. Dickerson courtesy
of Johnson Publishing Company, Inc.

Library of Congress Cataloging-in-Publication data
are available from the Library of Congress.

⊗ The paper used in this publication meets the
minimum requirements of the American National
Standard for Information Sciences—Permanence
of Paper for Printed Library Materials,
ANSI Z39.48-1992.

Northwestern University Press thanks The Chicago
Community Trust for its support of this book and
related efforts to promote Chicago's future by telling
the stories of Chicago's past. Thanks also to
Mr. Elzie L. Higginbottom for supporting this book
and for his efforts to preserve Chicago's rich history
of African American accomplishment.

*To Professor Leonard S. Rubinowitz,
who has shepherded this book ever
since his secretary found the manuscript in the Library of Congress*

CONTENTS

FOREWORD

John Hope Franklin

I first met Earl Dickerson in 1964. We may have met earlier than that, but I really got to know him when I moved to Chicago in 1964. I saw him at the Boule and at casual or social gatherings. I got to know, understand, and appreciate him.

My earliest recollections of Earl are of his talking about his own activities and struggles. He taught me about the early days of the civil rights movement. This was just during and right after the war. Through him, I first knew that the struggle was on as early as it was. He talked about going down to Alabama in the 1940s, helping people to sort out the problems in Birmingham, long before I knew him and long before we think of the civil rights movement as getting started in the 1950s and 1960s. I remember asking Earl how dangerous it was to be involved in civil rights struggles back then. Later, I marched in Montgomery with a group of historians and remember discussing these experiences with Earl.

Earl was a very strong advocate of equality in Chicago, especially on the South Side. He had a powerful impact on the effort to equalize housing and job opportunities. I knew about his involvement with the Supreme Life Insurance Company of America and his efforts to improve conditions on the South Side. I would put him right up there with the great people we think about such as Thurgood Marshall and others who functioned within the courts at the federal levels. Earl's activities were focused on Chicago. His impact in Chicago was immense, as he took on the restrictive covenants and ensured access to loans and mortgages. His activities were key to opening up both housing and employment opportunities for blacks.

We used to sit together at the Boule and have a great time. He had simply enormous charm and was very handsome. Earl could charm your pants off and leave you dumbfounded; it was a real gift.

Earl became familiar and friendly with the first Mayor Daley. Dick used to talk about Earl and how important he was to the city of Chicago. Earl was highly respected by Daley, though I never quite sorted out their relationship. I often heard Earl speak about Dick. There seemed to be a very high level of mutual respect. I'm sure Dick's respect had a lot to do with how effective Earl was. Daley himself was not well understood. He was a man of enormous capacity to see a problem and to work with it, accommodate himself to it. Dick often talked about problems of housing and employment, which of course were Earl's biggest concerns. Despite their differences, they had the interests of the city in common and were working toward the same end.

After I left Chicago, I did not have much to do with Earl but would see him occasionally when I visited Chicago, and I always looked forward to seeing him. I really enjoyed him and appreciated his willingness to serve the interests of the larger community and to make the world better.

FOREWORD

Alta M. Blakely

This book, *Earl B. Dickerson: A Voice for Freedom and Equality*, began as an oral history project of the Hyde Park Historical Society in Chicago, one purpose of which has been to record the history of the community through the lives of outstanding residents. One summer afternoon in 1983 the Oral History Committee, consisting of the Reverend Victor Obenhaus (chair), Jay Mulberry, and my husband, Robert Blakely, visited Earl B. Dickerson in his home at 4800 Chicago Beach Drive.

My husband had not known very much about Mr. Dickerson but was immediately impressed by the status and accomplishments of the man.

"Has anyone ever written about your life?" he asked.

"No."

"Why not?"

"Because no one ever asked."

My husband came home full of excitement. "I'm going to get in touch with John Hope Franklin"—who, I believe, was still a professor at the University of Chicago—"and ask that one of his students undertake the project." Thinking it over, however, he said, "No. It can't wait! Mr. Dickerson is ninety-two years old. I will have to do it myself."

As a former newspaper editor (including for the *Chicago Daily News*) and author of several books, Bob had been writing for much of his professional life. Mr. Dickerson was at first suspicious of Bob's motives, but he gradually came to trust him. And so began a close friendship between the two men.

Subsequently, there were thirty-eight taped formal interviews with Dickerson, as well as with thirty-nine colleagues, associates, and friends. Dickerson liked to call Bob his Boswell. Earl became like a member of the family.

Bob presented the completed manuscript to Earl at a small party at the Ritz-Carlton Hotel on December 30, 1984, in the presence of Earl's daughter, Diane (now deceased), her husband, Charles Montgomery, and a few other friends.

Earl had looked forward to seeing the publication of the book, but that was not to be. He died on September 1, 1986. My husband died in November 1994. Both men would have been pleased that this book is being published.

I WOULD LIKE to acknowledge Jay Mulberry of the Hyde Park Historical Society, who championed the book through many years and who searched for photos; Stephen Treffman, archivist of the Hyde Park Historical Society, and other members of the board for their backing; my three children, Cara and Roger Keller, Raye Farr, and Stanley and Cecilia Farr; my three stepchildren, Susan Shurin, Craig Blakely, and Steve Blakely (especially Susan for her conversations with Dr. John Hope Franklin); Dr. Franklin for his help in a busy time of his life; Marian Bennett; Dr. Donald B. Stewart; the Reverend Dr. Kenneth B. Smith; Earl Dickerson's grandchildren, Stephen G. Brown, Joshua B. Cohen, and Judith C. Cohen, for their generosity in lending their extensive collection of Dickerson photographs; Attorney Gary Fresen; Jesse A. Reid Jr. for opening the world of Kappa Alpha Psi; Jandava Cattron and Robert Colescott (a distant relative of Dickerson's) for information on William McWillie; Timuel D. Black Jr. and Leon M. Despres for their encouragement; Richard L. Wentworth of the University of Illinois at Urbana-Champaign for closely critiquing the manuscript; Marcus Shepard for his dedication to the project, his scholarship, and his uncounted hours of work with little remuneration; Professor Leonard S. Rubinowitz and his faculty assistants Laura Kessler and

Tim Jacobs and research assistants James Sayles (Yaki), Ben Thelen, and Slone Isselhard; Susan Betz, editor in chief of Northwestern University Press, and her staff; Demetrius Franklin and the office staff at Montgomery Place; and the many others who have believed in the importance of this book's coming to publication.

The story of Earl B. Dickerson's life traces the contours of African American experience through the entirety of the twentieth century and makes for a remarkable study of what African Americans have achieved at the beginning of a new millennium—as well as all that remains to be done. But this story is also testimony to the efforts of a single man committed to transforming African American experience. Dickerson understood from his own battles with racism that only when minorities are able to participate in the mainstream of American social, economic, and political life would the United States live up to its democratic potential. He had little tolerance for gradualist agendas and embodied this in his personal struggles to succeed as a lawyer, businessman, and political activist. Dickerson's convictions were fed by a pragmatic understanding of the vital importance of decent employment, fair business opportunities, and unrestricted political participation. This mercurial combination of roles—as both an uncompromising civil rights advocate and an ambitious businessman—is fundamental to the understanding of Dickerson's legacy.

Earl Dickerson labored behind the scenes of the civil rights movement, and his achievements often appear to be overshadowed by those of others. His efforts in politics were groundbreaking but not altogether successful. Dickerson was a one-term alderman in Chicago and ran a failed campaign for Congress, but he never gained a reliable foothold in politics. Dickerson was appointed to the first of Franklin Delano Roosevelt's Fair Employment Practices Committees during World War II but was evidently too radical in his commitment to swift and decisive change to be reappointed.

He was labeled something of a troublemaker by the political establishment, and upon finding the door to a career in government closed, he returned to the private sector in Chicago where his well-tested business skills were unmatched and could be used more effectively to further the cause of equality and justice for African Americans.

Dickerson is probably best known for his role in the *Hansberry v. Lee* U.S. Supreme Court case of 1940, which helped prepare the judicial ground for the final defeat of race restrictive covenant agreements as a legal tool of segregation in the North (and especially in Chicago). Although it did not achieve a decisive victory on constitutional grounds, Dickerson's involvement in this case is characteristic of both his skilled maneuvering and his remarkable abilities in the dual role of outspoken civil rights advocate and shrewd business leader.

Earl Burrus Dickerson was born in Mississippi in 1891, the very year Mississippi legally deprived African Americans of the right to vote. After the defeat of Reconstruction in the late 1870s, Mississippi led the South in establishing a system of strict racial segregation. This atmosphere of often severe deprivation shaped Dickerson's early experience. His grandmother was a former slave and had borne two children by her white master. After the death of Dickerson's father, Edward, his grandmother was reduced to running a boardinghouse for itinerant blacks and his mother to doing washing for the local white folks. One of Earl's schoolmates was shot dead by a white man whom he had accidentally bumped on the street. He saw his brother-in-law shot and crippled for life by the chief of police, whom he had unintentionally jostled while carrying packages.

Robert Colescott, the well-known African American painter, recalls that Dickerson used to pay frequent visits to the family's home in California when he was a child.[1] His mother, Lydia Hutton, was the daughter of Lydia Johnson, whose father was known to be William McWillie, owner of the Kirkwood plantation and the governor of Mississippi from 1858 to 1860. Lydia Johnson's older half brother was Edward Dickerson, Earl Dickerson's father. She had a half sister, Abigail, who was also known to be McWillie's daughter. It is likely that Edward was McWillie's son as well, making Earl Dickerson the descendant of a Mississippi governor who was an active supporter of the Confederacy.

In 1907, Earl, a stowaway on an Illinois Central train, fled to Chicago just as white racism was beginning to infect the North. Once in Illinois, motivated by a desire for learning and encouraged by his family, Dickerson worked his way through preparatory schools, through a year at Northwestern University, and to a bachelor's degree and a teaching certificate at the University of Illinois at Urbana-Champaign. He taught for a year at the Tuskegee Institute under Booker T. Washington and then completed two years of law school before enlisting in the U.S. Army.

After attending a segregated officers' training school, Dickerson was commissioned a second lieutenant in the Ninety-second Division and sent to France. There he acted as an interpreter and later commanded an infantry platoon in battle. In Paris, by chance, he attended a meeting of soldiers who were planning a veterans' organization, and on the way back to the United States, he persuaded the other black officers aboard his troop ship to sign a petition protesting the discriminatory quarters they had been given. This protest was reported in all the New York City newspapers.

During April 1919, the month he returned home, Earl became one of the founders of the American Legion and organized the first American Legion post of black veterans in Chicago. Dickerson soon resumed his law school studies and became the first African American to receive a degree from the University of Chicago Law School. When he was admitted to the Illinois bar in 1920, the dean of the law school recommended him highly to three of the leading law firms in Chicago, all of which turned him down because of race. Entering private practice, he soon became general counsel of the newly incorporated Liberty Life Insurance Company, the first insurance company owned and operated by African Americans to survive in Chicago.

Between 1939 and 1943 he was elected the first African American Democratic alderman to the Chicago City Council. In addition, during those four years he argued the first case challenging the enforceability of race restrictive housing covenants before the U.S. Supreme Court and won. He also served as a member of President Franklin Roosevelt's first Fair Employment Practices Committee. The only lawyer on the committee and its acting chairman for much of its two years, he was so skillful and aggressive that there is reason to believe Roosevelt appointed the second committee solely to get rid of him.

Dickerson led the movement in 1939 that broke the color barrier to membership in the Illinois State Bar Association, and in 1945 he was among the first African American members of the Chicago Bar Association. In 1947 he organized an independent ticket of candidates opposed to the "sweetheart" Coalition of Democratic and Republican judges in Cook County. This ticket made such an impressive showing that both parties soon began to include blacks on their slates for the county judiciary. During the height of the McCarthy period, as the first black president of the National Lawyers Guild, Dickerson successfully challenged the U.S. attorney general's attempt to destroy it.

In 1948, Dickerson ran for Congress on the Progressive Party ticket, whose presidential candidate was Henry A. Wallace, and in 1952 he was made chairman of the Platform and Resolutions Committee of the Progressive Party after Wallace had left. These activities were part of Dickerson's ongoing efforts, which began in 1923 and continued throughout his life, to give African Americans greater political independence from both of the two major political parties.

In 1955, Dickerson was elected president of Supreme Liberty Life Insurance Company. As its general counsel from 1920 to 1955, he had already saved that company three times from bankruptcy, and as president for over fifteen years, he made it profitable and built it into one of the three largest black life insurance companies in America.

Later in life Earl Dickerson continued to be active. He participated with A. Philip Randolph and Martin Luther King Jr. in the March on Washington for Freedom and Jobs. On August 28, 1963, with Randolph seated on his right and Dickerson on his left, King rose to proclaim, "I have a dream today!" When King was in Chicago for twenty-three months during 1966 and 1967, Dickerson led black businessmen in giving him financial and tactical support. From 1941 to 1973, Dickerson was a member of the national board of the NAACP. Here, he played such diverse roles as helping to prevent militant board members from firing Walter White because he had married a white woman and keeping the conservative board members from censuring a militant black member for criticizing the NAACP.

During the years when Paul Robeson and W. E. B. DuBois were being persecuted by the U.S. government, ostracized by most whites, and shunned by most blacks, Dickerson stood staunchly beside them both. His loyalty and commitment to these men is striking testimony to his unwavering defense of freedom of speech and conscience, even when the aspirations of these men proved to be at odds with his own convictions.

In this brief introduction to Earl B. Dickerson's public life we can begin to see why he is such a difficult figure to place historically and, consequently, why he has not received the attention he deserves in the annals of the American civil rights movement of the twentieth century. He played many and various roles in the course of his career and often combined them in a unique, resourceful, and occasionally quixotic manner. He was a successful businessman, a history-making lawyer, an outspoken community leader, and an uncompromising integrationist; he opposed the separatist agendas advocated by some black leaders of his time as vigorously as he fought the segregationist policies enforced by white authorities in both the North and South. Dickerson considered the question of assimilation or voluntary separatism as strictly matters of choice within a pluralistic society. This conviction, more than anything else, is witness to the depth of his commitment to the freedom of individual people to live as they choose, free from legal or social restrictions that would make them (or others) second-class citizens. Although he often stood in the shadow of others more visible on the national scene, the account of his life contained in these pages shows that he was a pioneering architect of the struggle for equal opportunity in American life.

EARL B. DICKERSON

Chapter One

THE EARLY YEARS: FROM MISSISSIPPI
TO CHICAGO

Earl B. Dickerson was an "affiliative" type of leader, to use a term coined by University of Chicago professor Allison Davis in his analysis of three categories of leadership. Davis suggests that this type of leader is "(1) relatively objective about the nature both of himself and society, (2) driven by *affiliative* rather than destructive feelings toward others, and (3) controlled inwardly by principles, which society recognizes as leading to its highest group goals."[1] If one can with confidence say that Dickerson fits this description, what, then, were the forces that formed him into the "reality-oriented" affiliative type of leader he became? One can identify several such important factors in his youth: his home, church, school, and community. To this one must also add the outrages perpetrated by white society on black Americans, which he regularly observed and experienced.[2]

Earl Burrus Dickerson was born on June 22, 1891, in Canton, Mississippi (a town of about three thousand, one-third of whom were black), located twenty-five miles north of Jackson on the main line of the Illinois Central Railroad. Dickerson's mother, Emma Garrett Fielding, and his father, Edward Dickerson, had been married in 1890.[3] Under slavery, no slave could be legally married. Henrietta Buckmaster in her book on Reconstruction noted that "more than anything else, the ceremony of legal marriage seemed to make freedom real to the former slaves."[4] The right to marry meant the legal right to have and hold children; no longer could sons and daughters be taken away like livestock. Emma's mother, Eliza, and father, Benjamin, had both been slaves. Emma also had a half brother and a half sister born into slavery, sired by Eliza's white master, and Emma and Edward's freedom to marry legally was too recent a change in their lives to be taken for granted.

In the transition from slavery to caste, both of Dickerson's maternal grandparents had gone from being property to being free people within a slave system and, later, from being free people during the brief period of Reconstruction to being members of a subordinated caste under what southern whites chose to call "home rule."

Dickerson's maternal grandfather, Benjamin Franklin Garrett, had come with his brothers from somewhere on the southern Atlantic coast well before 1855. His achievements mark him as an extraordinary man. He purchased his own freedom and that of two of his brothers. Later he purchased the freedom of Dickerson's maternal grandmother, Eliza Montgomery.[5] Eliza had been the slave of Charles Montgomery; in his household she had been a nurse, and she had borne two children by him (Charles and Ella). When Benjamin bought Eliza's freedom, they were able to marry and had two children of their own: Emma, born in 1855, and Benjamin Jr., born two years later.

After buying his freedom, Benjamin Sr. became a successful businessman. He owned a livery stable and operated a carriage service in Canton, taking white people to and from the railroad station and elsewhere; but this was lost to the Union army during the Civil War. Between July 1863, when Vicksburg fell, and February 1864, when the Confederate center was destroyed at Meridian, General William Tecumseh Sherman cut a wide swath through Mississippi. When Sherman's forces reached Canton, they commandeered all of Benjamin's horses and vehicles. Dickerson recalled that as a boy of five or six he went with his grandmother to a former township judge from whom she sought reparations. "I sat outside while

Grandmother filed a claim against the U.S. government. There never was any reimbursement."

However, Benjamin Garrett was not left destitute. He owned a house in Canton and also several pieces of property along its main street. His family lived well for blacks in Mississippi at that time. Dickerson recalled seeing a photograph of his mother before she married—"a fine-looking woman, fairly tall, well dressed. She must have been quite a belle."

Benjamin Sr. died sometime in the late 1880s, leaving to his widow, Eliza, his properties, including the house in Canton. Benjamin Jr., Emma's younger brother, who was graduated from Alcorn College (now Alcorn State University),[6] persuaded his mother to sell all her property except the house and give him the money to go into business. This sale and gift left Eliza and Emma without resources except for their home and the profit from their own labors. Eliza operated a "kind of boardinghouse, providing rooms and doing the cooking for itinerants such as bricklayers, plasterers, and carpenters." Emma did laundry for the white people in town.

Edward Dickerson, whom Emma married, was an upholsterer, and both Edward and Emma had been previously married. Edward had nine children by his first wife, who died, and Emma had a daughter named Luella, who was seventeen years older than Earl.

Dickerson's father was often away from home doing upholstering work in Vicksburg, Jackson, and elsewhere, and Dickerson had only a few sharp memories of him. "He was over six feet tall, perhaps seven-eighths white. My grandmother also was almost white. The black came through my mother from her father, Benjamin." Other memories concern his father's death at the age of fifty-six, in 1896 when Dickerson was only four. During the night of the visitation, he was sent to stay at a neighbor's house. He remembered that the next day he passed the open door of the room where his father's body lay. "I was frightened and ran away. I recall, too, the long, horse-drawn journey to the cemetery several miles away."

Thus, during his childhood and youth Dickerson was cared for by three women of three generations: his grandmother Eliza; his mother, Emma; and his half sister by his father's first marriage, Gertrude, who lived with them until she married. Dickerson described his grandmother as "a very strong woman," and so she appeared in a photograph taken of her with Emma and Earl. "My mother was a strong woman also," he said. In another photograph taken when she was forty, Emma appears as a handsome, full-bodied, youthful woman, dressed in a black Victorian gown and looking straight at the camera, candid and unafraid.

These three women took care of Dickerson with unqualified love. Grandmother Eliza and mother Emma both saw potential in him far beyond the scant opportunities available to a black child in Mississippi. They encouraged his curiosity, interests, and dawning ambitions. They protected him in every way they could. When Dickerson was seven or eight, a typhoid epidemic spread from the south along the Illinois Central Railroad. His grandmother and mother arranged with a man named Dawson to take the entire family in an ox-drawn wagon to his farm twenty-five or thirty miles away for several weeks until the danger passed.

The loving, protective, encouraging care that Dickerson received from the three women in his early life was undoubtedly the main influence that formed him into the "affiliative" type of leader he became. A distinguished lawyer and longtime associate of Dickerson's, Ruth Weyand, said:

> I cannot recall a single black whom I knew personally pre-1965 on a close basis, other than Earl Dickerson, whom I had not heard explode emotionally in terms of hostility to whites after some particularly heinous race atrocity by whites against blacks. I once asked Earl if the reason I had never heard such expressions from him was that he had been careful around me or that I had not happened to be present at a time he was so moved. Earl answered that one of his grandmothers was as fair as I am (I am as fair as they come). He had loved her dearly; how could he hate anyone because of a fair skin?[7]

Another influence in Dickerson's early life—that of the Methodist Episcopal Church and his mother's devotion to it—played "a tremendous part" in his development until he left for Chicago at the age of fifteen. At nine o'clock each Sunday morning, mother Emma and Earl would go to Sunday school where Emma taught a class, and at eleven o'clock they would attend services. On Wednesday or Thursday evenings, once or twice a month, they would go to "class meetings" where the women would bring pies, cakes, and cookies to sell in order to meet the expenses of the church or to buy a new suit for a pastor or an elder to wear when he attended an annual conference.

The church, a well-kept structure in the eastern part of town, could accommodate between two hundred and three hundred people. There were special programs at Christmas and Easter with music, pageants, and the recitation of poems. Throughout the year the congregation engaged in activities promoting the church both among its members and to other African Americans in the community.

The church had a choir and an organist, Mrs. Dogan. She taught Dickerson on the piano in his home when he was about five or six. He learned to play "ordinary tunes." He never went back to playing after he left Canton, but here was planted his lifelong appreciation of good music. In addition to church activities, the schools that Dickerson attended in the South had a great impact on him. The adults in his family, especially his grandmother who was not literate, had a deep respect for education. His uncle Ben and half sister Luella were college graduates, and both Luella and half sister Gertrude taught briefly in the Canton public school for blacks. Mother Emma taught a Sunday school class, and although she had not gone to college, she could read and interpret the Bible and was a faithful correspondent with members of the family.

The public school for blacks in Canton stood at the edge of town and included the first through ninth grades. The man who was principal, a graduate of Alcorn College, also taught the ninth grade. Seven or eight women taught the other grades. At recess the children played in a big open yard without equipment, and at both study and play the pupils were well disciplined. There were no special courses such as drawing, music, or foreign language, nor were there any organized sports or other extracurricular activities.

Dickerson entered the Canton public school in the fall of 1898 at the age of seven. He took the seventh and eighth grades together and was graduated from the ninth grade in the spring of 1906 — just short of his fifteenth birthday. He was valedictorian of his class and delivered the customary speech at the graduation exercises, which were held for this special occasion in the town's opera house.

Looking back on those years, Dickerson considered the Canton public school "about as good as any for Negroes in Mississippi at that time. All the basic subjects were taught, and the teachers were well prepared." This judgment seems to be confirmed by his subsequent educational experiences. At no time did he find himself at a disadvantage academically.

Dickerson was remarkably alert and intelligent as a child and read W. E. B. DuBois's *The Souls of Black Folk,* which had been published in 1903. This is a complex and subtle book for a twelve- or thirteen-year-old to read, and Dickerson read it several times since then. Its basic message is clear and is stated explicitly in the first sentence of the second chapter, entitled "Of the Dawn of Freedom": "The problem of the twentieth century is the problem of the color line—the relation of the darker to the lighter races of men in Asia and Africa, in America and in the islands of the sea."[8]

Another indication of Dickerson's alertness and desire to learn as a boy was his habit of regularly reading a northern newspaper "published somewhere in Pennsylvania," which he sold on Saturdays and which reported lynchings and other crimes against African Americans in the South. He also read the *New Orleans Daily Picayune,* which did not report such incidents but did report events on the national and international scene. In addition, Dickerson read books by the light of the wood fire in the front room at night until his grandmother or mother would order him to bed.

Dickerson was a keen observer of events around him as well. He would sometimes go to the Madison County courthouse to watch the trials, but no model for emulation was to be found there. "There were no Negro lawyers in Canton. If there had been, they would not have been permitted to practice. There was one Negro, Newton Handy, who ran errands for a white lawyer."

The only example of an African American professional who left a lasting impression on Dickerson was a physician who stayed at their boardinghouse in 1899 when Dickerson was eight years old. The young man, Dr. Miller, was a graduate of Meharry Medical School in Nashville, Tennessee. He established a practice and a drugstore and also drove a horse-drawn buggy. "He was quite the toast of the town. He was the first Negro professional to hit Canton, not counting the ministers." Dr. Miller provided a model of what a black youth might hope to become, and Dickerson early focused his ambition on becoming a physician. (He took courses toward that end until his third year at the University of Illinois.)

Unfortunately, another major influence on Earl Dickerson's early life was the pervasive intimidation of, and violence against, African Americans during this period. In the enforcement of the caste system that replaced slavery after the Civil War, violence was a principal instrument. John Hope Franklin explained, "White Southerners expected to do by extralegal or blatantly illegal means what had not been allowed by law: to exercise absolute control over the Negro, drive him from power, and establish 'white supremacy.'"[9] No record exists of all the physical outrages by whites against blacks in the South, either during or after Reconstruction, but the statistics on lynching—the ultimate form of organized violence—can be used as a litmus test of the racial environment in which Dickerson lived from his birth until his flight to Chicago. The figures for the years 1901 through 1907 show 2,267 lynchings in the United States, 1,611 of which involved black victims. Mississippi alone had a total of 561 lynchings, 517 of which were of African Americans, more than any other single state and nearly 23 percent of the documented total.[10] Studies of lynching during this period acknowledge that these figures are incomplete, and, of course, in addition to lynchings there were innumerable other crimes perpetrated against the black population of the South, such as rapes, murders, maimings, beatings, and the burning of houses, churches, and schools.

In 1903 one of Earl's schoolmates, a thirteen-year-old named Charles Stuart, was running on a Saturday morning with a package. He accidentally brushed against a white farmer in front of a saloon; the farmer turned, drew his gun, and shot the boy dead. No legal action was ever taken against this man.

One day that winter Earl was delivering some laundry that his mother had done for a white family in Canton. With no provocation, a gang of white boys assailed him in the town square. One hit Earl with a piece of ice or a snow-packed rock, knocking him unconscious. When he came to, his assailants and a policeman were standing over him laughing and treating the incident as a youthful prank.

At Christmastime in 1904, Earl's half sister Henrietta, a daughter of his father by his first marriage, arrived in Canton by train to return a visit that Earl and his half sisters Luella and Gertrude had made to St. Louis to see the World's Fair. Thomas Whiting, Luella's husband, took Earl to meet Henrietta at the station. As they were going through the crowded town square, Thomas accidentally brushed against the city chief of police, a man named Smith. Smith cried, "Nigger, don't touch me!" drew his gun and shot Thomas "like a dog," hitting him in the knee. No action was taken against Smith, and Thomas spent many weeks recovering. After he was able to get around, although permanently crippled, he worked to save enough money so that he and Luella could move to St. Louis where they lived for the rest of their lives.

This was the social environment from which Earl Dickerson yearned to escape—but how to do so? The answer came in a fortuitous series of events beginning in New Orleans in the spring of 1906.

Emma took Earl to see the Mardi Gras and to visit her cousin Florence. At the Mardi Gras was another cousin named Ben who was several years older than Dickerson. Ben was visiting a young woman he knew, then a student at Straight University. A short visit of half an hour or so with Ben was the first time Dickerson had been around such a school. "There I saw all those bright young men and women moving around so freely and happily." In the evening Ben took Earl to a big meeting of the Methodist Episcopal Church in the downtown area. The presiding elder was a minister, Robert Jones, who later became one of the first black bishops of the Methodist Episcopal Church. At that meeting Dickerson saw many other

> bright young kids from Straight University and the University of New Orleans. When I went home, I told my mother what I had seen and said, "I'd like to go to a place like that." She wrote to her cousin Florence in New Orleans. I graduated from the Canton public school in the spring of 1906. I worked that summer with some brick masons. Mother sent me to New Orleans that fall to the preparatory school of the University of New Orleans, which I attended from the fall of 1906 until the spring of 1907. That's where it all started.

Dickerson explained how his mother could afford to send him to a preparatory school: "It didn't cost much. With a little payment to a porter, I was a stowaway on the train. I stayed and did chores to pay part of my tuition, which wasn't much."

Two white teachers at the preparatory school in New Orleans had an important influence on Dickerson. One was a Miss Church from New Hampshire. The other was Miss Anna Parker from Grinnell, Iowa, who was working for her master's degree at the University of Chicago. "She thought I was something special for some reason. She used to wrap her arms around me. She taught a class on Sundays from the Bible, the Vulgate version. That was my first introduction to Latin." Miss Parker wrote to Earl's mother offering to pay his tuition at the University of Chicago's Laboratory Schools the next summer. Earl's mother accepted and made plans. "That's how the doors opened for me to that place that has been my greatest inspiration—the University of Chicago."

Dickerson found it hard to remember what particular subjects he was taught during this period. However, he did recall that the history he was taught in the ninth grade in Canton had much to do with Mississippi and Reconstruction. It emphasized the importance of slavery before the Civil War and the subsequent violations of states' rights. "I don't recall anything being taught about the history of the United States except that I studied the lists of the presidents through Andrew Jackson. It was a straight narrative history, friendly to the Confederacy. I do remember hearing about Abraham Lincoln for the first time." However, the aged Dickerson recalled, "as if from yesterday," a picture in Meyer's *General History of the United States* at the preparatory school in New Orleans. It depicted a slave bearing water in two buckets hung from a pole across his shoulders with the caption: "Hewers of wood and drawers of water." (In a 1984 interview Dickerson repeated this phrase softly, "Hewers of wood and drawers of water.")

Dickerson could now go where he had long wanted to go—Chicago. Why Chicago? As Dickerson said,

> Because of the trains. Chicago was the alpha and omega of the Illinois Central Railroad whose tracks were just a block away from our house in Canton. Every morning when I went into the backyard to cut faggots for Grandmother's stove, I would see those big trains, including the Cannon Ball Express. In winter the trains going south would often be covered with snow. I said to myself, "I want to go where those trains come from."

Dickerson's mother knew a porter on the Illinois Central trains, a Mr. Jones. By giving him two dollars "to pass on up the line," he would stow Dickerson away. The money was given, and on June 14, 1907, he slipped aboard an IC train going north. Many years later, on May 17, 1981, upon receiving the University of Illinois alumni's highest distinction, the Illinois Achievement Award, Dickerson said: "I left the desperate life of a black person in feudal Mississippi. I fled, clothed with little else than a burning sense of outrage and a driving resolve, cradled in the Declaration of Independence, not to be bullied, browbeaten, or held hostage, in fact or in spirit—ever again!"[11]

Mr. Jones took good care of the young stowaway. Whenever the conductor was due to pass through the coaches prescribed for black passengers, Jones would lock Dickerson in a compartment or toilet. But word soon came that an inspector was going to look into these areas of the train as well. One of Jones's successors on the line took Dickerson into the baggage car where he spent many jolting hours seated on a casket. Even there he was not safe from the inspector, and the porter was finally forced to put Dickerson in the blinds—the open space on the back of the coal tender of the locomotive. In the early dawn the train stopped at Centralia, Illinois, and a workman who had filled the tender and was wetting down the coal drenched Dickerson—still huddled in the blinds. Indignant, Dickerson, who had enough money for a coach seat the rest of the way, bought a ticket at Centralia and rode legitimately into Chicago. He arrived at Central Station at Twelfth Street and Michigan Avenue in the early evening of June 15, 1907—one week before his sixteenth birthday.

Upon arrival a fellow passenger in the Jim Crow car with whom Dickerson had been talking asked him, "Where are you going to spend the night?" Dickerson replied that he had friends at 2501 South Wabash. The man said, "Come with me. I'm going to stay at a cheap place just across from the station." And so Dickerson did; his rent was fifty cents. The next morning he walked to 2501 South Wabash, the home of Robert Covington, the husband of his half sister Gertrude. Dickerson soon got in touch with Miss Anna Parker, the teacher in New Orleans who had offered to pay his tuition, and a few days later he entered the Laboratory Schools of the University of Chicago.

Dickerson went to the Laboratory Schools part-time that summer and fall semester and found the racial situation in Hyde Park not much different from the one he had left in Canton. Often, when he was returning to his room after washing windows, scrubbing floors, or mowing lawns in Hyde Park, a policeman would stop him and ask, "What are you doing in this neighborhood?"

At University High (of the University of Chicago Laboratory Schools), on the other hand, "I was exposed for the first time in my life to a nonsegregated climate—a situation where I could share on an unequivocally equal basis the quest for education with others of different ethnic and religious backgrounds." Dickerson took courses in Latin and biology, pursuing his ambition to become a physician. On at least one occasion he saw John Dewey, founder of the University of Chicago Laboratory Schools (who must have been visiting from Columbia University, where he had moved in 1904). Unfortunately, both Miss Anna Parker's ability to pay Dickerson's tuition and her protégé's ability to earn enough extra money were soon exhausted.

In the fall of 1907, Dickerson went back to the New Orleans preparatory school for a quarter, but with no money to continue his schooling, he eventually returned to Canton. He stayed there for a month or so with his family and then went to Memphis for another month, staying with cousins while looking for employment. He had various short-term jobs, including a very brief period as a stevedore and a longer stint washing dishes in a restaurant. Soon, finding Memphis to be a blind alley, he went back to Canton to say his good-byes and then returned to Chicago with plans to enter Wendell Phillips High School. Back in Chicago, he roomed in the house of Mrs. Lucile Preston at 3134 Forest (now Giles) Avenue where black teachers studying at the University of Chicago often stayed. He did chores for Mrs. Preston such as scrubbing and sweeping to cover his room and board.

One Saturday morning as Dickerson was scrubbing the steps of an English-type basement apartment, there occurred a momentous encounter—one of several such in Dickerson's life that illustrated both the role of chance and young Dickerson's extraordinary effect on perceptive people. Out of his room in the apartment house came John Faulkner. Dickerson soon learned that Faulkner was a native of Glencoe, Illinois, and a teacher at Walden University in Nashville (which no longer exists). Upon hearing of Dickerson's plan to enroll the following Monday in Wendell Phillips High School, Faulkner said he was a graduate of Northwestern University in Evanston, a Chicago suburb and a place friendly to African Americans where Dickerson would be able to live cheaply and get plenty of work. In addition, Evanston Academy was located there—the prep school for Northwestern University. Faulkner was acquainted with the principal and offered to introduce Dickerson to see if something couldn't be worked out. On Saturday morning Faulkner and Dickerson went to Evanston Academy (founded in 1900 on the model of Phillips Exeter, a prestigious private school in New Hampshire). Faulkner took Dickerson to see the principal, Dr. Wilde, at his office in Fisk Hall and recommended him as a candidate. In the ensuing conversation the subject of tuition, ninety dollars a semester, came up. Faulkner informed the principal that Dickerson had no money but suggested that he might be given a scholarship on a probationary basis. After further conversation, Dickerson took examinations and was admitted as an advanced third-year student. No further mention was made either of a scholarship or of having to pay any tuition.

In what must have been an accelerated schedule, Dickerson took Latin (Cicero and Virgil), English, and mathematics (advanced algebra, plane and solid geometry, and quadratics). He was graduated from Evanston Academy in the spring of 1909, and in the school's yearbook, *The Bear*, are his picture and name. Underneath is the caption "A Latin and English shark of the first water." (The aged Dickerson added softly, "The exact language.") In all his classes at the academy Dickerson was the only black student, although there had been others before him (including William Prince, who will figure in Dickerson's life at the University of Illinois).

During the summer of 1909, Dickerson worked "doing everything" in the dining and Pullman cars on special trains between Chicago and other points, including Minneapolis, Los Angeles, and Oakland, California. On a trip to Oakland, before passing over the bridge, he saw San Francisco, still in ruins from the earthquake of 1906. During his free time Dickerson took a ferry back to San Francisco and wandered around. (Thus began his lifelong fondness for that city, which influenced the decision to send his daughter, Diane, to Mills College in Oakland.)

Dickerson found Evanston congenial. The people there, both black and white, were friendly to him. Most of the African American families in Evanston had come from the South in the 1880s and 1890s and were well acclimated to the culture of the North. In addition, the university's welcoming attitude toward black students and residents had a positive influence on the white community. Dickerson lived in a room on the second floor of a house on Dempster Street owned by a black woman named Mrs. Conners. (Dickerson remembered how cold his room was in the winter; he used to huddle over the register when there was heat and put on his outdoor clothing when there was none.)

He enrolled as a freshman at Northwestern University in the fall of 1909 and continued Latin (Cicero, Ovid, and Terence under Professor Long) and English (under Professor John Dill Scott). He also took a course in speech at the Cummock School of Oratory. ("Great teachers! Great days!")

The only person who knew Dickerson from that period and who was available for an interview for this biography is Lovelyn Evans, who recalled:

> When I was a student in Lake View High School, he was a student at Northwestern. We Negro girls looked up to him and the other Negro students at Northwestern because they were college men. They had an informal fraternity, which they called Theta Beta Delta. Twice a year they would have parties in the home of Mrs. Conners. Minnie, her daughter, would play the piano. We high school girls felt highly complimented when we were invited.
>
> The members of Theta Beta Delta were all fine young men, working very hard both at their studies and to support themselves at any honest jobs. Earl used to say he ate Wheaties three times a day because he couldn't afford anything else. He didn't mind doing hard work because he had a goal. He was a very handsome

man. All of the girls had a crush on Earl, but he was so busy, he didn't have much time for fooling around. We girls would talk to him, and he would tell us of his plans. We would look at him and say to ourselves, "Hmph! He thinks he's going somewhere, but he isn't going anywhere!"[12]

No matter how hard he worked and despite the dollar bill his mother enclosed in her weekly letter (one-third of her earnings), Dickerson did not have enough money to pay the tuition at Northwestern after three semesters. Dr. Roy Young of Evanston told him that tuition at the University of Illinois was low, so he considered that option among others.

Dickerson moved back to Chicago from Evanston in the spring of 1911, rooming again in the house of Mrs. Preston on Forest Avenue. He took the U.S. Postal Service exam for the job of clerk and passed. While waiting for a regular appointment, he worked as a substitute clerk from five o'clock in the evening until one o'clock in the morning.

During those months when Dickerson was pondering his future, he would observe the regular employees and make an effort to get acquainted. He met African Americans who were already professionals—doctors, lawyers,[13] and architects—and would wonder, "Even if I become a professional man, will I have to work like this in order to get along?" In the daytime at Mrs. Preston's he would study the university catalogs he had requested. ("They were from all over the country; they covered the walls of my room.") He wanted to go to Harvard, made an overture, and received an encouraging reply, but he knew he could not afford the tuition.

One of the men with whom Dickerson became acquainted at the post office was Claude A. Barnett, a graduate of Tuskegee Institute, who told him he had started a newspaper-clipping service in his home and was organizing the Associated Negro Press (which he later did successfully).[14] Barnett also told Dickerson that he was a dealer of drawings, pictures, and books by and about famous

African Americans such as Crispus Attucks, Frederick Douglass, Sojourner Truth, Phillis Wheatley, Booker T. Washington, and Paul Laurence Dunbar. Learning that Dickerson was considering various universities, Barnett told him more about the University of Illinois at Urbana-Champaign and suggested that if Dickerson went there, he might sell Barnett's books and pictures on commission. Details were discussed, such as a way by which, with a small payment to a porter, the materials could be slipped aboard a train and thrown off at a designated place and time to avoid freight charges.

In the middle of August 1911, Dickerson received notice that he would be appointed as a regular clerk on September 1. The day before he was to report, he was given a scheme from which he was to learn how to sort letters and packages. He took it home and studied it. On the afternoon of September 1, he walked into the post office with the scheme in hand and, instead of reporting for work, left it on a table and walked out impulsively.

Dickerson's abrupt change of mind was a rejection of what he saw before him in the post office and an affirmation of what he intended to do. "I will become a professional so successful that I won't have to be subjected to double employment like so many of the professional men I see here. To become such became an obsession with me, which ripened into a vow." When Dickerson walked out of the post office, he was at the same time crossing his personal Rubicon.

During the next few days, Dickerson made preparations to go to the University of Illinois. He wrote his friend William Prince, who had gone there directly from Evanston Academy. He borrowed thirty-five dollars from a man named Andrew Johnson who lived in the same house and, with another thirty-five out of his own pocket, boarded the train for Champaign at Forty-third Street and Indiana Avenue. Andrew Johnson's money was not the only help Dickerson received from friends. He also took with him an ROTC uniform given by a young black man named Hale Parke who had attended the University of Illinois but who had decided not to return.

William Prince met Dickerson at the railroad station. They made the long walk to Prince's rented room in a house at 408 East Stoughton Street in Champaign. The landlady, who was a cook at the Zeta Pi fraternity house, told Dickerson that the fraternity needed help. She took him over, and the next day he started waiting tables. Besides waiting tables for his meals, he did many other things to earn money, including selling pictures, drawings, and books for Claude Barnett. He picked up the contraband packages at agreed-upon locations and sold them in black neighborhoods, often on an installment plan. If a book cost a dollar and a half, he would take fifty cents as a down payment and make two or more visits for the remainder.

Dickerson entered the University of Illinois in the fall of 1911. He received his bachelor of arts degree in June 1914, but with credits transferred from Northwestern University and additional summer courses, he had already finished his degree requirements by the fall of 1913. Concerning his intellectual development Dickerson later commented:

> I entered the University of Illinois seeking signs and guideposts that would assist and offer directions in my personal quest to erase the injustices that were so pervasive in my early life. However, in those days of 1911 and after, Champaign-Urbana offered little change in the totally segregated community from which I had recently migrated. On the other hand, the university itself was a haven of comfort and challenge—offering the prize of intellectual freedom through the application of discipline, universal knowledge, and books.
>
> It was at the University of Illinois that I first met those great minds of antiquity that shaped Western philosophy and laid the groundwork for all democratic societies. It was at the University of Illinois through the study of Latin, Greek, and French that my intellectual pathways were formulated. It was at the University of Illinois through the study of political science, history, and economics that I received the stimulus that set in motion my struggle for equality and justice that remains unabated to this day.

It was the inspiration and influence of the University of Illinois
that led me into the study of law. It was here that I made the lone
dissent by Justice John M. Harlan in *Plessy v. Ferguson* my cause
célèbre. He wrote: "In the view of the Constitution, in the eye of
the law, there is in this country no superior, dominant class. Our
Constitution is color-blind. In respect to civil rights all citizens are
equal before the law."[15]

Dickerson's experience at the University of Illinois changed his
professional goal from medicine to law. During his third year he
took biology, zoology, and calculus in preparation for medical
school. He also took an elective course in public speaking under a
young instructor just out of Harvard. During a conference the instructor asked Dickerson what he planned to be. When Dickerson
said a physician, the instructor replied, "Dickerson, you ought to
be a lawyer. Think about it." Dickerson became increasingly convinced that he wanted to work in a field that had a more direct impact on issues of social justice and concluded that law was best
suited to these ambitions. In order to support himself and save
money for law school, he needed to qualify in another field. The
obvious choice was teaching. Undoubtedly Dickerson's youthful as-
piration to become a physician had already been modified by his
discovery of alternative goals and emerging abilities, but this conversation with his public speaking instructor was an important
turning point in his life.

In his final year at the University of Illinois, Dickerson enrolled
in liberal arts courses in psychology, sociology, and education, and
as part of his work, he visited various state institutions—the prison
at Joliet, the hospital for the insane at Kankakee, and the poor farm
in Sangamon County. In the summer of 1913, in addition to completing his degree requirements, he took courses in education to become certified as a teacher.

One day in the winter of 1913, during an interval between semesters, a man approached Dickerson on campus asking where he
could meet other African American students. He was Elder Watson

Diggs from the University of Indiana. He was on the campus to promote the idea of a national fraternity of black students. Dickerson took him to a room where a number of students were playing whist. Diggs explained the idea of a black fraternity, but the groundwork had already been laid. At the University of Illinois there was an organization of black students called the Illini Club, with Dickerson as president, and out of that meeting with Diggs on February 8, 1913, came the chartering of the Beta chapter of Kappa Alpha Nu (later changed to Kappa Alpha Psi) at the University of Illinois. Dickerson was elected the chapter's first polemarch (president).

Elder Watson Diggs and nine other students at the University of Indiana, Bloomington, had founded Kappa Alpha Nu on April 11, 1911. It was the first undergraduate college fraternity to be incorporated by African Americans as a national body. Kappa Alpha Nu came into being for the same reason that other black organizations did: discrimination on racial grounds. At the University of Indiana white students ignored their black counterparts, and the university administration was indifferent to their needs. They were denied the use of entertainment and recreational facilities, they were not permitted to participate in swimming or contact sports, and they had difficulty getting housing or even finding places to eat. They also had no organized way to meet by themselves.[16] The situation at Champaign-Urbana was the same as at Bloomington. For example, there was no restaurant in Champaign where blacks could eat and only one in Urbana. At the University of Illinois, as previously at Northwestern University and later at the University of Chicago, while other black students were enrolled, Dickerson was usually the only African American in his classes. In the face of these circumstances, he became a pioneer in a fraternity in which he was to play an important role nationally.

In his personal life at this time, Dickerson was deeply grieved by the death of his grandmother, Eliza Garrett. He received word in the winter of 1911 that she was seriously ill. He took a train to Canton during the Christmas break, stayed two or three days, but had to return to classes before she died. After the funeral, Mother

Emma then went to St. Louis to live with her daughter, Luella, and her son-in-law, Thomas Whiting.

On the very evening that Dickerson returned to Champaign, William Prince introduced him to Mrs. Moss, a widow, and her daughters, Myrtle and Inez. Prince and Dickerson were frequent guests in the Moss home and often dated the two sisters. One weekend in 1912, Dickerson was going to St. Louis to visit his family. He and the two Moss sisters went by way of Peoria where the girls had friends. There he and Inez were married. ("I don't know what got into me," he said.) Upon returning to Champaign, the couple lived apart and did not tell anyone of their marriage for quite a long time. Upon finding out, Mrs. Moss insisted on a public announcement as soon as Dickerson finished his course requirements and was prepared to leave town to teach elsewhere.

Having been certified to teach, Dickerson applied to several schools, but his opportunities were limited by segregation. One of his professors at the University of Illinois told him that he was going to recommend him to teach Latin in the public schools of Peoria. Dickerson asked, "Sir, do you think they will hire a Negro teacher?" The professor responded, "You know, this is the first time I have regarded you as a Negro." The professor wrote a letter of inquiry, but Peoria school officials replied that they would not employ African American teachers.

In time Dickerson did receive a favorable reply from Tuskegee Institute (historically a black institution). He arrived there early in September 1913. The next day he interviewed with Principal Booker T. Washington. Dickerson related in 1983: "Some communication had reached Mr. Washington that I was married and was trying to leave my wife. Mr. Washington offered to give her a job teaching physiology. She went to Tuskegee, taught for a semester, and then returned to Champaign."

Dickerson taught English, debate, and mathematics at Tuskegee Institute during the 1913–14 school year. He did not know Washington except as the principal but heard him speak many times at chapel exercises. Dickerson said:

Mr. Washington was deeply devoted to the advancement of colored people. His constant message was that the colored students had to learn to enter industrial life; to use their hands skillfully; to acquire the habits of cleanliness and health, of acceptable deportment, dress, and speech. I saw those raw youngsters from the country learn these things, and I helped them learn some of them. I never heard Mr. Washington oppose higher education for colored people. He must have applauded it, because all his faculty members were college graduates from good schools, including Harvard, Brown, Dartmouth, and the University of Illinois.

Some Sundays, Washington invited faculty members to go with him through the big dining hall. Dickerson related, "If he saw a student leaving food, he would say, 'Eat it all up. Don't throw it away.' He insisted on the complete use of all resources. In his speeches in chapel he would emphasize thrift, industriousness, decency, and perseverance. He was a great man, and I'm glad I had some moments in his presence."

In the spring of 1914, Washington called Dickerson in, complimented him on his work, and said, "I'd like so much to have you here another year." But Dickerson was planning to go to law school. He had written to Harvard, which had responded favorably, and to several law schools in the Midwest. "So I said I could not return. That was the last I saw of him."

After Tuskegee, Dickerson went back to Urbana to receive his bachelor of arts degree. There in the front row, watching him march across the stage, was his mother, Emma. He later remarked, "It was one of the happiest moments of my life to see her there. As I looked at her, tears came to my eyes remembering that each week when I was getting educated in the North, she sent me one dollar. This was one-third of her weekly earnings. Here she had been living on two dollars a week for my sake. Such love overwhelmed me."

After graduation and hearing about available summer jobs, Dickerson went to Detroit and signed on to work on summer excursion boats on the Great Lakes between Buffalo and Duluth. On his last trip he left the boat at Port Huron, Michigan, where he had his mail addressed, intending to go from there to Ann Arbor for law school at the University of Michigan. Waiting for him was a telegram from his wife, Inez, reporting that her mother had died. He went to the funeral in Champaign, stayed a few days, and somehow managed to spend most of the money he had saved for his education.

Again Elder Diggs entered Dickerson's life. He knew that Dickerson had received his degree and was certified to teach. Diggs, who for several years had been principal of a black school in Vincennes, Indiana, was moving to an elementary school in Indianapolis and asked Dickerson to become his successor. Dickerson went to Vincennes that very week. He took examinations all day Saturday and was quickly appointed. One woman taught first through third grades, another fourth through sixth, and Principal Dickerson seventh and eighth grades as well as the four grades of high school. In the 1914–15 school year there was no pupil in the eleventh grade, and in the spring only four students graduated.

Dickerson hated segregated schools and the accompanying lack of adequate books, materials, equipment, and opportunities. His eyes were constantly on the horizon beyond which was a law school education. The University of Chicago, to which he had applied, wrote back that he could get a reduction in tuition by working in the law library, and so in the fall of 1915, Earl Dickerson resigned as principal and enrolled at the University of Chicago.

Toward the end of his second year as a law student, after the United States had entered World War I, he and all other male members of his class received telegrams from the War Department informing them that they could apply for acceptance at the officers' training school at Fort Sheridan, Illinois, if found to be physically fit. Dickerson was one of the first to apply and to be pronounced fit for military service. He and the others who had passed the physical examination received telegrams ordering them to report to Fort Sheridan on or before June 15, 1917.

Chapter Two

WORLD WAR I AND ITS AFTERMATH:
THE PROMISE OF FREEDOM

In his war message to Congress on April 6, 1917, President Woodrow Wilson said: "We shall fight for the things we have always carried nearest our hearts—for democracy, for the right of those who submit to authority to have a voice in their own governments, for the right and liberties of small nations, for all universal dominion of right by a concert of free peoples as shall bring peace and safety to all nations and make the world itself at last free." Earl Dickerson read this speech while sitting in the smoking room of the University of Chicago Law School. "It lifted me to the skies, close to my dreams. Here was an opportunity for me to take a direct part in the struggle to bring freedom and equality to the world—a world in which blacks could take their rightful place as a result of this magnificent triumph."[1]

After volunteering and receiving a telegram to report by June 15 at Fort Sheridan, north of Chicago, Dickerson received a second telegram with a countermanding order to report by the same date to a newly established segregated officers' training school (OTS) at Fort Des Moines, Iowa. Earl was surprised and angry to discover that as a fighter for the cause of freedom and democracy, as expressed so eloquently in Wilson's war message, he, an African American, would remain a second-class citizen subjected to the continuing injustice of segregation. Wilson's exclusion of African Americans from world democracy was consistent with his personal racial prejudice,[2] with the political base of the Democratic Party in the South, and with white supremacist dogma, which was then more widely accepted throughout the nation than at any other period.[3] It was clear that the decision to establish a segregated officers' training school was part of a larger racist policy governing the deployment of black Americans in World War I.

Soon after the United States declared war on Germany, fourteen officers' training camps were operating, but not one was open to African American candidates. The first draft call, which included Negroes, was due in a few weeks. How were the drafted black soldiers to be officered? Was this to be accomplished entirely by white officers or partly by black officers? And if the latter, where were they to be trained?

Joel Spingarn and James Weldon Johnson (two men that Dickerson would have much to do with later), acting for the NAACP, proposed to Secretary of War Newton D. Baker that he establish a separate OTS for African Americans since they would not be permitted to enter any other.[4] Baker's decision depended on whether enough suitable candidates could be found. The Central Committee of Negro College Men found fifteen hundred qualified candidates, but many were immediately disqualified because of their youth when the War Department set the qualification for both whites and blacks at twenty-six to forty years of age. The committee made another drive, this one successful. The army reluctantly agreed to the black OTS with the secret provisions (unknown to the committee) that no more than 2 percent of the total officer candidates would be black (although at least 13 percent of the draftees were African American), that few of the officers would be given command assignments, that these few would be washed out as quickly as possible on the grounds of incompetence, and that there would be no black officers of the rank of major or above.[5]

One of the remaining 1,250 candidates was Earl B. Dickerson, who would be twenty-six years old on June 22, 1917. About one thousand of his fellow candidates were civilians, and the rest were from the four "Colored Regulars," many of them noncoms. During the three-month course, the candidates were deeply shaken by external events. On June 29, Colonel Charles Young, the third African American to be graduated from West Point (class of 1889) and the highest-ranking officer in the U.S. Army, was put on inactive duty on the grounds of "ill health" by Secretary of War Baker. To prove his fitness, he made a dramatic but fruitless ride on horseback from his home in Chillicothe, Ohio, to Washington, D.C. In addition, on July 31 the pogrom against African Americans in East St. Louis began, and on August 23, members of the Twenty-fourth Colored Infantry rose up in Houston in response to the alleged mistreatment of black troops by the city police.[6]

The knockdown blow came a few days before the class was scheduled to graduate on September 15 (the same day Earl's white classmates were graduated from the OTS at Fort Sheridan). The army announced, without explanation, that the black candidates would not be graduated until October 15. The reason for the postponement was that the War Department, not knowing where to send black draftees for basic training (in view of the affair in Houston and its aftermath), had delayed the draft of blacks until October 3. Joel Spingarn, who more than any other person had brought about the decision to have a segregated black OTS, said, "The army officers want the camp to fail. The last thing they want is to help colored men become commissioned officers."[7] Not knowing what to do with more than half the candidates to be recommended for commissions, the army assigned them to further training with the insulting implication that they needed more work than their white compatriots. The remaining candidates who were not recommended for commissions were released from service.

Earl Dickerson was one of those recommended for a commission. But indignant over the insult implied by this delay of black officers only, he refused his commission, left the army, and returned to Chicago planning to resume his third year at the University of Chicago Law School. Dickerson soon decided, however, that his resignation was a mistake because he was still inspired by Woodrow Wilson's war message. Returning to Fort Des Moines, he applied for and was appointed as an assistant to a man named De France who was head of the YMCA at the OTS in Fort Des Moines. During his previous three months of OTS, Earl had become acquainted with him when he had been secretary of the black YMCA in Indianapolis. While working for De France, Earl wrote Emmett J. Scott in Washington, D.C., to see whether his commission could be reinstated.

Because of increasing racial friction and German propaganda being circulated to blacks in the United States, Secretary of War Baker appointed Scott as his special assistant to serve as "confidential advisor in matters affecting the ten million African Americans in the United States and the part they are to play in connection with the present war."[8] Scott had been secretary of Tuskegee Institute for eighteen years and for fifteen was secretary of the Negro Business League (organized in 1900 by Booker T. Washington). After Washington's death in 1915, Scott became secretary-treasurer of Howard University. When Earl was an instructor at Tuskegee, he came to know Scott casually. Baker appointed Scott on October 3, and the OTS graduation was set for October 15. During those twelve days, through Scott's influence, Dickerson was permitted to withdraw his resignation. On October 15 he was one of 639 black men commissioned at Fort Des Moines—106 captains, 329 first lieutenants, and 204 second lieutenants. He was commissioned a second lieutenant and was told that he would have been a first lieutenant if he had not resigned. One of those 329 first lieutenants was William L. Dawson, who was later to become a prominent politician both in Chicago and nationally and who played an important role in Dickerson's career.

More than thirty thousand of the hundred thousand black men who served overseas in World War I were originally slated for combat duty. This was in accordance with Secretary Baker's assurance to W. E. B. DuBois.[9] The other seventy thousand were to be army laborers. (A euphemism, Service of Supply [SOS], was coined for labor battalions.) The War Plans Division of the army wanted to use an additional twenty-five thousand of the African American soldiers as laborers, but General Lytle Brown wrote to the chief of staff that "on the other hand, they desire combat service and public sentiment, to a certain extent, demands their organization."[10] By the end of the war, however, 80 percent of the black troops in France were at labor duties and only 20 percent saw combat duty—not the 65 to 35 percent ratio that Baker had pledged DuBois.[11] Thus, the disposition of the drafted blacks, like the commissioning of black officers, was determined by racial bias and political expediency.

Approximately twenty-five thousand of the most qualified black draftees were organized into the Ninety-second Division with four infantry regiments and all the prescribed units of artillery, engineers, and support personnel. The white commander was General Charles C. Ballou who had also commanded the OTS at Fort Des Moines.[12] The army cautiously split up the Ninety-second Division into six camps in the North, and General Ballou's headquarters were at Camp Riley, near Manhattan, Kansas. Both Second Lieutenant Earl Dickerson and First Lieutenant William Dawson were assigned to Company E, Second Battalion, 365th Infantry Regiment, Ninety-second Division, stationed at Camp Grant, near Rockford, Illinois. There, Dickerson trained with the drafted black troops for the rest of 1917 and the first two months of 1918.

Toward the end of Dickerson's stateside training, a notice was circulated in the camp that officers who were conversant in French should report for examination as interpreters. Dickerson reported. The chairman of the examining committee was Colonel Albert A. Sprague, a white man who would play a significant role in Dickerson's life in Chicago after the war. Dickerson was chosen as one of eight black officers who spoke French to be in General Ballou's advance party. On the train between Chicago and Hoboken, New Jersey, the port of embarkation, Dickerson came to know General Ballou—at least to the limited extent that a black second lieutenant could know a white general.

The voyage from Hoboken to Brest, France, was made under constant alert against attacks by submarines. Some ships in the convoy were sunk. Every morning from three o'clock until dawn—the time of greatest danger—the American troops would be summoned to stand on deck in their life jackets.

The ship landed at Brest in the early spring of 1918. That very evening Dickerson and the other black officers in the general's advance party had their first experience with the difference between American and French racial mores. All the white officers of General Ballou's party were billeted in a first-class hotel. The black officers were assigned to the "Old Napoleon" barracks, but these did not yet have accommodations for officers, so Earl and his fellow officers secured their own accommodations in a second-rate hotel. Going out for dinner, they asked the concierge to recommend a good place to dine, and he recommended a first-class hotel. They went there and were seated by the headwaiter in the dining room—where General Ballou was also dining. The aged Dickerson laughed when recalling the consternation of General Ballou and his party at seeing the black officers seated nearby.

After a week or two, the Ninety-second Division was sent to Saint-Dié, about fifty miles southeast of Nancy in northern France, near the German border. There they trained for another two or three weeks and then marched about one hundred miles northwest through Lorraine into the Argonne Forest. Dickerson acted as an interpreter for the Americans with the French, whom they were relieving. He and his fellows witnessed the curiosity and occasional fear that the French civilians exhibited toward the black troops. White Americans had warned them that the black soldiers were like wild beasts and would rape the French women.[13] Some of the French civilians watched the black troops closely and were surprised that they had neither horns nor tails. "After we got acquainted with them, they treated us magnificently. It was at a dinner for Negro officers given at the home of a mayor of a French village that I first heard Debussy's 'Clair de Lune.'"

On the other hand were the German propaganda leaflets aimed specifically at African American troops. These flyers, which were dropped from planes over the trenches, asked the black soldiers what they were fighting for, given that they did not enjoy democracy at home but instead suffered injustice and violence at the hands of their fellow Americans: "Don't be cannon fodder; come to the German lines where you will find friends who will like and respect you."[14]

With his duties as interpreter and as defense counsel in several courts-martial completed, Lieutenant Dickerson reassumed charge of an infantry platoon in Company E of his battalion. After further training in the Argonne Forest, the Ninety-second Division moved to the front lines in September and remained in the trenches until the final drive. The German lines were about a hundred yards away. Here Dickerson experienced the miseries and perils of trench warfare, including artillery and mortar barrages, gas shells, and constant sniping. Like most combat soldiers he learned the random nature of death and survival in battle—a shell here rather than there, some men blown to bits while others remained uninjured—so that for the rest of his life Dickerson would be fatalistic concerning death, emotionally if not intellectually.

During all his time in France, Dickerson knew of no black officer who was promoted. He later learned of one: Adam Patterson, a lawyer from Oklahoma who was promoted to captain three months after OTS and later to major in the judge advocate general's office.[15]

In September 1918, soon after the Ninety-second Division had moved into the trenches and suffered its first casualties, the War College issued a new table of organization for the division that effectively blocked the advancement of black officers and resulted in their being transferred or replaced by whites. The Ninety-second Division, which had started with 82 percent black officers, ended the war with only 58 percent.[16]

On the afternoon of November 10, 1918, Major Mason, a white man now commanding the Second Battalion, which included Company E, gave instructions that the next morning the division was going "over the top" for the final drive to capture the fortress Metz. The next morning Company E was ordered to move out. Preceded by an intense artillery barrage, they crossed to the German trenches. At eleven o'clock came word that an armistice had been signed. "The troops on both sides jumped up and walked out in joy," Dickerson reminisced.

After Germany surrendered, the Ninety-second Division remained for several months in France. Dickerson's unit was stationed near Le Mans, about 150 miles west-southwest of Paris. During this period Dickerson enjoyed the hospitality of several French families with whom he had become acquainted.

Dickerson recalled that one day over the radio he heard a eulogy delivered by Theodore Roosevelt Jr. upon the death of his father.[17] In that eulogy the son quoted Edwin Markham's passage on the death of Abraham Lincoln:

> And when he fell in whirlwind, he went down
> As when a lordly cedar, green with boughs,
> Goes down with a great shout upon the hills,
> And leaves a lonesome place against the sky.

Sixty-five years later Dickerson would remember this passage and use it in a eulogy for his close friend Dr. Metz Lochard, who for more than half a century had been editor and editorial writer for the *Chicago Defender*.

Early in 1919 in Le Mans an unofficial meeting was held of members of Kappa Alpha Psi, the African American fraternity that Dickerson had helped found on the campus of the University of Illinois at Urbana-Champaign in 1913. Irven Armstrong, a sergeant in the 351st Field Artillery, an early member of the fraternity at Indiana University in 1911, and in 1919 its second "grand polemarch," issued the call. Despite problems of communication and transportation, twenty-five Kappa men responded, including Elder Watson Diggs and Earl B. Dickerson. Sloshing through the icy mud, they came together to sing their fraternity song and make plans for building up their chapter after the war.[18]

Walking down the Champs-Élysées while on furlough in Paris, Dickerson met an army buddy from Camp Grant who told him that at a certain address some soldiers were meeting to discuss the formation of an organization of veterans after the war. Dickerson attended this meeting and listened to speeches by such men as Marshall Field III and Theodore Roosevelt Jr. but then did not participate actively. Nevertheless, his presence was noted and led to his becoming one of the founders of the American Legion later in the year.

At this time serious charges were being made against the Ninety-second Division and against black soldiers in France generally. Washington had received reports that the Ninety-second Division had failed in battle and that black troops in France were unbridled in their sexual behavior toward French women. Some American whites openly expressed their fear that the black troops had developed habits and attitudes that would cause trouble when they returned home.

On December 3, 1918, President Wilson and Secretary Baker asked Robert R. Moton, Booker T. Washington's successor as principal of Tuskegee Institute, to go to France to investigate these reports. The president and the secretary made every facility available to Moton. The commanding general of the Ninety-second Division asserted that rape was prevalent and that there had been twenty-six cases in recent months. From records the general himself furnished, Moton found that in a division of twelve thousand men, only seven cases involved rape, only two of the accused soldiers had been found guilty, and one of these convictions had been reversed at general headquarters. Moton also found that the Ninety-second Division had performed creditably in combat; only one company of one battalion had failed, and General John J. Pershing himself had judged that under similar adverse circumstances any officer would have failed.[19]

While in France, Moton made many speeches to the black soldiers, one of which Dickerson heard. The speeches all said much the same thing: they had achieved a magnificent record, they must not spoil it when they went home, they should not expect the kind of social freedom they had enjoyed in France, and they should remain content with the same position they had occupied before the war. Moton's corrections about the performance of the Ninety-second Division and the behavior of black troops in France, like most such corrections, did not catch up with the lies. But his speeches to the black soldiers, remembered or misremembered, brought him harsh criticism from African Americans, both soldiers and civilians.[20]

In March 1919, Earl Dickerson's unit boarded a Cunard liner embarking for the United States. Soldiers from several divisions were on the ship. The rule was that soldiers who had been the longest in France would get accommodations in the preferred areas of the ship. But when the members of Dickerson's unit went aboard, they found that although they had been in France longer than many of the white soldiers who were being shipped home, all African Americans, both officers and troops, were assigned to makeshift quarters constructed on the decks. Dickerson agitated among the black officers to protest this discrimination, but many felt that if they made demands for better treatment, they would be put in the brig. Dickerson responded that if every one of them protested, there would not be enough room in the brig. "I wrote a petition," he said. "It was signed by all of the about 250 Negro officers on board, and I presented it to the officer commanding the contingent on the ship. It had no effect either way. But when we reached the harbor of New York City, newspaper reporters, who had somehow heard about the situation and the petition, came out to the ship in boats. The headlines in the New York evening papers that day covered stories about discrimination and injustices on the ship."

Once home, a parade was held on Fifth Avenue in New York City and another on Michigan Avenue in Chicago. "Everybody treated us royally. It was thrilling." Dickerson's unit went back to Camp Grant, near Rockford, for demobilization. From Camp Grant, Dickerson returned to Chicago.

Before the black soldiers went overseas, a white speaker in New Orleans had told some of them: "You niggers are wondering how you are going to be treated after the war. Well. I'll tell you, you are going to be treated exactly like you were before the war; this is a white man's country and we expect to rule it."[21] But millions of blacks, especially in the North, had different ideas and different expectations. There were talks and writings about "the new Negro." One of the characteristics of "the new Negro" was that he would fight back. History gives an instructive example of the difference this would make.

A pivotal moment in the defeat of Reconstruction was the attack by whites on blacks in Meridian, Mississippi, in 1871. Whites learned from this massacre that blacks offered no effective resistance to violence, encouraging them to further unrestrained acts of brutality.[22] The situation changed after World War I, at least in the North. People who have the will to fight back will sooner or later find the means to fight back, and African Americans in the North were now acquiring that will. W. E. B. DuBois and Claude McKay gave two of the most militant expressions of this will.

In the May 1919 *Crisis*, an organ of the NAACP, editor DuBois[23] wrote, "*We return. We return from fighting. We return fighting.* Make way for Democracy! We saved it in France, and by the Great Jehovah, we will save it in the U.S.A. or know the reason why." That same year Claude McKay wrote in *The Liberator* (successor to *The Masses*):

> If we must die, let it not be like hogs
> Hunted and penned in an inglorious spot,
> While round us bark the mad and hungry dogs,
> Making their mock at our accursed lot.
> If we must die, O let us nobly die,
> So that our precious blood may not be shed
> In vain; then even the monsters we defy
> Shall be constrained to honor us though dead.

The Earl Dickerson who returned to Chicago in April 1919 was a changed man—toughened and matured in the crucible of war, more keenly aware of what the world and America were like and what they should be like, more conscious of the barriers to democracy that had to be removed, and more militant in his determination to work for the achievement of full equality and freedom for his own people and for all people. Dickerson reminisced:

> When I was a second lieutenant at Camp Grant, I took a young lady into a Chicago restaurant. The waiter refused to seat us. I asked, "Why?" He answered, "The guests would object." I asked the guests if they would object to our presence. They said, "It's okay." So we sat down and were served.
>
> One Sunday I took a young lady to see a movie in the Chicago Theatre. When our turn to go in came, an usher said, "Step aside." I brushed past him and we sat down. He came to me and said, "I'll call the police." I said, "You do that, and I'll have you arrested for violating the state civil rights act." He went away.

The Chicago that Dickerson returned to was changing as well. It was vastly different from the Chicago he had first entered a dozen years earlier. When Earl first came from Mississippi to Chicago in June 1907, the attitude of whites toward blacks had already changed from indifference to hostility.[24] Less than five months after he returned from France in March 1919, hatreds exploded into one of the worst race riots in American history. By fighting back, blacks demonstrated that they were in Chicago to stay and that the two races had to find a better way to live together.

In the summer of 1919, Chicago was without experience in large-scale racial violence and was not prepared to avoid it.[25] Warnings of racial tensions were abundant around the country. The most serious of these were the riots in East St. Louis, Illinois, on May 28 and June 2, 1917. Between the East St. Louis and the Chicago violence, major riots occurred in five other cities. Warnings were abundant in Chicago as well. Between July 1 and July 27, 1919, twenty-four bombs were thrown at the homes of African Americans and the real estate agents who sold or rented to them in racially contested neighborhoods; no arrests were made. The so-called Black Belt and its surrounding areas, which had absorbed almost fourteen thousand African Americans between 1900 and 1910, could take no more. Residential building had stopped with the outbreak of war, and the Black Belt had to expand into adjacent areas to the south, with the whites in those areas fleeing and whites in all other "threatened" areas strengthening the barriers of segregation.

On the night of June 21 white hoodlums murdered two black men just "to get a nigger." A white gang posted notices along the boundaries of the Black Belt proclaiming that it would "get all the niggers" on July 4 and soliciting help to do so. Ida Wells-Barnett, a black activist, warned in the *Chicago Tribune* of July 7: "Will the legal, moral and civic forces of this town stand idly by and take no notice of these preliminary outbreaks? . . . I implore Chicago to set the wheels of justice in motion before it is too late and Chicago is disgraced by some of the bloody outrages that have disgraced East St. Louis."[26]

But it was too late. On the afternoon of Sunday, July 27, a very hot day, Eugene Williams, an African American youth of seventeen, entered Lake Michigan at Twenty-sixth Street, the southern side of an imaginary line separating black and white beaches. Holding on to a railroad tie, he drifted farther south to the Twenty-ninth Street "white" beach. A group of white men and boys began throwing rocks at him until he was knocked unconscious and drowned. African Americans who witnessed the event demanded of a white police officer that he arrest the man accused of throwing the fatal rock. He refused to do so and instead arrested an African American man based on another white man's complaint.

Thus began a riot in which many policemen sided with the white rioters and fired indiscriminately into black crowds. For three days Mayor William Hale Thompson did nothing, and Governor Frank O. Lowden could not do anything without the mayor's request. Finally, at 10:30 on Wednesday night, Thompson asked Lowden for help. Several companies of the state militia, which the governor had stationed in nearby armories, took up posts throughout the South Side. In contrast to the state troops who had aided the white mobs in the East St. Louis riots, the militia was well trained and performed its duties with fairness and skill. By Friday, August 1, the rioting had abated. On August 8, Governor Lowden withdrew the militia (but kept them handy)—thirteen days after the beginning of the riot. Active, intermittent rioting had taken place in the first seven days, most of it on Sunday through Wednesday. During the remaining six days the city returned to normal, which is to say the bombings of African American homes continued.[27]

After he was demobilized, Dickerson reentered the University of Chicago Law School in the spring of 1919. He would walk east on Forty-ninth Street to Cottage Grove, take the streetcar to Fifty-eighth Street, and then walk to the university. Because the streetcar system had been struck by the rioting, Dickerson now had to walk all the way. He took to wearing his service Smith and Wesson revolver under his coat. On one occasion at Fifty-eighth Street and Cottage Grove he saw a truck stop and two white men get out. He paused, revolver hidden but ready, and waited. Fortunately the men were only delivering a package. In class or in the smoker of the law building, he was careful to keep his coat buttoned. During the violence, he saw several instances of white gangs beating African Americans, one at the corner of Thirty-fifth Street and South Parkway and another in the Loop business district. He said, "The whole atmosphere was charged with fear and madness."

DURING THE SPRING of 1919, Dickerson became a founding member of the American Legion. Shortly after he returned to Chicago, Dickerson received a message from Colonel Albert A. Sprague (who had chaired the committee at Camp Grant that tested his ability to speak French). The message stated that as an attendee of the meeting in Paris, during which an organization of the veterans of World War I was planned, Dickerson was invited to be a member of a caucus to meet in St. Louis. Dickerson told Captain Myron Adams, Sprague's secretary, that he had no money, but Sprague took care of his expenses. Dickerson was one of a contingent of ninety ex-soldiers from Illinois who helped found the American Legion that spring. When the constitution was being drafted in St. Louis, Dickerson recognized that because it was based on the federal-state principle, some state departments, particularly those in the South, would segregate or even refuse to grant charters to black posts. He therefore proposed to the Illinois contingent that black posts have the right to appeal ultimately to, and receive charters directly from, the national body. He proposed also that the American Legion condemn the Ku Klux Klan as being contrary to the words and spirit of the national charter. He was not supported in either of those proposals, nor was he supported when he made the same proposals at subsequent national conventions. (Sixty-two years after the St. Louis caucus, the American Legion designated the original organizers as "founders." A certificate naming Dickerson as one hung on the wall of his study.)

Returning to Chicago, Dickerson immediately set about organizing a post of African American veterans as the St. Louis caucus had authorized him to do. Most of the black soldiers who had been with him in the Ninety-second Division came from all over the country, while most of the black veterans in Chicago had been in the Ninety-third Division of the Eighth Illinois Infantry, which made up the 370th Regiment.[28] Dickerson therefore wanted to appeal directly to the veterans of the Eighth Illinois. When the organizing group discussed what to name the proposed post, a man asked, "Why don't we name it after somebody killed in the war?" Dickerson suggested the name of George Giles. He explained: "I knew about him because I was acquainted with Colonel Franklin Dennison who had commanded the Eighth Illinois." Giles, who had been in the Eighth Illinois, was one of its first fatalities. The name was unanimously approved and the post was organized.[29] Dickerson was elected temporary commander, and the Illinois Department of the American Legion recognized it as Post 87. Dickerson persuaded Colonel Dennison to accept the command of the post for a year, and when his term was up, the post elected Dickerson commander for four years.

IN MARCH 1920, Dickerson received his law degree—the first to be awarded to an African American by the University of Chicago. Before he took his diploma in hand, he paused to exchange a loving glance with his mother, Emma, who had come from St. Louis for an occasion that was momentous to them both.

He had been such an outstanding student in the law school that Dean James Parker Hall and Professor Ernest Freund wrote letters recommending him to three major law firms in Chicago, which, of course, meant white firms. Ruth Weyand, an Order of the Coif (an honorary scholastic society) cum laude graduate of the University of Chicago Law School and later an eminent attorney in Washington, D.C., recalled how she had first heard of Earl Dickerson. She related that on Thanksgiving Day 1929, Alice Greenacre, J.D., University of Chicago Law School, 1910, had invited all women law students attending the university who were unable to go home for Thanksgiving to her suburban Palos Park lodge for dinner and to meet the women members of the Chicago bar. Ruth Weyand was among them, and in 1984 she wrote:

> The women lawyers spent the day giving the students a lesson in the sex discrimination we would face, with extensive analogies to the fate of black lawyers. Alice Greenacre said there was an outstanding and brilliant black man who had graduated from the University of Chicago Law School, that Dean Parker Hall, Dr. Ernest Freund, and other members of the law school faculty often spoke of Earl Dickerson's having the best mind of any student they had ever had. Alice Greenacre went on to tell how she had heard Dr. Freund and other faculty members describe their repeated and unsuccessful efforts to find some established firm that would give him a chance.[30]

With a gentle smile, the aged Dickerson remembered:

> In the first firm I was courteously received. A senior member interviewed me, then took me around and introduced me to his partners. They had a conference in private. Then the senior partner took me into his large office. "Mr. Dickerson, we would so much like to have you with us. But we are so sorry. My partners

feel that our clients would object to our having a colored lawyer in the firm." The story was the same with the other two firms.

On January 3, 1921, therefore, Dickerson opened a law office at 184 West Washington Street. This was the same day that Governor Frank O. Lowden wrote to Edgar A. Bancroft, chairman of the Chicago Commission on Race Relations, stating:

> I have received and read with great interest your letter of January 1, transmitting to me a detailed statement of the work of the Chicago Commission on Race Relations. . . . I suggest that the Commission arrange for its publication as soon as possible, in order that your findings and recommendations may be made available to all students of race relations in our country.[31]

The commission did not indicate, of course, how those in power could be induced to make the recommended changes. That task was left to people like Earl Dickerson.

Chapter Three

YEARS OF EMERGENCE

On Thursday afternoon, June 21, 1919, his classes at the law school over for the day, Dickerson met Charles Smith, a lieutenant in the Ninety-second Division and the son of a bishop in the African American Episcopal Church in Detroit. After personal exchanges, Smith told Dickerson that the previous evening at a bar in the 3100 block of Indiana Avenue he had overheard a speech in the adjoining dining room. A large, heavyset, middle-aged man was telling a small group that he had recently founded the first African American life insurance company in the North and that he intended "to build it around young men." His speech finished, the man went into the bar and passed around his card. He was Frank L. Gillespie, and the newly incorporated company was the Liberty Life Insurance Company of Illinois at 3517 Indiana Avenue. (In 1929 the company's name was changed to Supreme Liberty Life Insurance Company when it merged with two other insurance companies.) Gillespie gave the card to Smith, who gave it to Dickerson.[1]

Dickerson went to that address on Saturday, June 22, 1919, his twenty-eighth birthday. ("What is so rare as a day in June?" Dickerson quoted to the board of Supreme Liberty Life Insurance Company in 1983, on the sixty-fourth anniversary of that day.) He climbed the stairs above a funeral parlor, introduced himself to Gillespie, and announced: "I want to be one of those young men you said you want to build your company around." Gillespie told him that the company had to raise a hundred thousand dollars in capital and another five thousand dollars in surplus before June 3, 1921, as a deposit with the Illinois Insurance Department in order to get a license to do business. He suggested that Dickerson "come around from time to time."

Dickerson did so. He wrote advertisements and took on various other chores. Shortly after receiving his law degree, he was admitted to practice by the state bar. In December 1920, Gillespie scheduled a meeting of stockholders to persuade them to help raise the additional money needed for licensing. He told Dickerson, "I want you to write the agenda for that meeting. I'm going to have fifteen directors." Dictating, he started with himself as president and went down the list. Finally, Gillespie dictated: "Number 15: General Counsel, Earl B. Dickerson." Thus began Dickerson's official relationship with a company through which he made what he considered his most outstanding contribution, not only to the black community but also to American society as a whole.

In addition to his work for Supreme Liberty, on January 3, 1921, Dickerson opened a law office at 184 West Washington Street. He shared this office with a fellow 1920 graduate of the University of Chicago Law School, Wendell Green.[2] It was not a partnership but an arrangement to share office space and expenses. Green practiced criminal law, and Dickerson had a civil practice.[3] At that time there were only about one hundred black attorneys in Chicago serving an African American population of over eleven thousand—a ratio of 1 to 1,100. (The ratio of white lawyers to the white population was then 1 to 570.)[4] These figures might suggest a demand for more black lawyers, but the large discrepancy between white and black income, and consequently the limited ability to pay for good quality legal services, indicates the opposite, particularly for young black attorneys without connections.

AFTER DICKERSON OPENED his law practice in 1921, his wife, Inez, joined him in their apartment. The next year his mother died in St. Louis at the age of sixty-seven. When he went to St. Louis for the funeral, his half sister Luella told him that their mother had wanted to be buried in Canton, Mississippi. They dutifully took her body there, but Dickerson would never again return to his hometown.

Earl and Inez lived in a rented apartment until 1923 when Dickerson bought a house at 4807 South Prairie Avenue for $6,000, with a mortgage of $4,000 from Liberty Life Insurance Company. In May 1924, Dickerson bought a two-flat building at 4528 South Parkway (previously named Grand Boulevard, now King Drive). He paid $22,500 for it, $10,000 of which was his own capital. "It was a beautiful house, built about 1904," he said. "I bought it from the original owners. This was the first time an African American had owned property in that neighborhood."

Lovelyn Evans, who as a high school girl had attended parties given by Earl and his classmates when he was a student at Northwestern University, recalled the Dickersons during this period: "Inez was a very refined lady. She and Earl entertained beautifully. They had a rumpus room. Everybody wanted to be invited. The last time I was at their house it was for a Valentine party. We had a wonderful time."[5]

Although the Dickersons hosted many such enjoyable gatherings, they were not happily married. Dickerson said, "The marriage was never a steady, ongoing thing. We continued in that sort of relationship until we separated in December 1926. I gave her the house and stepped out. A year later, in 1927, we were divorced."

After staying for several months in the Vincennes Hotel at Thirty-sixth Street and Vincennes Avenue, Dickerson moved in with Robert Dickerson (half brother by his father's first marriage) and his wife, Carrie, at 3848 South Calumet Avenue. He lived there until he and Kathryn Kennedy Wilson were married on June 15, 1930.

Kathryn Kennedy was born on November 4, 1904, in Greenville, South Carolina. When Kathryn was about one year old, her parents separated, and she and her mother relocated to York City. One summer Kathryn's mother took her to Chicago to visit Mother

White, a close friend from South Carolina who had a daughter about Kathryn's age. Kathryn's mother was persuaded to let her stay in Chicago with Mother White, where she attended Drake Elementary School, was graduated from Englewood High School, and took a job. Good with her hands and artistic by temperament, she enrolled in courses at the Art Institute of Chicago and became expert in sewing and fashion design. In 1922, Kathryn married C. Rodger Wilson.[6] They had a son, Rodger, born in 1925, but were divorced in 1927.

Earl Dickerson and Kathryn Kennedy had met at the Kappa Alpha Psi fraternity house, often called Calumet Castle, in the 3100 block of Calumet Avenue, before she and Rodger Wilson were married. She and Dickerson became reacquainted later after they were both divorced. ("I came to know many other women at that time. I think it was the first part of 1930 that I finally asked Kathryn to marry me.") Earl and Kathryn were married on June 15, 1930, and moved immediately into an apartment in the Rosenwald Building, between Forty-sixth and Forty-seventh Streets and Michigan and Wabash.[7]

Their daughter, Diane, was born at Provident Hospital on May 13, 1934,[8] and they soon moved to 3840-42 South Parkway. There, Dickerson had half interest in a six-flat building acquired in a foreclosure proceeding. The Dickersons lived on the third floor, which Kathryn remodeled extensively.

Although Dickerson's services as counsel to Supreme Liberty Life Insurance Company filled much of his time, his private cases were few. Yet one case in 1923 was to have a considerable impact on his life. A member of the board of Liberty, Frank Preer, confided that the attorney for his wife, Evelyn, who was suing him for divorce, had filed for half interest in two pieces of property Preer owned. Evelyn's attorney was the venerable Edward H. Morris.[9] A few days later Preer became seriously ill. Visiting him in Provident Hospital, Dickerson learned that Preer was dying. Dickerson saw that transferring his interest to somebody else could void the joint tenancy that Preer held with his wife. Preer wanted to transfer it to his brother. Dickerson prepared a quitclaim deed and explained the matter to Preer. He then propped the dying man up in bed, guided his hand to mark his signature, with the physician and the head nurse as witnesses, and rushed downtown to register the document. When word came that Preer was dead, Morris asked the court to assign the entire property and its proceeds to the widow. At that moment Dickerson produced the quitclaim deed of transfer to the brother. Morris was dumbfounded that a young lawyer could be so imaginative. After Preer's affairs were settled ("It was the first time I received a thousand dollars, or thereabouts, in fees"), Morris said, "How would you like to be in partnership with me? We'll be Morris, Cashin, and Dickerson." And so they became the only partnership of black attorneys in Chicago at that time. It was a big step up for the young, solitary Dickerson to be the partner of a man "regarded as the dean of colored lawyers."[10]

The other partner, James B. Cashin, a few years younger than Dickerson, eventually became jealous and took his opportunity for redress early in 1927. At the urging of others, Dickerson ran as an independent candidate in the primary for alderman in the Second Ward against Louis B. Anderson, the incumbent since 1917. In the campaign Dickerson urged black voters to declare their independence from the "machine" politics of both parties in Chicago. He said, "I threw some darts at the Negro politicians as tools of the Republican machine." The main target was Louis B. Anderson, but behind him was Oscar De Priest, a close friend of Edward Morris. Cashin told Morris that Dickerson was "disturbing their clientele." Morris called Dickerson into his office and said, "I understand you have been criticizing Mr. De Priest and his colleagues." The day after Dickerson lost in the primary, Cashin told him, "Mr. Morris and I are moving our offices, and unfortunately we don't have room for you."

Dickerson rented a double office at 35 South Dearborn Street, where he shared office space with William E. King until 1942.[11] Dickerson then moved to an office at Supreme Liberty, where, continuing as counsel, he also became officer in charge of loans.[12]

BY 1923, REPUBLICAN William Hale "Big Bill" Thompson, mayor of Chicago from 1915 to 1923, had so mismanaged the city that the Republicans nominated Arthur C. Lueder, the postmaster of Chicago, who belonged to a faction that opposed Thompson. The Democrats nominated William E. Dever, an impeccable candidate who had served in the appellate court and had long tried to break the alliance between Thompson and organized criminals such as Al Capone. (In fact, when Thompson withdrew from the race, Capone moved his headquarters to Cicero, where he soon took over the city government.)[13] But the Democrats faced a problem: how to persuade a substantial number of black voters to switch from "the party of Lincoln" to the party that represented the hated South? A major obstacle here was that Thompson had given many minor offices to African American politicians who supported him.[14]

This was the political background of another chance encounter that Dickerson had in early 1923, which led to his serving as an attorney in the city government. He met Captain Myron Adams, secretary to Colonel Albert A. Sprague. Adams took Dickerson to Sprague's office where he was invited to head a drive for black votes in the Servicemen's Organization on behalf of Dever. Dickerson accepted the offer of a salary of fifty dollars a week, an office, and an expense account. He worked so effectively that after Dever won the mayoralty, Sprague recommended him for the first of eight appointments to the office of the new corporation counsel, Francis X. Busch. Sprague also asked Dickerson to write the recommendation himself, and he did so on Sprague's personal stationery. ("I sometimes wonder if I was the fellow I wrote about.") Dickerson was appointed assistant corporation counsel at two hundred dollars a month. He was assigned to the section that defended the city in damage suits and wrote briefs to the appellate court. He was also able to continue his private practice, which wasn't much, as well as his work for Supreme Liberty Life. Three other African American assistant corporation counsels worked in the office with Dickerson, one of whom was Adam Patterson, the only black officer in the

Ninety-second Division known by Dickerson to be promoted during World War I.

One incident worth noting illustrates both the social status of African Americans in Chicago at this time and Dickerson's characteristic response. Soon after the election, City Corporation Counsel Busch was honored at a banquet in the Congress Hotel to which all the assistant corporation counsels were invited. The hotel management set up a separate table near the kitchen for the four black attorneys. White waitresses served the other tables, while a black waiter served Dickerson's party. Dickerson left in disgust. The other three remained.

Nevertheless, Dickerson continued as assistant corporation counsel for nearly four and a half years, until 1927. His work, which involved writing legal briefs in damage suits, was occasionally brightened by cases closer to his heart. One day in 1926 a young black man, Edgar Brown, came to him with a grievance. He was a supporter of George E. Brennan, the party boss of the Chicago Democrats, in his race for the U.S. Senate against Republican Charles E. Deneen. Attempting to go to Brennan's headquarters on the top floor of the Bismarck Hotel, Brown had been ordered to take the freight elevator. He asked Dickerson whether he had any legal redress. Dickerson told him that under the Illinois Civil Rights Act, he could either bring a civil suit for damages against the owners of the hotel, the two Eitel brothers, or he could file a criminal action, which he, Dickerson, would handle as assistant city corporation counsel. Brown chose criminal action, and Dickerson sought a judge who would sign a warrant for the arrest of the Eitels. None would comply until he came upon a judge who was both Jewish and dark-complexioned. The judge said, "I know what it is like. Because of my dark complexion I have been denied accommodations at Michigan summer resorts several times. Give me the warrant. I'll sign it." So the Eitel brothers, much embarrassed, were brought into court. The facts were established, and the presiding judge apologetically told the indignant brothers, "I have no choice but to find you guilty. I fine each of you twenty-five dollars."

Because he believed that African Americans would fare better in a two-party system, Dickerson worked to build up the black Democratic electorate in Chicago between 1923 and 1932. In 1932 almost the entire Democratic slate was elected in Illinois and Chicago, with Henry Horner as governor and Otto Kerner Sr. as attorney general. Democrat Anton J. Cermak had been elected mayor of Chicago in 1931.

In 1933, Dickerson, as the chairman of the NAACP's Legal Redress Committee, led a group to Mayor Cermak's office protesting the showing of *The Birth of a Nation,* which was then being revived around the country. Their business done, the mayor asked Dickerson whether he could stay to talk about another matter. The mayor took Dickerson into an inner office and said, "You've been with us all these years, yet you've never asked for anything. I'd like to do something. What would you like?" Dickerson responded, "Mr. Mayor, there is one thing I wouldn't mind having: an appointment by your man Kerner as assistant attorney general. But I've known some Negro lawyers in that office, and all they're given to do is shuffle paper. If I'm appointed, I want to be treated like the other assistant attorneys general." The mayor put in a call to the attorney general. "I have a young colored lawyer here, Earl Dickerson. He has been with us for a long time but has never asked for anything. I'd like to have you appoint him assistant attorney general. But he says that if you do so, he wants to be treated like the others, and I want it that way, too." Kerner said he would call back after a trip to Springfield, which he did. The next week Earl was appointed to the Chicago office. He was assigned to the liquidation of insurance companies in Chicago, on the instruction of the Springfield office, and also to the removal of the licenses of offending doctors and lawyers. He argued several of these cases before the Illinois Supreme Court. "It was a great experience—for almost seven years," he said. "I had the complete cooperation of the attorney general and also of his first assistant in Chicago."

Leadership in Professional Associations and in Legal Redress for the NAACP

In one sense the Cook County Bar Association (CCBA), organized in 1914 by African American lawyers, was just another of the twenty organizations of ethnic lawyers in Chicago; but in another sense it was quite different. Whereas other such organizations had members in the Chicago Bar Association (CBA), the Cook County Bar Association did not because the CBA refused to admit African Americans.

Since the American Bar Association (ABA) also refused to admit black lawyers, the National Bar Association (NBA) was organized in Des Moines, Iowa, in 1925. One of its founders was Wendell E. Green, with whom Dickerson had shared his first office. Like the Cook County Bar Association, the NBA had no color or religious barriers but was nevertheless almost entirely black.

The National Lawyers Guild was organized in 1936 by a group of liberal lawyers and legal scholars who were opposed to the pre-dominantly conservative positions taken by the American Bar Association and also to its racial restrictions.

Dickerson joined the Cook County Bar Association in 1920, immediately after law school. He joined the National Bar Association when it was organized and the National Lawyers Guild soon after it was organized. He was twice elected president of the CCBA, for the years 1938 and 1939. In his inaugural address of February 1938, he focused on racial discrimination and exclusion in the profession, stating:

> I raise a matter that may be considered new business. It is unrea-
> sonable that a bar association [the Illinois State Bar Association]
> that passes on the character and fitness of everyone who practices
> law in the state, that has the power to approve or disapprove can-
> didates for the judiciary and other high legal offices, that can dis-
> cipline any member of the bar—it is unreasonable that this body
> should deny membership to a significant segment of the legal

profession representing a significant segment of the people of Illinois.

An aged white lawyer from Springfield then took the floor. He said he was surprised that the association was discriminatory in its membership. He knew a fine African American lawyer in Springfield, and he was outraged by the association's policy. He urged that it be ended quickly. Before long the Illinois State Bar Association issued a notice that applications for membership by qualified black lawyers would be accepted. Dickerson suggested that one of his colleagues, Theophilus Mann, apply. Mann did so and was accepted. Thus the barrier to the Illinois State Bar Association was broken.

Dickerson's leadership had consequences in the legislative process as well. For example, the *Chicago Defender* of March 18, 1939, carried a headline: "Cook County Bar Acts on Pending Bills." The story specified eight pending bills, including one that would void racially restrictive housing covenants. The story ends: "Under the presidency of Dickerson, the various committees of the association have luncheon meetings on Saturdays to discuss important laws and bills dealing with Race."

AFTER THE 1919 riot in Chicago, black organizations tended to fall into one of two groups: those who shared the philosophy of Booker T. Washington supported the Chicago Urban League, while those who shared the philosophy of W. E. B. DuBois supported the NAACP. Followers of Washington emphasized economic self-sufficiency within the black community through assiduous labor in modest work and the fostering of mutual respect through personal and moral development. Followers of DuBois emphasized the struggle to achieve legal, social, and political equality through education and activism. Although liberal white leaders could support both organizations, black leaders usually chose the group with which they preferred to be identified.[15] Earl Dickerson, however, joined both organizations—the NAACP in 1920 and the Urban League in 1921.

In appealing for support from African Americans, the NAACP

was at a disadvantage because most blacks who joined such organizations were more likely to join those that stressed economic and social gains rather than civil and legal rights.[16] Dickerson constantly struggled to overcome the weak appeal the NAACP had for most African Americans at the time. His struggle is illustrated by an anecdote related by Elmer Gertz, who for more than half a century was one of the foremost Chicago lawyers fighting for social and economic justice. In the 1930s he and Dickerson were on a committee opposing the legal status of restrictive housing covenants (written neighborhood agreements signed by a majority of property owners to exclude racial or religious minorities from occupancy or home ownership). Gertz was very annoyed that many of the black lawyers would either be late for the meetings or would not show up at all. He commented, "I was close enough to Earl to speak frankly about this. He said, 'You've got to remember that we are dealing with people who have many personal, social, and economic problems. They can't take these matters, which seem to them to be abstract, as seriously as you and I do. They can't afford to.'"[17]

In 1926, Dr. Herbert Turner, president of the Chicago chapter of the NAACP, brought Dickerson onto its board of directors and appointed him chairman of its Legal Redress Committee. This was at a time when neighborhood improvement associations in Chicago had begun to draw up restrictive housing covenants.[18] Under his chairmanship the Legal Redress Committee fought many battles against restrictive covenants, evictions, discrimination in public accommodations, police brutality, and inequities in the law. The committee had few victories and many defeats. Even when the Illinois Civil Rights Act had been clearly violated, a civil suit usually resulted in an award too small to cover the plaintiff's court costs or to deter the defendant from further violations. In addition, criminal prosecutions before Chicago juries almost always failed.

Among his many cases during this period, Dickerson recalled with pleasure a victory in the 1930s that freed a black man and woman from prison. A white man from Evanston met a young white woman from Iowa in a Chicago Loop restaurant. He took her to the house of a female black acquaintance on the South Side. He then persuaded the acquaintance, with the white woman's consent, to procure a black man for her as a sexual partner. The white woman later told her version of the incident to her sister, who then went to the office of State's Attorney Robert E. Crowe. The black man was indicted for rape and the black woman as an accessory. They were tried, convicted, and sentenced to prison. Hearing about the case from the attorney for the convicted pair, Dickerson, with the approval of the Legal Redress Committee, appealed the conviction to the Illinois Supreme Court. There he proved the facts of the case and got the conviction reversed. "I took the order to release to the prison," he said. "It was on a holiday, Memorial Day or the Fourth of July, and got those people freed. It was one of the happiest moments of my life."

Member of the Chicago Urban League

The Chicago Urban League met the needs of both whites and blacks during World War I because employers needed workers, and both whites and African Americans needed jobs. But after the war, the scarcity of jobs and labor unrest posed a difficult problem for the league: How could it meet the demand for stability and gradualism made by whites, whose cooperation and major financing were needed, and also the increasing demand for rapid change being made by African Americans, whose cooperation was equally needed? This tension developed into a serious dilemma when the depression hit, the horns of which became ever sharper from 1939 through World War II as it came to an end for most whites but remained unabated for the vast majority of black Americans. This was the challenge that Earl Dickerson faced as the president of the Chicago Urban League during this period.

Dickerson was elected to the board of directors of the Chicago Urban League in 1925, only four years after he became a member. He served on various key committees and played a role in the founding of two major affiliated groups, the Chicago Council of Negro Organizations in 1935 and the local Negro Chamber of Commerce in 1937.[19]

He was elected vice president of the Chicago Urban League in 1937 and immediately began to press for more vigorous action to open up job opportunities for blacks, saying: "We do not feel that we have made satisfactory progress in breaking down employment barriers in public utilities and such private industries as the dairies, bakeries, and the large distribution industries whose products are used in large amounts by Race[20] citizens. By abolishing our placement section we shall be able to give more time to the development of group pressure."[21]

Dickerson was elected president of the Chicago Urban League in March 1939 and was reelected in 1940, only the second African American (after Dr. Midian O. Bousfield) to be president of the Chicago branch. He became increasingly forceful in his demands. In November 1940 he called upon the National Urban League to mobilize countrywide agitation to pressure President Franklin Roosevelt to issue an executive order requiring equitable employment of black workers in government and defense industries.[22] This was more than two months before A. Philip Randolph proposed a march on Washington to secure this end and more than eight months before the threat of such a march by a hundred thousand African Americans finally led Roosevelt to issue an executive order establishing the first Fair Employment Practices Committee (FEPC), of which Dickerson proved to be the most aggressive member.

Lawyer for the Burr Oak Cemetery Association

One day in 1927, W. Ellis Stewart, secretary of Supreme Liberty Life, told Dickerson that a young man had proposed a cemetery be established to meet the needs of the increasing number of African Americans in Chicago. Suitable land was available in Alsip, a white suburb south of the city. Dickerson discovered that the group that owned the land was represented by a lawyer whom he had known at the University of Chicago Law School. From a meeting of the two former schoolmates came a proposal that forty acres of land be sold for fifty thousand dollars. Dickerson took with him Alexander Flowers, president of the Roosevelt State Bank, to inspect the property. Flowers agreed to lend forty thousand dollars provided that Supreme Liberty could raise the balance. Stewart, Dickerson, and several others raised the remainder by subscription, incorporated the Burr Oak Cemetery Association, and purchased the land. The law stipulated that for a cemetery to be officially dedicated, a human body had to be buried there. The association acquired an unclaimed body from an undertaker. As a legal and ceremonial group they took the body to the cemetery for the interment and dedication. The people of Alsip resisted the idea of a black cemetery in their community, however, and, assisted by armed police, drove the group out of town. The body had to be returned to the morgue. Dickerson went to Robert E. Crowe, then the Republican state's attorney, and told him what had happened.[23] Crowe sent a protective deputy sheriff with the group, which returned to Alsip, buried the corpse, and legally dedicated the Burr Oak Cemetery (incurring much enmity from the people of the town, of course).

During the depression the mortgage for Burr Oak came due. The cemetery association defaulted, and the bank was forced to foreclose. A Republican judge, Robert Gentzell, appointed a receiver and gave him authority to sell the cemetery at the very low price of fifteen dollars a lot. Because the receiver was the brother-in-law of a member of the law firm that planned to sell the lots, Dickerson, representing the Burr Oak Cemetery Association, persuaded the appellate court to set aside the receiver's authority. Bonds on the remaining mortgage of about nineteen thousand dollars ("We had paid a lot on the mortgage by then") were then sold in open bids. Supreme Liberty Life, the only bidder, redeemed the bonds at the rate of about ten cents on the dollar, thereby becoming the sole owner. The group accepted Dickerson's suggestion to reorganize the bankrupt Burr Oak Cemetery Association as the solvent Chicago Burr Oak Cemetery Association. This new corporation, with a mortgage from Supreme Liberty, bought the cemetery. In time it paid off the mortgage and thus became the sole owner of the property.

Dickerson continued to serve the organization as general counsel for many years. "It is still going strong," Dickerson said in 1983. "Saving that cemetery was one of my great achievements as a lawyer." He was speaking of his lifelong commitment to giving vitality and continuity to worthwhile human endeavors. In this case, vitality and continuity have a poignant personal meaning. In that cemetery are buried, among others, W. Ellis Stewart, who was secretary of Supreme Liberty; Truman K. Gibson, who was chairman of the board of Supreme Liberty; the son of John H. Johnson, also a chairman of the board; and Kathryn Dickerson. Earl Dickerson is buried beside her.

Member of the American Legion

Dickerson remained an active member of the American Legion throughout his life. In 1920, soon after returning from the war, he approached Victor O. Lawson, owner and publisher of the *Chicago Daily News,* for a contribution to aid needy black veterans. Lawson invited him to dinner in his home as the sole guest. Dickerson remembered the capacious dining room, the immaculate and crisp linen, the silver service reflecting the dazzling lights of the chandelier, the excellent dinner served by a liveried butler, and the wide-ranging conversation. This was a brief introduction to a way of life that was much appreciated by the young man who as a youth had once lost out to a dog in competition for a sandwich left over at a picnic ground. But most of all Dickerson appreciated the culmination of that evening: Lawson wrote a check for a thousand dollars to the Giles Post of the American Legion.

Despite acts of generosity such as this, the plight of black veterans remained largely what it had been before the war. African Americans returned from Europe with the expectation of a better life but soon discovered that the old order of segregation and poverty would not be budged. Their courage in battle and their sacrifices for their country were not to be acknowledged at home, and frustration quickly mounted. Despite their contribution to the war effort in Europe, black veterans continued to be treated as second-class citizens.

Although he was an educated professional and had been an officer in Europe, Dickerson often faced the same discrimination and ill treatment that his fellow veterans suffered in America after the war. In 1925, Marshal Ferdinand Foch, who was commander of the unified British, French, and American armies from April 1918 until victory in November, visited Chicago and was feted at a banquet in the Drake Hotel. As commander of the Giles Post, Dickerson was invited. He and two other members of the post went to the hotel in their uniforms but were refused admittance until a telephone call was made confirming that they were indeed guests. (Marshal Foch repeated to Dickerson one of his favorite sayings during World War I, advice he gave throughout his life: "The command is, 'Forward!'")

Dickerson viewed his role in the American Legion as an integral part of the struggle to achieve equality for all African Americans. The contribution of black soldiers to the war for democracy in Europe would have to be recognized before the war for equality at home could truly be won.

The October 1, 1937, *New York Amsterdam News* carried a two-column picture of Mr. and Mrs. Earl Dickerson aboard the SS *Normandie*. (Kathryn was seeing Earl off.) The caption read:

> The Legionnaires sailed last Friday for five weeks in Europe— London, Paris, Brussels, Germany, Italy, Switzerland, Gibraltar, North Africa, and the Azores. The trip is being made in connection with the American Foreign Legion Pilgrimage, commemorating the twentieth anniversary of the American Expeditionary Force in France. The contingent will be the guests of the French government for a week.

Dickerson had a special reason for remembering this date. On that very day he read in the newspaper that President Franklin Roosevelt, at the ceremony opening the Outer Drive in Chicago, had delivered his "Quarantine the Aggressors" speech against Nazi Germany, Fascist Italy, and Imperial Japan. It was an ironic coincidence—the start of a commemoration of the twentieth anniversary of the American Expeditionary Force and the first day of America's step-by-step entrance into World War II. By that time Dickerson himself had long been making speeches about foreign policy—calling for the League of Nations and the United States to aid Ethiopia against the invasion by Italy and arousing Americans to oppose Nazism and Fascism and to support the Loyalists in the Spanish civil war. Two years later the *Chicago Defender* of March 25, 1939, reported the burden of the speech Dickerson made commemorating the twentieth anniversary of the founding of the American Legion and of the Giles Post.[24] Dickerson was quoted as saying: "Fight Hitler racism, both abroad and at home. The only way to defend America from the menace of Hitlerism abroad is to use the full strength of the American people by removing the shackle of racial segregation and discrimination at home."

Member of Kappa Alpha Psi

In 1923, Dickerson and several of his fraternity brothers organized the first alumni chapter of Kappa Alpha Psi (the first black fraternity to be incorporated as a national body). "We sought to bring into that chapter men who had gone to college at a time when there was no fraternity that would accept blacks," Dickerson explained. He persuaded Robert S. Abbott, owner and publisher of the *Chicago Defender* and a graduate of Kent College of Law, to join the alumni chapter. That chapter wanted the national fraternity to recognize Abbott for his contribution to journalism. The national body voted to give him its highest award, the Laurel Wreath, and Dickerson was asked to make the presentation at the fraternity's Fourteenth Grand Chapter in St. Louis, December 27–31, 1924.

Dickerson did so on a Friday. He was then called back to Chicago on business. On Saturday evening he received a telephone call informing him that the fraternity had elected him grand polemarch. He had been nominated from the floor partly because of his eloquent presentation of the Laurel Wreath to Abbott. (In 1948, Dickerson was to receive the Laurel Wreath himself.)

Dickerson was reelected grand polemarch in 1925 and again in 1926. The Grand Chapter of 1926 was to be held in Washington, D.C., and the fraternity wanted its representatives to be received by the president of the United States. For that reception Dickerson was asked to address the convention. He arranged the meeting through Edward H. Wright, Republican committeeman of the Second Ward, and Republican Congressman Martin B. Madden of the First Illinois Congressional District. On June 16, 1926, Dickerson as grand polemarch, W. Ellis Stewart as past grand polemarch, and Mortimer H. Harris, a ranking fraternity member, visited President Calvin Coolidge in the White House. The president declined the invitation to speak, and after what Dickerson described as "a delightful half hour of conversation," the grand polemarch suggested that a photograph be taken. The four moved to the Rose Garden. Something went wrong with the photographer's equipment. "Be patient, Mr. President," Dickerson advised. The president laughed and said, "Don't worry. They are always like that." Dickerson's copy of the photograph has been lost, but the fraternity's history preserves it with the comment: "The President, Calvin Coolidge, stood with the delegates for a picture, and in so doing honored a group of college men whose forebears had been in servitude little more than two generations earlier. It was quite appropriate that the achievements of these men should come to the attention of the president."[25]

Dickerson's major contribution to his fraternity is to be found not in its official history, however, but in the lives of the brothers whom he influenced and aided. The account of U.S. District Judge James B. Parsons is typical:

When I was a student at Millikin University, Decatur, Illinois, I refused to follow through on my application to Kappa Alpha Psi because I considered the hazing to be demeaning. When I was a teacher at Lincoln University, Columbia, Missouri, in 1936, I changed my mind and reapplied for membership. I waived the faculty exemption from hazing and decided "to cross the burning sands." Two officers of the national fraternity came to Lincoln University for the induction. One was J. Ernest Wilkins.[26] The other was Earl Dickerson; it was the first time I met him. They spent a good deal of time with me before I went through the proceedings. They knew why I had not gone through the initiation at Millikin, but they wanted to hear about it from me, because they were weighing whether changes should be made in the proceedings.

When I entered the University of Chicago Law School after World War II, Dickerson became a kind of model for me. I used to visit with him and ask him questions about lawyers and the law. Later, Earl and Kathryn and my wife, Amy, and I became close friends and engaged in many civic activities together.

Earl gave me a lot of help, including advice and a substantial financial contribution, when I ran in 1960 for a judgeship on the Superior Court of Cook County. I won. The door had been opened to Negro judges by the campaign that Dickerson led against the Democratic-Republican Coalition ticket for judges in 1947.

In 1961, President John Kennedy appointed me U.S. District Judge for the Northern District of Illinois.[27] Earl was behind the gigantic testimonial banquet that was held for me in the grand ballroom of the Sherman House. The main speaker on that evening was William Hastie.[28] On the platform also were Governor Otto Kerner, Mayor Richard Daley, and Earl Dickerson.

Afterward we went to the Kappa House on Ellis Avenue, sat down at the bar-grill, and Earl lectured me on how to be a good judge.[29]

The Citizen in Politics

Dickerson's participation in politics must be viewed as his rejection of "the Gentlemen's Agreement." In 1924, W. E. B. DuBois applied that term to

> a tacit if not expressed agreement between the two major parties by which Negro voters in the North are almost completely eliminated as a political force. This agreement provides that the Republican Party will hold the Negro and do as little for him as possible and the Democrats will have none of him at all. . . . It is possible because practically every Negro vote is labeled, sealed, delivered and packed away long before elections. How can the Negro expect any worthwhile consideration for his vote as long as the politicians are reasonably sure as how it will be cast? The Republicans feel sure of it and the Democrats don't expect it.[30]

Dickerson's involvement in politics—it could not be called a career—was an attempt to arouse black voters to use what power they held both independently and intelligently in the service of their legitimate interests, free from bondage to any political party.

Between 1924 and 1936, Dickerson worked to build up the Democratic Party in Chicago and the North because he believed that African Americans should have leverage in both parties. By the time he was elected alderman, a nonpartisan post, he was as harshly critical of the Democrats' manipulation of the black vote as he had previously been of the Republicans'.

In 1983, Elmer Gertz, looking back on more than half a century of association with Dickerson, offered this judgment: "He was not a politician, but he was intensely political."[31] He was intensely political because he was deeply concerned about the basic issues of politics. He was not a politician because he followed no political leader (even for strategic reasons) whom he did not believe was right.

Dickerson's political activity continued during the 1924 presidential race between Calvin Coolidge and John W. Davis. Two distinguished black lawyers, William H. Lewis, who had been assistant U.S. attorney general under President William H. Taft, and Ferdinand Q. Morton, chairman of the Civil Service Commission of New York City, asked Patrick A. Nash, Democratic national committeeman, to recommend a young African American to head the Midwest regional organization in order to persuade black voters to support Davis. Nash recommended Dickerson, who went to the Blackstone Hotel to be interviewed. (According to Dickerson, Lewis and Morton had to enlist the aid of top white Democrats to be permitted to stay at the Blackstone, and Dickerson had to get special permission to enter the hotel, which did not permit blacks to serve even as busboys.) The Midwest region, which Dickerson organized and ran, was made up of Illinois, Missouri, Wisconsin, Michigan, Indiana, Ohio, and West Virginia. (Dickerson said, "It was a busy summer. We got about 25 percent of the Negro vote in that region in November.")

Dickerson himself was a candidate in the primary election of 1927 for alderman (an event, it should be recalled, that led to the breakup of his law partnership with Edward H. Morris and James B. Cashin). During this period Dickerson resided at 3848 Calumet Avenue. Next door lived the veteran and venerable Edward H. Wright who had been elected Republican committeeman of the crucial Second Ward in 1920—the first African American to be elected a ward committeeman in Chicago.[32] Wright and Dickerson got to know each other. (As Dickerson said, "He seemed to like me. He and Mrs. Wright used to invite me over for Sunday dinners.") Wright was caught in a political quarrel between William Hale Thompson, who was making his comeback in a third term as mayor of Chicago, and Governor Len Small. A part of the Thompson-Small quarrel was one also between Wright, as ward committeeman, and the incumbent alderman of the Second Ward, Louis B. Anderson. Wright proposed to Dickerson that he run in the primary against Anderson. Dickerson explained: "It was a nonpartisan post. Wright pledged three thousand dollars. I agreed. He started the campaign off. I ran as an independent." Dickerson lost, and his defeat played a small but significant part in Wright's downfall.

Dickerson's next political venture was in the presidential race of 1928: Herbert Hoover against Alfred E. Smith. A wealthy lawyer from Boston, William Gaston, formed the national "Smith for President Colored League." He selected Dickerson to head the Midwest region (the same states as in 1924, with the addition of Nebraska). Despite Hoover's poor record concerning civil rights and Dickerson's energetic work for ten weeks, only between 25 and 30 percent of the black vote in the region went to Al Smith.

The big political news of 1928 for African Americans in Chicago and around the nation was the election of Republican Oscar De Priest to Congress from the First Congressional District of Illinois. De Priest, who in 1915 had been the first African American to sit in the city council of Chicago, would now be the first to sit in the U.S. House of Representatives since January 29, 1901, when the last of the Reconstruction representatives left Congress. Moreover, De Priest was the first African American from the North ever to sit in Congress. Thus, on April 15, 1929, De Priest fulfilled the prophecy made by the gentlemanly George H. White of North Carolina, who had been defeated in 1900:

> This, Mr. Chairman, is perhaps the Negro's temporary farewell to the American Congress; but let me say, Phoenix-like, he will rise up some day and come again. These parting words are in behalf of an outraged, heart-broken, bruised, and bleeding, but God-fearing people, faithful, industrious, loyal people—rising people, full of potential force. . . . The only apology that I have to make for the earnestness with which I have spoken is that I am pleading for the life, the liberty, the future happiness, and manhood suffrage for one-eighth of the entire population of the United States.[33]

De Priest was reelected in 1930 and again in 1932. But in 1934, during the era of Franklin D. Roosevelt, a black Democrat—the first African American congressman from the Democratic Party—defeated him.

As we will see in the next chapter, that Democrat might have been Earl Dickerson. He had supported Democratic candidates since

1923, and as a member of the Democratic organization in the Second Ward since 1930, he brought many young blacks into the organizations of both the Second and Third Wards. In 1932 he was chosen as an alternate delegate to the Democratic convention in Chicago that nominated Franklin Roosevelt. The members of the Second and Third Ward organizations pressed Edward J. Kelly (who had succeeded as mayor when Cermak was assassinated in February 1933) to give Dickerson the recognition he had earned through hard work for the party. But Kelly and Patrick Nash, the chairman of the Cook County Democratic Committee, named Arthur W. Mitchell as their candidate, and in November 1934, Mitchell defeated De Priest by a vote of 27,963 to 24,820. Harold Gosnell writes:

> The election of Mitchell . . . was an event of greater national than local importance. As compared with De Priest, Mitchell was a novice in Chicago politics. At the time of De Priest's first election to Congress in 1928 this little-known lawyer from Washington, D.C., who had just come to Chicago, was Republican in politics. Four years later he shifted to the Democratic Party and took an active part in the Democratic national campaign. The Democratic Committeeman from the Second Ward, a white man, supported him for the congressional nomination. Mitchell's candidacy was not taken seriously and his election viewed with amazement and even alarm by many Negroes in Chicago [because he was not nearly so militant as De Priest]. However, in the national field the election was an outstanding event. Several spells had been broken. Northern Democrats had given national recognition to the place of the Negro in their party. The Democratic caucus in the House of Representatives was compelled to admit a Negro. The Republican Party could no longer claim that it had the Negro vote in its vest pocket.[34]

It is probable that the Democratic Party in Chicago knew what it was doing in passing over Earl Dickerson. His political activities had not been primarily as a member of the Democratic organization but as an activist for civil rights. In mid-1938 he had formed the

South Side Legislative Commission. Under his chairmanship it was formulating a series of bills to be presented to the General Assembly. The *Chicago Daily Record* of Sunday, October 30, 1938, carried a column under his byline. He began by referring to the race riot of 1919, the immediate cause of which, he reminded readers, was the murder of a black youth on the lakefront. He continued:

> But back of this tragic incident lies a history of jim crowism, segregation, police terror, and persecution against the Negro people. An investigation under the Chicago Commission on Race Relations took place. The report of that commission was an indictment of American democracy in high places.
>
> The Negro population of Chicago has doubled since those fateful days. Yet the evils that the commission sought to eliminate remain.
>
> Segregation has spread until now it covers the entire metropolitan area. Race restrictive housing covenants prevailed in every section of the city. Property owned by the University of Chicago is covered by these vicious covenants, which run with the land.[35] Discrimination is rampant in every first-class hotel and restaurant.
>
> These are problems Chicago faces. The question that confronts us is: Will we solve them now or leave them as a mortgage for our children?
>
> The South Side Legislative Commission believes that these problems can be solved here and now. It believes that the concerted efforts of an outraged community turned in the direction of remedial legislation offers a way out.
>
> The South Side Legislative Commission calls on Chicago's great South Side to work together with it so that the New Deal aims and purposes may be realized by all.

It should be clear from these comments and from his role in bringing the black vote to the Democratic Party that Dickerson was first and foremost an activist for civil rights and only secondarily a politician and political operative on the Chicago scene.

Chapter Four

ALDERMAN DICKERSON

Between April 1939 and late May 1943, Earl Dickerson played three major roles in the struggle for civil rights: as alderman of the South Side of Chicago's largely black Second Ward, as a member of President Roosevelt's first Fair Employment Practices Committee (FEPC), and as the attorney who in 1940 won the first decision before the U.S. Supreme Court that ruled against a racially restrictive covenant. For Dickerson these roles could never be separated; they formed three fronts in the ongoing battle against racism and exclusion in America. Ideally, Dickerson's story during this period should be told as a continuous and overlapping narrative, but for the sake of clarity, a separate chapter will be devoted to each role. The present discussion covers his four years as alderman.[1]

In February 1939, Dickerson, an independent candidate affiliated with the Democratic Party, ran in the primary race for Chicago alderman against two veteran black politicians, and in April he won the runoff election. Yet early in 1943 the Democratic organization of the Second Ward rejected him as its candidate for reelection. How could this have happened to such a committed and energetic man? At least seven factors were at work, all of which contributed either directly or indirectly to Dickerson's rejection: (1) In Chicago politics during this period, both the Democratic and Republican parties roundly ignored the basic problems of the black population. (2) Although theoretically aldermen were elected on a nonpartisan basis, all members of the city council had to secure the backing of either the Democratic or Republican Party.[2] (3) The Democratic machine (an alliance of Edward J. Kelly, mayor of Chicago, and Patrick A. Nash, chairman of the Democratic Cook County Committee) had a near monopoly on key posts by 1936.[3] (4) The real source of political power in the wards was the ward committeeman, who might also occupy some other office. In 1936, fourteen of the ward committeemen were also aldermen.[4] (5) Most of the financing of African American political organizations in the Second and Third Wards came from the white political bosses.[5] (6) While politicians, including those who were black, would often join forces within or between the parties when it served their interests, they were always in keen competition with one another. (7) The competition to be ward committeemen and aldermen of the Second and Third Wards were intertwined because the two together made up the majority of the voters in the First Congressional District; hence a black committeeman or alderman in one ward had to gain influence in the other in order to have a reasonable chance of electing the congressman from the First District.[6] All these factors will be discussed in this chapter.

Dickerson believed that African Americans should have leverage in both political parties and had been working almost continuously since 1923 to build up the black Democratic electorate. In addition, he formed and chaired the South Side Legislative Commission, whose purpose was to end all racial discrimination in Chicago.

In 1938 the Democratic organization of the Second Ward urged him to run for alderman the following year, and he did so in the nonpartisan primary race of February 28, 1939. The other two candidates were William L. Dawson, who had been Republican alderman of the Second Ward since 1933,[7] and William E. King, also a Republican, who had served three terms in the Illinois House and one term in the Illinois Senate.

Both Dawson and King had developed as politicians under Republican Oscar De Priest, but De Priest and Dawson had split.

De Priest sent King into the Second Ward both to wrest control from Dawson and to defeat the growing Democratic organization there.[8] The big question at this time was, Who would Democratic Mayor Kelly support?

Kelly told the Second Ward's Democratic committeeman, Joseph F. Tittinger, a white man, that he wanted the reelection of Dawson who, although a Republican, had worked closely with the mayor. Yet many members of the Democratic organization in the Second Ward were urging Kelly to support Dickerson. For weeks Kelly refused to do so, but the Second Ward members persisted. Finally, through Tittinger, Kelly passed the word that he wanted Dawson reelected but would not take patronage away from those precinct workers who supported Dickerson.[9] In the primary, Dickerson ran first and Dawson ran third; Dawson was thereby eliminated from the race.

On the morning after the primary, Dickerson stepped out of his house to find Dawson waiting in a car at the curb. "Come for a ride along the lake. I want to talk with you," he said. During the ride Dawson asked whether there would be any objection if he received the patronage of the Second Ward by switching to the Democratic Party. Dickerson answered, "I have no objection. I don't want to be committeeman." In response, Dawson said, "Then I will support you in the runoff, and if you win, I will work with you. Moreover, if I get to be acting Democratic committeeman and you get to be alderman, I will see that the district committee selects you as the Democratic candidate for Congress in 1940." (Dickerson learned long afterward that Dawson, by threatening to throw his support to Dickerson, was able to cut a deal backing Congressman Arthur W. Mitchell for reelection in 1940 in exchange for Mitchell's promise to step down in favor of Dawson in 1942.)

Between the primary and general elections, Dawson told Mayor Kelly that he would switch to the Democratic Party and swing his Republican votes to support Kelly for reelection if he was made the acting Democratic committeeman of the Second Ward with control of patronage. Kelly agreed, and Dawson promptly switched parties.

By gaining patronage Dawson became the most powerful Democratic politician in the Second Ward, and in the campaign for the April general elections, he supported both Kelly and Dickerson. In the runoff election on April 14, Dickerson defeated William E. King by 19,141 votes to 16,690, thus becoming the first black Democratic alderman of the Second Ward. He immediately issued a public statement, which was printed the following day in the *Chicago Daily News:* "The whole theme of my campaign was based on the New Deal programs—adequate housing for the people of the Second Ward and all people with low incomes, medical facilities in community centers close to the people with low incomes, additional recreational centers, and continued improvement in the public schools."

In 1965, Arthur Waskow wrote that the Chicago Commission on Race Relations failed to indicate in its report on the 1919 riot how those in power could be induced to make the much admired changes it recommended.[10] Dickerson sought by efforts within the city council and by mobilizing citizen action to induce those in power to make these changes. John H. Johnson, who was Dickerson's political secretary for most of this period, claimed that although all the Democratic aldermen were expected to clear their speeches with the mayor's office, Dickerson refused to do so.[11] Lovelyn Evans recounted:

> Earl made a speech to the city council demanding fair employment by a proposed municipal traction system. He said, "I want everyone to understand that if you don't employ Negroes as conductors, ticket-takers, and drivers, I will lead a group to stop every streetcar and bus that goes through our area." Mayor Kelly stood up and said, "Alderman, I told you to leave that alone!" Kelly then walked out but Earl kept on.[12]

Dickerson himself described a similar event that took place when a group of blacks was scheduled to testify concerning the public schools. "I happened to be sitting in range of Kelly's voice. I heard him say to his corporation counsel, 'Let the Hottentots come in.'" Such racial slurs demonstrated to Dickerson that neither the mayor nor the city council had any intention of taking the Chicago Commission on Race Relations report seriously. Dickerson's efforts within the council must therefore be understood in the context of his relationships with Mayor Edward Kelly, Acting Democratic Committeeman William Dawson, and his fellow aldermen, all of whom were white, except Benjamin A. Grant of the Third Ward.

Dickerson's personal relations with Dawson after the April 1939 election were few. He recalled that

> Dawson used the word "power" more often than anyone else I ever knew. All he wanted was power, but he was always subject to the dictates of Kelly and other white people. And he treated the people in his own organization as though they were children. I was the only one who would challenge him.
>
> I made a speech the first night Dawson was presiding as acting ward committeeman. I said I was pleased that he was there and went on, "Now we ought to be able to make our own decisions in the ward, pick our own candidates, and be independent in every respect."
>
> The next day when I went to my office, Dawson was there. He said, "You made a fine speech last night, but let me tell you something. You told those people that they will be able to make the decisions. I make the decisions with the mayor. And I don't want to hear that kind of speech again." He didn't call on me much the rest of the time I was alderman.

Dickerson's marginal status as a black council member confronted by persistent racial discrimination is revealed in two episodes from this period. Alderman Roger J. Kiley had invited all members of the council to be his guests at the Butterfield Country Club, and both Dickerson and the only other black alderman, Benjamin Grant, accepted this invitation. Then in two conversations, one of which was with Alderman George Kells of the Twenty-eighth

Ward, Dickerson was informed that the club would not receive him and Grant because of their race. Dickerson wrote Kiley on October 5, 1940:

> The effect of the two conversations is that you have withdrawn or cancelled your invitation to me to be one of your guests. I accept this good-naturedly, but I want it understood that I am very much disappointed in the fact that you have done like most of my other white friends in such cases—acquiesced in the denial of civil rights to me and my colleague on the basis of color or race, contrary to the laws of the state. . . . I stated my position to Alderman Kells, which is: that if I were inviting members of the City Council to have dinner with me as my guest, I would countenance no refusal from the club hired to do the entertaining on the ground that certain members of the council were of the Caucasian race. I feel the same in the present case.[13]

In 1939, when Archbishop Samuel A. Stritch of Milwaukee was appointed archbishop of the Archdiocese of Chicago, Dickerson was one of five members of the council selected by Mayor Kelly to escort him by special train to Chicago. The members of the delegation were expected to dress appropriately, and Dickerson, along with two of the white aldermen selected, went to Marshall Field's department store to be measured. The other two were allowed to charge their purchases even though neither had an account, while Dickerson was forced to pay in cash.

In 1939 the Second Ward extended from Wentworth Avenue on the west to Lake Michigan on the east and from Twenty-third Street on the north to Forty-seventh Street on the south. The Third and Fourth Wards were adjacent, respectively, to the west and the south. These three wards made up the heart of the Black Belt. The following table represents the growth of the black population of the Second Ward; of the Second, Third, and Fourth Wards combined; and of the city of Chicago as a whole during the four years when Dickerson was an alderman.[14]

	Second Ward	Second, Third, and Fourth Wards Combined	Chicago
April 1939	85,000	165,000	275,000
April 1943	100,000	200,000	335,000

These figures show a rapid acceleration of the black population in Chicago during this period and their concentration in the Second Ward specifically. Between 1930 and 1940, the black population of Chicago increased by 44,828, while the total remaining population of the city increased by only 20,370.[15]

Taking the growth of the African American community into account, the city lost 24,458 white inhabitants during the decade. Yet the areas in Chicago where blacks were permitted to live were ever more tightly throttled. Racially restrictive covenants were a noose tightening around the Black Belt. The percentage of neighborhood improvement associations that drew up restrictive covenants increased from about 69 in 1939 to about 88 in 1943 and reached 100 in 1945.[16] The result was that the areas where blacks were permitted to live became nearly completely segregated, more congested, and more deteriorated, with all the attendant evils.

As the United States entered World War II, the living conditions of African Americans in Chicago and throughout the nation became worse in every way. The depression was ending for most white Americans but continued without relief for most blacks. Indeed, it was becoming deeper because they were often shut out of war-related jobs, inflation was mounting, and welfare programs were being cut. As President Roosevelt put it, "Dr. New Deal is dead. Dr. Win the War is here."

Dickerson responded to this increasingly desperate situation both as alderman and later as a member of the Roosevelt administration's first Fair Employment Practices Committee. In the city council Dickerson was appointed to seven committees: utilities; judiciary and state legislation; consolidation, reorganization, and taxation; recreation and avocation; housing; health; and special assignments. The new alderman of the Second Ward went immediately into action.

The *Metropolitan Post* of April 15, 1939, reported that at his first city council session he introduced two resolutions, one calling for a report from a building inspector on a fatal fire in his ward, the other calling for the Committee on Schools to investigate, report on, and make recommendations for the improvement of the public schools in the black areas of the city.

Dickerson maintained this rapid pace throughout his four years as alderman and was responsible for important initiatives in the areas of education, housing, safety and health, employment in the traction system (public transportation), and welfare in the African American community of Chicago.

Schools

During the Great Migration following World War I, the black population in the Chicago public schools increased sharply and was being ever more tightly segregated. According to the Chicago Commission on Race Relations, in 1920, ten elementary schools were at least 70 percent black and twelve more were between 13 and 70 percent.[17] According to another study conducted in 1931, at least twenty-six public schools were more than 85 percent black, including one senior high school and two junior high schools. That study reported that the "census volumes show that the number of Negro children attending public schools in the city increased from 11,140 in 1920 to 43,385 in 1930."[18] By 1939 the number was about 50,000.[19]

The depression forced a general cutback in support for public schools, which resulted in many "double-shift" and even "triple-shift" schools (with shortened school days conducted in relays). In 1938, thirteen of the fifteen schools running in shifts were in the black areas.[20] Discrimination in facilities, supplies, faculty, and hiring was also pervasive. On May 24, 1939, the city council approved Dickerson's resolution authorizing the Committee on Schools to investigate and offer recommendations. The *Chicago*

Daily News of May 25 reported that, speaking on behalf of his resolution, Dickerson stated: "This resolution is closely related to one which I introduced last week calling for the Wagner-Steagall housing bill by Congress in order that Chicago might receive sixty million dollars in housing projects. Overcrowded housing conditions such as exist on the South Side inevitably lead to overcrowded schools."

A column in the *Chicago Daily Record* of June 20, 1939, read: "Feathers in the fedoras of Alderman Dickerson (2nd) and Mayor Kelly is the announcement by the Board of Education that it will spend $1,265,000 for one new Negro school and six additions."

The *Chicago Defender* of January 10, 1940, reported an example of Dickerson's mobilization of public groups to bring about action. It described a meeting of representatives of the National Negro Congress, the Chicago Council of Social Agencies, the Chicago Urban League, the Douglas PTA, and the National Education Association. Dickerson was quoted as urging the group to "put on the heat" to improve education for black children. That same day the *Chicago Daily Times* stated:

> After a public hearing the board of education today passed its 1940 budget of $71,443,560, which included $1,050,000 to finance the fortieth week of school. Two Negro aldermen, Earl B. Dickerson and Benjamin Grant, also appealed for additional facilities for Negro children. Dickerson declared that the school board should permit Negroes to attend Washburne Trade School or stop making appropriations for it.

Later, Dickerson did achieve the admission of black students to the Washburne Trade School by threatening to block appropriations.

A closely related issue was to get African American representation on the Chicago Board of Education, which was comprised of eleven members appointed by the mayor. The black press in Chicago had argued for representation since 1909,[21] and Dickerson had previously led delegations to urge Mayor Thompson to appoint an African American member. As alderman, he again led a delegation to Mayor Kelly, who in October 1939 appointed Dr. Midian O. Bousfield as the first African American on the school board.[22]

Housing

At the Mayor's Conference on Race Relations in 1944, the chairman of the Chicago Housing Authority addressed the increasingly critical problems of the Black Belt:

> In 1939 there was an excess population of 87,300 persons, measured by citywide standards of density. Since then an estimated 60,000 or more persons have moved into the area to accentuate an already bad condition.
>
> The race relations problem of Chicago resolves itself around the question of living space for Negro citizens. A major revision in public opinion on race relations must be effected before private and public agencies can make any substantial contribution to the activities of this problem.[23]

Of Alderman Dickerson's many efforts to relieve the housing problem for blacks in Chicago, the most important were his work on the subcommittee to investigate the shortage of housing, breaking of the deadlock on the Ida B. Wells housing project, his effort to have the Illinois General Assembly require racially open housing in the city's exercise of eminent domain, and his unsuccessful attempt to have the General Assembly declare race restrictive covenants against public policy.

Newspaper stories also related Dickerson's activities in the related field of safety and health.

> Dickerson asked delegates to the Chicago Housing Council to "send a ringing memorial to the city authorities demanding adequate enforcement of the building and sanitary laws of the city to

eliminate the blighted areas of Chicago." (*Chicago Sunday Times,* June 9, 1940)

A two-year campaign for health centers in Chicago was won by Alderman Earl B. Dickerson with the setting up of a station on the South Side as an experiment which may bring such centers on a citywide basis soon. The new Ida B. Wells station—the first in the city—is expected to open by January 1. (*Chicago Daily News,* December 5, 1941)[24]

Subcommittee on Housing

Soon after he became alderman, Dickerson, as a member of the Committee on Housing, introduced a resolution calling for a study of housing conditions in Chicago, to be followed by a report and recommendations for action. The resolution was passed, and a subcommittee of three members was appointed: Dickerson, Paul Douglas of the Fifth Ward,[25] and Patrick Sheridan Smith of the Sixth Ward. The members of the subcommittee went into every community where African Americans lived and held six public hearings. They also secured information from the Metropolitan Housing Council and the Chicago Urban League. Dickerson, as chairman, signed the Report of the Subcommittee to Investigate Housing Among Colored People, which was submitted to the city council's Committee on Housing on April 10, 1941:[26]

At the last census (1934) there were 236,305 colored residents, making up 7 percent of the total population of Chicago.[27] Today over 75 percent of these live in an area roughly from Twenty-sixth Street to Sixty-ninth Street, from Cottage Grove [800 block east of State Street] to west Wentworth [200 block west of State Street].

According to an estimate several years ago, there was an excess of 50,000 Negro people over accommodations. Since then, beginning in 1934, many houses have been torn down. There has been no accompanying program of construction, except for the Ida B. Wells housing project, not yet completed; when it is completed, it will accommodate 1,662 families—less than two-thirds of those removed by demolition between 1934 and 1937.

The subcommittee's proposed remedies included subsidized housing for low-income groups, Federal Housing Administration–financed housing for higher income groups, rehabilitation, and better enforcement of housing codes.

The subcommittee also recommended the coordination of agencies and the codification of laws, the creation of a department of housing in the municipal government with a commissioner to take over enforcement of all housing laws, and "a petition by the City Council that the Illinois General Assembly investigate the enactment of a comprehensive multiple dwelling law such as is at present in force in New York."[28]

The Ida B. Wells Housing Project

Federal money for low-cost public housing in areas that were predominantly white came quickly under the New Deal's Works Progress Administration (WPA). The Jane Addams Homes, Julia Lathrop Homes, and the Trumbull Park Homes were ready for occupancy before the end of 1938. But federal money for low-cost public housing in black areas on the South Side was not available until early 1936. This was to be, in effect, a segregated housing program that favored white over black neighborhoods. The first site chosen for black public housing was a six-block area between Vincennes Avenue (700 block east of State Street) and South Parkway (now King Drive, 400 block east of State Street). Land was purchased and houses in which more than twenty-six hundred black families lived were demolished by August 1936. But then the land lay vacant for three years. One obstacle after another was put up, removed, and then replaced by new difficulties.

> Obstacles included a court decision against the use of the power of eminent domain, the difficulty in getting state and local tax exemption, and a series of court injunctions. In these injunctions attorneys for the Chicago Tribune Company were active. The

primary objective was to defeat low-cost public housing. Also, Alderman Arthur G. Lindell of the Nineteenth Ward, chairman of the City Council's Committee on Housing, was opposed to public housing projects in the Negro areas. Secondary attacks were made to hold up construction until contracts were given to favored construction companies, jobs were multiplied for union members by limiting the use of large machines and other labor-saving devices.[29]

Newspaper stories during this period told of a complicated situation.

> A restraining order was issued by Judge John J. Lupe to Robert Geigel, an insurance broker, who entered a suit to compel the Chicago Housing Authority to split contracts for construction to various companies. (*Chicago Daily Record*, July 25, 1939)

> A big mass meeting will be held Sunday afternoon at 2:30 on the site of the proposed project where it is expected that more than 5,000 Negro citizens, led by Alderman Earl B. Dickerson, will register their protests against the judge's alleged un-American actions. (*Pittsburgh Courier*, July 29, 1939)

Dickerson filled in the details: "I started an agitation to get the injunction lifted. I organized a large group of people to protest the delay. We held a public meeting of some 10,000 people on the ground that had been vacant for so long. We had some important speakers. I was the first speaker. We passed resolutions; we sang songs of protest. The whole crowd cried out in protest. As a result, the lawyers who had got the injunction called me into their office and agreed to have the injunction dissolved."

Open Housing in the Eminent Domain Context
One of the reasons the Ida B. Wells housing project was delayed was that a federal court in Louisville, Kentucky, declared unconstitutional the federal government's use of eminent domain to secure sites for new housing. Consequently, Chicago housing officials

"turned to the slower process of direct purchase from property owners."[30] When federal funds became available for public and private housing projects, Chicago needed the Illinois General Assembly to give it the power of eminent domain to acquire slum housing for sale in order to permit private developers to proceed with new construction. When the General Assembly was drawing up legislation giving cities the power of eminent domain for this purpose, it sent the draft legislation for endorsement, as was the practice, to the Chicago City Council, which referred the draft to its Committee on State Legislation. The first draft of the proposed legislation contained no provision requiring racially open policies for the purchase and rental of the new housing to be developed. As a member of the Committee on State Legislation, Dickerson so vigorously opposed endorsement without an open housing provision that the first draft was not endorsed. A second draft containing such a provision was endorsed, and the General Assembly passed the legislation. Thus, when the large private housing projects of Lake Meadows and Prairie Shores were developed in the late 1950s and early 1960s, they were interracial.

Efforts Against Racially Restrictive Covenants
A significant obstacle to the improvement of housing for African Americans in Chicago and other U.S. cities was the racially restrictive covenant. Dickerson strove in many ways to tear down this barrier. As an alderman he tried to get the city council to petition the Illinois General Assembly to declare such covenants against public policy, but this effort was in vain. As a member of the city council's Committee on State Legislation, he was influential in having two antirestrictive covenant bills introduced in the state legislature, and both had strong public support; but the opposition by property owners and real estate interests prevented their passage. Meanwhile, Dickerson was working to make such legislation unnecessary by getting the courts to declare restrictive covenants unenforceable. The first step in achieving this end was winning *Hansberry v. Lee* before the U.S. Supreme Court in 1940 (as discussed in chapter 5).

Fair Employment in Public Transportation

Until the 1940s, Chicago had three privately owned and operated transit systems: Chicago Surface Line (rails), Chicago Motor Coach Company (buses), and Chicago Rapid Transit Company (elevated). For several years, the city council had been weighing whether to consolidate these three systems into one, and if so, how? By giving a franchise to one private company or by municipal ownership?

As alderman, Dickerson vigorously opposed increases in fares under private ownership and advocated municipal ownership. His major concern, however, was to get a fair employment policy enacted by the system, private or public. Soon after he was elected alderman, Dickerson and Oscar De Priest dramatized the intensity of their feelings on this issue. The Chicago Surface Line, laying tracks on Fifty-first Street from Cottage Grove east to Lake Park, was employing only white men. One day Dickerson and De Priest went to the digging and wrested the tools from two of the white employees.[31]

Finally, in mid-1940, the city council gave serious consideration to consolidation under municipal ownership. Dickerson, though not on the Committee on Local Transportation, took advantage of his right to speak on all issues. Here, too, he had done his homework. He had written for information to other cities that had municipal ownership—among them Detroit, New York, and London—and then used what he had obtained both in his proposals and to mobilize public action. Again, newspaper stories recount the main episodes.

> South Side citizens descended upon the aldermanic council hearings in City Hall Tuesday, February 4, and refused to leave until they had fulfilled the purpose for which they came. They heard Alderman Dickerson put dynamite into eloquent words when he told the transit committee that Race citizens [African American civil rights activists] meant business about seeing that there shall be adequate safeguards against discrimination in the proposed traction setup. (*Chicago Defender*, February 8, 1941)

Last week Alderman Dickerson introduced in the City Council a resolution asking for public ownership of traction in this city. "Under private ownership in Chicago," he said, "Chicago Surface Line employs some 15,000 persons and only 41 are Negroes. These 41 are employed as manual laborers. The proportion and nature of the work of Negroes are the same with Chicago Rapid Transit and Chicago Motor Coach Company." (*Chicago Bee*, March 9, 1941)

Chicago's long-debated $102,000,000 unified traction ordinance was scheduled in the City Council today, with the expectation that it will be called up for passage February 11. The ordinance includes a provision that no person may be refused employment by the new company because of race, color, or religion. This was insisted upon by Aldermen Earl Dickerson (2nd) and Benjamin A. Grant (3rd). (*Chicago Herald American*, January 9, 1942)

The Unification Traction Ordinance passed, but municipal ownership depended on approval by the citizens of a bond issue, which the voters rejected the first time. Therefore, the contract with the private companies was renewed until the bond issue could be approved, and the renewal had a provision against discrimination in employment and the establishment of a review committee to hear complaints of discrimination.

Hailing the signal victory which last week smashed the color barriers in Chicago's vast transportation system, *The Bee* recalls the drive for transit jobs, which reached the concerted stage with the election of Earl B. Dickerson as alderman of the Second Ward and Benjamin A. Grant as alderman of the Third Ward. It culminated in the employment of Plato Biggs, 5335 Indiana Avenue, last week. Biggs began a fifteen-day trial period, at the end of which he will be assigned to a run as Chicago's first Negro streetcar conductor. His training period ends next week.

This week another victory on the traction front was revealed in the announcement that the Chicago Motor Coach Company will take on Negroes as drivers. Interviews will start soon. (*Chicago Bee,* October 31, 1943)

Dickerson's account ties these items together, particularly the crucial moment when the city council took up the final draft of the proposed ordinance on February 11, 1942:

> I had prepared Section 18 of a certain chapter in this ordinance providing that there should be no discrimination in hiring and that there should be a committee to review complaints of discrimination. The hearings went on for two years before the ordinance was presented, and each time I insisted that my section be included. When the ordinance was finally presented and was being passed on by the full council, chapter by chapter, I noticed that my section had been omitted. I made a speech at some length for the inclusion of my Section 18. Some alderman moved that it not be included. I got the floor again and declared that if the ordinance went to the citizens for approval of the bond issue without my section, I would oppose it; I would appear before every organization possible in the city and enlist all the liberal people to defeat the bond issue. The council chamber was packed. Everyone listened intently to my threat.
>
> When I finished, Mayor Kelly, who was a member of the council as a committee of the whole, arose and said: "Gentlemen, I have heard what Alderman Dickerson has said. It makes good sense. I ask that the Council reconsider their opposition and approve this amendment." At that point the alderman who had moved that my section be rejected moved that it be reconsidered. It was passed unanimously.

Health and Welfare

Dickerson sought to bring relief to the many needy people of Chicago in many ways, three of which were by organizing concerned citizens to bring pressure on the city council, by forming the Illinois

Conference on Social Legislation to seek relief from the state legislature, and by creating and managing the Second Ward Community Fund. Several newspapers recounted these efforts:

> Resolutions calling on Governor Horner to include relief in his special session and demanding that the legislature provide $6,000,000 a month for relief were passed last night by the Illinois Conference on Social Legislation. The conference was held in the Council Chamber at City Hall Saturday, January 6. Alderman Earl B. Dickerson, chairman, pointed out that thousands of Chicagoans are living on a starvation budget and that a fight must be made to increase the relief appropriations. The conference brought 500 delegates representing 61 social organizations to the City Council chamber to discuss the relief crisis. (*Chicago Sunday Times*, January 6, 1940)

> The City Council last Thursday passed a resolution introduced by Alderman Earl B. Dickerson favoring passage of Illinois House bills 399 and 400, which provide a promise of aid to dependent children. (*Chicago Defender*, May 14, 1941)

The most direct aid Dickerson gave to the needy was though his creation of the Second Ward Community Fund. It was supervised by a ward advisory council and regularly audited. The *Chicago Daily News* of August 31, 1940, reported its beginning and purposes:

> To finance the project a ward community fund has just been established. One of its main objectives will be to aid needy people to buy food and clothing. Another is to help needy property owners to buy garbage cans in the effort to control rats. Other purposes will be to improve cultural and recreational facilities. The first contribution to the fund, one of fifty dollars, was announced this week, from Alderman Earl B. Dickerson, who launched the civic responsibility program.

By the end of 1940, Dickerson had broadened the program, blanketing the city in the solicitation of money and extending its benefits beyond ward lines. That year he organized the first of three annual benefit shows to create "a continuing Community Service Fund." The *Chicago Defender* of December 21, 1940, stated: "The first show was at the Regal Theatre on December 14, for the needy of the Second Ward and adjacent communities. It featured Duke Ellington, Roy Eldridge, popular trumpeter, and Fats Waller and his orchestra."

Activities in the Early War Years

An influential member of the Democratic Party, Dickerson supported two main planks in the national party's 1940 platform: aid to the Allies and full democracy at home. The July 15, 1940, *Chicago Tribune* reported:

> Alderman Earl B. Dickerson headed a delegation of Negro leaders at yesterday's public session of the Democratic platform committee and submitted their proposal for platform pledges. Dickerson wanted the party to go on record for abolishing the poll tax in the southern states, for adoption of cloture in the U.S. Senate in order to pass the Wagner-Gavagan anti-lynching bill, and for safeguards against discrimination on account of race, color, or creed in the administration of relief, the national defense program, and all tax-financed projects.

When Franklin D. Roosevelt was inaugurated on January 20, 1941, Dickerson was an official guest, in stand 1, section G, row 9, seat 6.

Earl and Kathryn Dickerson were also the main organizers of the American Negro Exposition in Chicago. The *Chicago Herald American* of July 5, 1940, reported: "More than 20,000 persons crowded into the Coliseum to attend the American Negro Exposition. President Roosevelt turned on the dedicatory lights by remote control from the White House. More than 120 exhibits trace the achievements of the Negro in religion, music, sports, science, industry, the arts, and on the stage."

In addition, the Dickersons were leaders in the founding of the

South Side Community Art Center at 3837 South Michigan Avenue. Mrs. Eleanor Roosevelt attended the dedication on May 10, 1941, and Dickerson was her official escort.

Dickerson was also a member of the Illinois State Commission on the Condition of the Urban Colored Population. Governor Henry Horner appointed the commission in May 1940, made up of members of both the House and the Senate and also of private citizens. The chairman was Senator William Wallace, an African American from Chicago. Dickerson was appointed as a private citizen and was chairman of the committee that selected the staff. He selected Elmer Henderson, then a graduate student in sociology at the University of Chicago, as head of the staff and, as his assistant, St. Clair Drake, then a graduate student in anthropology, also at the University of Chicago. Many years later Henderson recalled: "Dickerson was the driving force. He set the agenda and kept the commission on it."[32] The commission made its preliminary report to the Illinois Senate on February 25, 1941.[33] (The longer, final report did not differ in substance.) Both reports were broken down into headings such as housing, employment, health, and public accommodations. In all areas they found that needs were great and that discrimination was rampant throughout the state. The Illinois Civil Rights Act was, in effect, "a dead letter." When asked years later whether the report had any impact, Henderson replied, "I think so, though I don't point to any specific legislation. The climate of opinion was somewhat affected. The results of the study were used widely by various citizens' groups because it was primarily factual. It was very helpful to the Urban League, the NAACP, and other groups. In all of these Dickerson was active."[34]

Dickerson's many and diverse roles during his years in the Chicago City Council were specified in his weekly newsletter put out by John H. Johnson, political secretary, dated January 9, 1942:

> Member, President Roosevelt's Fair Employment Practice
>   Committee
> President, Chicago Urban League

General Counsel, Supreme Liberty Life Insurance Company
Chairman, Annual Conference on Negro Problems
Chairman, Legal Redress Committee, Chicago NAACP
Member, National Board of NAACP
On Executive Committee, Chicago Council of Social Agencies
Chairman, Chicago Council on Race Relations
Member, Metropolitan Housing Council
On Executive Committee, National Lawyers Guild
Chairman, National Negro Stop Hitler Committee

Through the National Negro Stop Hitler Committee, Dickerson fought for "a double victory": victory over America's racist enemies abroad and over racial discrimination at home. As committee chairman he made a coast-to-coast address over the Columbia Broadcasting System's *Wings over Jordan* program on Sunday, January 4, 1942. The speech marked the seventy-eighth anniversary of the Emancipation Proclamation. In his speech Dickerson pledged black America's full support for the United Nations' efforts to achieve universal human liberty. He saw the war against racism abroad and at home as a single struggle and demanded "no restriction or limitation on the Negro's role in the current battle for human liberty."

Dickerson Versus Dawson for Congress

William L. Dawson had offered Dickerson after the primary election in February 1939 the promise of a First Congressional Democratic Committee endorsement over the incumbent Arthur Mitchell for Congress in 1940. However, when the time came, Dawson supported Mitchell for reelection in exchange for Mitchell's promise to step down in favor of Dawson in 1942. In 1940, Dawson also told Dickerson that he would support him for Congress in 1942. In the meantime, a Draft Dickerson for Congress Committee had been formed. The *Chicago Defender* of February 17, 1942, reported:

In a letter to the Draft Dickerson for Congress Committee Alderman Earl B. Dickerson this week refused the offer of the group to sponsor him as nominee for Congress from the First Congressional District. . . . In this letter Dickerson said he appreciated the offer, but "I have decided that the people of my ward need a representative in the City Council who will wage, as I have, a relentless fight against the many injustices faced by our people."

In 1942, when Patrick Nash, chairman of the Cook County Democratic Committee, asked Dawson, the acting committeeman of the Second Ward, who should be endorsed as Democratic nominee for Congress from the First Congressional District, Dawson replied, "I have your candidate," and pointed to himself.[35] Dawson received the endorsement of the Second and Third Ward organizations. Enraged by Dawson's breaking of his promise and by the Second Ward organization's endorsement of Dawson, Dickerson decided at the last moment to accept the support of the Draft Dickerson for Congress Committee and challenged Dawson for the Democratic nomination in the April 14 primary.

Dawson's campaign against Dickerson was vicious. He paid senior citizens in ragged clothes to allege that Dickerson had not performed legal services for which they had paid, and he circulated pictures of those people and copies of their allegations. He called attention to Dickerson's light brown skin. He spread the rumor that Dickerson was married to a white woman. He publicly asked Dickerson, "What did you do with the charity funds?" He called Dickerson "silk stocking" and "high hat" because he had held seminars in the Second Ward on social problems, with professors from the University of Chicago as guest speakers.

The Kelly-Nash machine gave Dickerson no financial support, and the many ministers, lawyers, doctors, teachers, and poor people who supported him could not raise substantial funds. But Dickerson made the race ("I couldn't live with myself if I hadn't"). He went five thousand dollars into personal debt and campaigned vigorously.

A Dickerson election flyer states: "Attend the Dickerson for Congress Campaign Rally, Wendell Phillips High School, Sunday, April 12, 3:00 P.M." Referring to Dawson's question, "What did you do with the charity funds?" the flyer's head is: "Here's Where Ours Went—How About You, Bill?" Beneath the head is an accounting of the funds, including photocopies of many of the checks. Then the flyer turned to attack:

> How about you? The Second Ward is still talking about the boxing show you staged with a take to you of some 200 pages of advertising at $24 a page and $5,000 paid admissions. Comes Christmas and "Wee Willie" pulls Santa's beard. Instead of the usual 20 baskets per precinct for needy families, the Dawson diet is only five per precinct. And not long after that "Wee Willie" pops up with a brand new Chrysler. That's bad politics—but not bad business, at least for you.

Dickerson and his supporters also produced a campaign poster with a picture of Franklin Roosevelt looking up at Dickerson with the caption: "Roosevelt needs him." They had another with a picture of Joe Louis, the heavyweight champion of the world, in a boxing stance and a letter from Fort Dix, New Jersey (where Joe was a soldier): "Dear Voter, Right now in the scrap we've got on our hands with Hitler, we need a fellow like Dickerson to talk up for the Negro people in Congress and help us win this war." [Signed] Joe Louis Barrow.[36]

At the final campaign rally, Dickerson invited his wife and their six-year-old daughter onto the platform. He said: "Mr. Dawson says I am married to a white woman. In law there is a Latin phrase 'Res ipsa loquitur,' which means 'The thing speaks for itself.' Look at my wife and daughter and decide whether I am married to a white woman."

Recalling this campaign, John H. Johnson commented years later:

> In the old days the machine ran the precinct captains and the precinct captains controlled the voters. All was based on jobs,

favors, getting people into hospitals, out of jails, or onto welfare, which were needed by a great many people. There was no non-political social mechanism to provide such services. There was no television. A candidate like Earl could not see all the people in meetings or by going from door to door. You needed another vehicle, and that was the precinct captain. He was acquainted with all the people in the community, and he colored the thinking of the people about whom they should vote for. Earl was a victim of the circumstances of his times, and there was no way to change that because the people downtown truly dictated who ran for public office throughout the city.[37]

Elmer Gertz recalled: "One day I had lunch with William Dawson. He said, 'When I ran against Earl I had a real problem. How do you compete against a man whom you admire and whose views are your own? I ignored our issues and ran against 'High Hat Earl.'"[38]

At the April 14 Democratic primary, Dawson decisively defeated Dickerson, and in November, Dawson ran against William E. King, the Republican candidate. (Mitchell had kept his promise and stepped down in favor of Dawson.) Dickerson supported Dawson, who won by a narrow margin. Had he not done so, Dawson might well have lost.

Dickerson Rejected as Alderman

In 1943, when in Washington on business for the Fair Employment Practices Committee (FEPC, which will be discussed in chapter 6), Dickerson called upon the new congressman Dawson. Dawson told Dickerson that he was going back to Chicago in a few days for a meeting of the Second Ward organization, at which its nominee for alderman in the primary elections would be named, and once again he promised that he would support Dickerson. But when Dickerson returned to Chicago, a Democratic colleague said, "You told me that Dawson was going to endorse you for reelection. But Dawson came back yesterday. He took one of his flunkies, William Harvey, down to Mayor Kelly and got Kelly's approval to have the Second Ward organization endorse Harvey instead of you. That's the way it's going to be tomorrow night." And so it was. Dickerson recalled the event: "The room was crowded. Dawson was chairman. He talked. Then his lieutenants talked. They all spoke of the 'silk stocking alderman,' referring to the seminars I had held for the people in our ward with professors from the University of Chicago. They did everything but use my name. They said, 'We want a candidate who will be meeting with the common people.' Then they called on me." Dickerson later reconstructed what he said in response:

> I recognize what is happening here. I have been trying to use the political weapons as alderman of the Second Ward to place the Negro people in a structure where they would have an equal chance to move forward with white people, to make them independent and self-moving in that direction, not slaves to the political system that dominates this city. Therefore, I organized and promoted programs to enlarge the thinking of our people by bringing to them views and ideas, and also to enlist as our allies thinkers from the larger community. I did that. You don't want that.
>
> The time perhaps is not yet here when the group of people I represented will support me. I can see now that you gentlemen know what I am doing. In your sense of values you don't consider what I have done as important to our people. Someday you will see it. I am willing to go back to my Tiber farm, like Cincinnatus, and carry on. I will carry on as a lawyer, as an executive of an insurance company, and as a citizen. I will do so in the churches, on the streets, everywhere people live. Wherever there are people, you will hear my voice asking them to join the parade of our people for full equality.

After Dickerson spoke, the vote was taken. With one or two exceptions every member of the organization voted to sponsor Dawson's candidate, William Harvey, a temporary apprentice fireman who had not been active in the Democratic organization. Dickerson never returned to the party organization after that evening.

Later, Dawson came to Dickerson and said, "I want you to keep on in the organization. I want you to be nominated for election as municipal judge." Dickerson recalled:

> Kelly called me in and told me he was going to recommend me for nomination for the municipal court the next time. At the same time he had supported two or three other aldermen, white, for the superior court. I said, "You know from the debates they are no brighter than I am. Why are you going to recommend me for the municipal court?" Then I told him he could take the job and stick it where he wanted to.

At the final meeting of the city council during his term as alderman, Dickerson delivered his valedictory. Weathers Y. Sykes, a high school student in a class visiting the city council, heard this speech. Forty years later he said: "Earl Dickerson stood up like a Lincoln, tall, slim, erect."[39] Dickerson said:

> I hope you will see the wisdom in supporting and carrying forward some of the things for which I and others have striven during this past term. Though you come from different sections of the city and are elected by people from the various wards, your responsibility must be not to your ward commitments alone—it must be to all of the people.
>
> When the people of my community are refused equal job opportunities; when they are hemmed into ghettos by restrictive covenants and left to die in disproportionate number because of inadequate health and medical facilities, an improvement in their welfare should be the concern not just of their own representatives, but of every member of the elected body of the city; for we

cannot have a great city free from disease, poverty, and crime if we permit one large group to grow up and live under substandard conditions.

Our concern for the underprivileged people should not end with the City of Chicago. If we can find sympathy in our hearts for the people in far-off countries being overrun by dictators—and I believe we should—then certainly we should have feeling for the citizens of our country who are being lynched, kicked around, and denied the right to vote.

When I view the paradox of our democracy and the gross injustice perpetrated on some of its citizens, I find myself in complete agreement with Thomas Jefferson, the author of the Declaration of Independence, who said: "I tremble for my country when I reflect that God is just and that his justice cannot sleep forever." . . .

Whether America wins the war and loses the peace, as she did in 1918, or wins them both this time, as she should, will depend in a large measure on the attitudes that men like you all over the country take toward working for complete democracy and full integration of all people into the democratic process.

Democracy is not just something that we go abroad to fight for every twenty-five years. It is a spirit and attitude toward our fellow men that should be practiced at home as well as abroad. The fight for complete democracy for all people—whether in the city council of Chicago or in the cotton fields of Mississippi—is becoming increasingly rooted in the hearts of a growing number of white and colored people. . . .

In closing I should like to quote Jefferson again. He said then, and I say now: "The hour of emancipation is advancing in the march of time, and it will come."

Chapter Five

THE FIGHT AGAINST RACIALLY
RESTRICTIVE COVENANTS

While serving as a Chicago alderman, Earl Dickerson engineered and argued the first case against racially restrictive housing covenants to be won in the U.S. Supreme Court. The Court decided the case, *Hansberry v. Lee,* on November 12, 1940, and although Dickerson's victory was based largely on a legal technicality, *Hansberry v. Lee* helped establish the groundwork for subsequent cases that would finally put an end to the enforceability of restrictive covenants. Eight years later, on May 3, 1948, in *Shelley v. Kraemer,* the Supreme Court finally ruled that no such agreement is enforceable by state courts.[1]

A racially restrictive housing covenant is a mutual agreement entered into by a group of property owners not to sell, rent, lease, or otherwise convey property to minorities, often African Americans.[2] The agreements were said "to run with the land"—that is, to be attached to the property deed and transferred to heirs and assigns of the owner or succeeding owners, all of whom were bound by the restriction. Such covenants usually remained in force until a certain date "and thereafter" unless abrogated by written agreement of the owners of 75 percent of the frontage included in the original document.

Until 1948 the racially restrictive housing covenant was a powerful instrument of racial segregation and was used extensively in Chicago to segregate a growing African American population within the so-called Black Belt. Such contracts, based on the weight of authority and practice and if properly processed, were legally binding upon all parties; were enforceable by injunction or suit for damages against any member breaking the agreement; and were enforceable through the charge of "conspiracy" against any person (individual or corporate) acting to break the agreement. The restrictive covenant was therefore among the most pernicious legal tools for maintaining racial separation. The assumption that such agreements were legal and enforceable provided an intellectual and ethical rationalization for racism, and to challenge their enforceability was therefore to strike at the very heart of segregation.

By the end of the nineteenth century African Americans had begun to move into urban areas in ever-increasing numbers. Although violence would remain the primary bulwark against integration, a number of cities instituted racially restrictive zoning ordinances to legally segregate their black populations. By 1916, Baltimore, St. Louis, Richmond, Dallas, and Oklahoma City, to name but a few, had either enacted or were considering racially restrictive zoning ordinances to reverse the trend of white urban flight and declining property values. But these efforts did not last long. Louisville, Kentucky, was to become the test case after it passed a restrictive ordinance in April 1914. William Warley, branch president of the NAACP in Louisville, arranged to purchase property from a white realtor, Charles Buchanan. Their plan was to test the Louisville ordinance in the courts by including a provision in the deed stating explicitly that either Warley could take immediate occupancy of the property or he would not be required to accept the deed or to make payment. In this way they would purposefully run afoul of the Louisville ordinance. Warley, of course, refused to pay for a property he could not occupy by law, and Buchanan then brought suit against Warley, claiming in addition that the ordinance had deprived him of his livelihood.[3] The *Buchanan v. War-*

ley case worked its way slowly through the courts, and in 1917 a unanimous U.S. Supreme Court declared the Louisville ordinance unconstitutional. The court stated: "The Fourteenth Amendment and these statutes enacted in furtherance of its purpose operate to qualify and entitle a colored man to acquire property without state legislation discriminating against him solely because of color."[4] This meant that state legislatures could no longer require residential racial segregation. Yet it left open the question whether state authority could constitutionally enforce private agreements to segregate housing on the basis of race. One legal means to residential segregation may have been closed off by the Supreme Court decision in *Buchanan v. Warley,* but another quickly sprang up to take its place.

In the 1926 case of *Corrigan v. Buckley,* the U.S. Supreme Court ruled that racially restrictive housing covenants were not unconstitutional as contract agreements,[5] and this decision was often cited in defense of restrictive covenants. However, the court did not rule on the vastly different point of whether the use of court injunction to enforce such contract agreements is constitutional. Consequently, racially restrictive covenants were to become one of the predominant means for perpetuating racial segregation in American cities until 1948.

Hansberry v. Lee

In 1937, Carl Hansberry, who was on the board of the Chicago NAACP with Earl Dickerson, mentioned that he wanted to buy a property at 6140 Rhodes Avenue.[6] He needed money and hoped that Supreme Liberty Life Insurance Company, of which Dickerson was general counsel, would lend him forty-four hundred dollars with a mortgage for security. Dickerson informed him that the Woodlawn Property Owners Association, which had a restrictive covenant in the area, would take him to court and asked whether he was willing to endure the inevitable legal battle. Hansberry answered yes, and Dickerson warned that Dr. James Hall had bought a property in the same area but was forced out by the Woodlawn Property Owners Association in the case of *Burke v. Kleiman.*[7]

Isaac Kleiman had leased a property at 6018 Vernon Avenue, within the area covered by the covenant, to James Hall, an African American. Olive Ida Burke, the wife of the president of the Woodlawn Property Owners Association, which held the covenant, brought suit against Kleiman. Unknown to Hall, this was a "dummy proceedings to establish the integrity and invulnerability of the covenant."[8] In plain language, Hall had been swindled. Kleiman had cooperated with the Woodlawn Property Owners Association to get the court to accept, by stipulation only, that the covenant had met its own terms and, without examination, that the neighborhood had not changed so much racially as to render the covenant unenforceable even if valid.

Hansberry nonetheless chose to go ahead with the purchase despite the covenant issue, and Dickerson recommended that Supreme Liberty make a loan with a mortgage on the property. The other officers and directors of the company were reluctant to do so, knowing that the company would be sued and fearing that it would lose both the suit and the money. But Dickerson eventually persuaded the company that the risk was consistent with its social goals and, in addition, that the chances of winning the suit were good. Hansberry received the loan, bought the property, and moved in. Harry H. Pace, an officer of Supreme Liberty, also bought a property in the same area but did not take up residence. In response, Anna Lee (the named plaintiff in the suit), along with other members of the Woodlawn Property Owners Association, applied to the circuit court for an injunction against Hansberry, Pace, and Supreme Liberty. Hansberry engaged C. Francis Stradford as his attorney, and Pace engaged Dickerson, who also represented Supreme Liberty and the Chicago NAACP as chairman of its Legal Redress Committee.

Over the objections of Stradford and Dickerson, Judge Michael Feinberg issued a temporary injunction ordering Hansberry to vacate the property and to convey title within thirty days "to any person other than a Negro for any consideration of its choice."[9] The injunction also ordered Pace to sell his property within the same period and on the same terms; enjoined the previous owners from selling or leasing the properties to African Americans; and also enjoined Supreme Liberty from making any further loans to African Americans for the purpose of buying property in the covenanted area. In response, Stradford and Dickerson went to the appellate court, which, without hearing the case on its merits, maintained the injunction.

Stradford and Dickerson then returned to the circuit court to have the case heard on its merits. Because *Burke v. Kleiman* was being used as a precedent to make the *Hansberry* case res judicata (a matter already decided), Stradford and Dickerson argued that in the precedent case the prospective seller of the property, Isaac Kleiman, had been induced to sign the covenant by trickery and fraud; that the owners of only about 54 percent of the frontage had signed the covenant, not the 95 percent required by law; and that *Burke v. Kleiman* was a "dummy proceedings." Judge George Bristow, the chancellor, accepted all this as proved. Nevertheless, he "reluctantly" sustained the injunction on the grounds that *Burke v. Kleiman* made the case of *Hansberry* already decided and that consequently the orders of injunction were final. By this time the thirty days Hansberry had been given to sell his property had passed, and the order provided him no compensation. (Hansberry and his family had posted bond and consequently remained in the contested property throughout the proceedings.)

During the progress of the case, Dickerson, Irwin C. Mollison, and Loring B. Moore, all graduates of the University of Chicago Law School, spoke with Robert M. Hutchins, president of the university, in an attempt to persuade him to keep the university from siding with the Woodlawn Property Owners Association. But this effort was in vain. Because the covenant was protecting its west flank, the University of Chicago paid a part of the association's legal fees, according to Dickerson, who also said, "Hutchins expressed the fear that if blacks moved into that neighborhood, the value of the property of the university would depreciate and the whole university would suffer. I have no grudge against Hutchins for this. In fact, I admire him for much that he did. But I can't give him any bouquets for the position he took on the restrictive covenant."

Stradford and Dickerson then appealed to the Illinois Supreme Court, which affirmed the injunction without a hearing. Finally, on March 11, 1940, Stradford and Dickerson filed a petition for a writ of certiorari asking the U.S. Supreme Court to hear the case. The U.S. Supreme Court granted certiorari on April 22, 1940.[10]

In preparation for their oral arguments before the Supreme Court, Dickerson and his colleagues held practice court presentations at Howard University Law School attended by students, members of the faculty, and also by several interested attorneys. Attorney Ruth Weyand, who was present at the first practice presentation and later at the actual arguments, said:

> It is my impression that this was the first in a long line of such moot court dress rehearsals in such cases, which preceded by a day or two the real thing in the Supreme Court. They were thereafter repeatedly used in subsequent civil rights cases. These sessions were not only helpful to the lawyers arguing the case at hand before the Supreme Court but also helped train a large group of black lawyers who later were appointed to the federal courts. I always gave Earl credit for this method.[11]

The case was argued on October 25, 1940.[12] The full court was present: Chief Justice Charles Evans Hughes and Associate Justices Harlan Fisk Stone, James Clark McReynolds, Owen Josephus Roberts, Stanley Forman Reed, Felix Frankfurter, William O. Douglas, Frank Murphy, and Hugo Lafayette Black.[13] Dickerson argued:

> The Illinois Supreme Court had denied [Dickerson's] clients due process of the law and equal protection of the laws that were

guaranteed by the Fourteenth Amendment. It did so by merely affirming the judgment of the lower courts that the enforceability of the covenant had already been decided in the previous case of *Burke v. Kleiman.* That affirmance was wrong because the case of *Burke v. Kleiman* did not apply to the case of *Lee v. Hansberry,* and the covenant had failed to meet its own legal requirements. Therefore, decrees enforcing it were null and void in both *Burke v. Kleiman* and *Lee v. Hansberry.*[14]

Dickerson said the covenant was unenforceable because the requisite percentage of owners had not signed the agreement. The plaintiffs in the suit argued, in response, that this issue was already determined in the *Burke* case and consequently could not be raised again. The Illinois Supreme Court had agreed, but the question now turned to whether the *Burke* case actually constituted an applicable class action, which would determine whether this matter was, in fact, res judicata. The U.S. Supreme Court determined that it was not and that the interests of the parties in both cases did not involve property in common, but only a common issue. Consequently, the presumed class in question was inapplicable, and the parties in the *Burke* case could not now represent the parties in *Hansberry v. Lee.* The issue of percentages (and consequently the enforceability of the covenant) was thereby opened to adjudication. The main question here was whether the decision in the *Burke* case, which upheld the original restrictive covenant, precluded the efforts of Dickerson to reexamine the agreement in order to determine whether it had met the necessary conditions for enforceability. If it did not, the Woodlawn covenant could once again be brought into question directly in the *Hansberry* case.[15]

Dickerson also made a second and broader argument that the enforcement of the covenant was unconstitutional, but this was not given sufficient priority by either Dickerson or by the Court. It would seem that Dickerson felt he stood a better chance of winning the case by emphasizing the technical issues. The Court therefore focused the greatest part of its attention on issues involving class suits and neglected the underlying constitutional questions.[16] For this reason the key issue of constitutionality and enforceability was left unresolved until the 1948 decisions in *Shelley v. Kraemer* and *Sipes v. McGhee.*

The U.S. Supreme Court decided *Hansberry v. Lee* on November 12, 1940. Justice Stone delivered the opinion for a unanimous Court. The following is a summary of the Court's findings: *Burke v. Kleiman* was not a class suit in which Carl Hansberry and the other petitioners were represented, and therefore they were not bound by the injunction in the *Burke v. Kleiman* case;[17] the Illinois Supreme Court's decision that the issue in *Hansberry v. Lee* had already been decided in *Burke v. Kleiman* was in violation of due process.

The immediate effect of the Supreme Court's decision in the *Hansberry* case was to terminate the racially restrictive covenant attaching to all properties extending from Sixtieth Street on the north to Sixty-third Street on the south and from South Parkway (now King Drive) on the west to Cottage Grove on the east. Consequently, a new and better residential area became available for the first time to African Americans in the city of Chicago, and this helped to relieve the congested housing situation.[18]

CARL HANSBERRY'S DAUGHTER, Lorraine, who was only ten years old at the time of the decision, later portrayed the human cost of these events in her play *A Raisin in the Sun.* The play premiered on March 11, 1959, on Broadway and was received as one of the most important American literary works of its time. Critics ranked it with the plays of Eugene O'Neill and Arthur Miller, and it was hailed as inaugurating a new era in black theater. *A Raisin in the Sun* won the award for best play of the New York Drama Critics' Circle in 1959, and a subsequent film adaptation (also written by Hansberry) received a Cannes Film Festival award in 1961. But controversy also accompanied acclaim, and for a time the play was a lightning rod in some circles for the tensions and controversies emerging within the civil rights movement of the 1960s. In 1961 an interviewer asked Lorraine Hansberry, "Someone says, 'This is not really a Negro play.' What do you say?" She answered:

> They are trying to say something very good—that the characters in our play transcend categories. However . . . I believe that one of the most sound ideas in dramatic writing is that to create the universal, you must pay very great attention to the specific. . . . Not only is this a Negro family, specifically, definitely, and culturally, but it's not even a New York Negro family or a Southern Negro family. It is specifically a South Side Chicago family. . . . I think people, to the extent they accept the family and believe them as they are supposed to be, to that extent the family can become everybody.[19]

There were those within the more radical branch of the black activist community who misconstrued these comments to mean that Hansberry was concerned less with the distinctiveness of African American experience than with universal themes that could just as easily apply to the struggles of any other beleaguered social or ethnic group.[20] The importance of affirming a uniquely black American identity, with its roots in African heritage and culture, was presumably given short shrift by the play in favor of a predominantly integrationist vision rooted in the promise of white middle-class entitlement and mainstream values. Although this argument did not take stock of Lorraine Hansberry's wide-ranging views on race in America, it was nevertheless to cause her some grief and probably contributed to her gradual radicalization in the 1960s prior to her tragic and premature death in 1965.[21]

The legal battle to defeat restrictive covenants on Chicago's South Side was spearheaded by upwardly mobile, middle-class African Americans such as Carl Hansberry, Harry Pace, and Earl Dickerson. Yet by the early 1960s such efforts to achieve integration were viewed as fundamentally "assimilationist" by a small but growing number of radicalized black activists and intellectuals and were increasingly criticized for neglecting the importance of African

American identity, heritage, and, most important, self-reliance. The rise of radical separatist groups such as the Black Muslims and the Black Panthers in the 1960s, which emphasized the intractability of racism in America, and the corresponding need for black autonomy and self-sufficiency began to cast a growing shadow over the efforts of groups such as the NAACP and the Urban League, which were committed to integration through sanctioned legal, political, and economic means. In addition, the success of Martin Luther King Jr.'s strategies of direct action, although integrationist, also challenged the idea that equality for African Americans could ever be won wholly through legal reform within the established white political, institutional framework.

A new generation of educated blacks in the late 1950s and 1960s were rediscovering both their African heritage and unique African American identity and at the same time were responding to the failures of the civil rights movement up to that point. The charge of assimilationism was sometimes leveled against their predecessors, who were perceived as having rejected African American history and heritage in pursuit of a dream of social and economic equality that never seemed to materialize for the majority of black Americans. These are the sorts of charges to which Lorraine Hansberry found herself responding. By 1961 (roughly two years after the play first opened) she was becoming a controversial figure in some radical circles for whom her play had come to embody the failed promise of equality and the social and cultural costs that this failure threatened to exact on African Americans.

The misunderstanding and misrepresentation of Lorraine Hansberry's appeal to "universalism" in defense of *A Raisin in the Sun*[22] must therefore be viewed within the context of the increasing friction within the black activist community of the 1960s, supported by two key personal issues. First, Hansberry's portrayal of the Younger family bore a rather limited resemblance to the circumstances of her own family, who were upwardly mobile, middle-class African Americans. Lorraine's father, Carl, was a fairly successful businessman who owned apartment buildings on Chicago's

South Side that were rented to blacks. Some people regarded him as a slumlord (perhaps unfairly) whose aspirations to personal success and wealth had eclipsed his concern for the plight of his fellow African Americans. His reputation eventually became so tarnished in Chicago that he moved his family to the West Coast. The Youngers in *A Raisin in the Sun,* on the other hand, were portrayed as a working-class black family struggling at a subsistence level in a tiny kitchenette apartment in the Chicago ghetto—a far cry from the circumstances of Carl Hansberry and his family. James Baldwin makes a brief and disparaging reference to this accusation in his introduction to Lorraine Hansberry's memoir *To Be Young, Gifted and Black.*[23]

Second, Hansberry was married to a white man named Robert Nemiroff whose success as a songwriter allowed her the leisure to write *A Raisin in the Sun* and whose connections were said to have contributed to its success. Malcolm X wrote a widely circulated article in *Mohammed Speaks* condemning interracial marriage, which cited Hansberry's marriage to Nemiroff as an example of the divided loyalties perpetuated by such unions within the black community. Although Malcolm X later famously changed his views, for the time being the damage was done.[24]

Behind personal attacks such as these loomed a larger issue concerning the very means and objectives of the civil rights movement in America. On the one side were those (often older figures in the movement) who believed that full civil rights would be achieved gradually through legal reform guided by the ideals of the U.S. Constitution. For them the battle was to be waged primarily in the courtroom and through patient but firm negotiation. On the other side were those who believed that the roots of racism in America were too deep to be overcome by working strictly within the law; they advocated a more resistant and even combative stance. Dickerson grasped the legitimate claims of both camps, and any effort to understand his role in the history of the civil rights movement must take this into account. He was certainly a political idealist who believed in the universal promise of established democratic institutions, which could only be realized step-by-step through persistent legal and social reform. But he was also a pragmatist who recognized that challenging racism in America also meant confronting an obdurate social and economic system, often supported by law, and that this sometimes required more radical measures. This is especially evident in his activist stance as a Chicago alderman and his subsequently being rejected, both by white city government officials and by many of his fellow black politicians. Also, his work on the Fair Employment Practices Committee, which again ended in his effective dismissal, shows him to have been a more radical and uncompromising figure than many of his contemporaries. By the same token he was intolerant of racial separatism of any sort, and this perhaps distanced him from a generation of more militant activists.

Dickerson believed firmly that the advancement of the black middle class was crucial to the advancement of African Americans as a whole, and his representation of Carl Hansberry before the U.S. Supreme Court underscored his commitment to this view. That this commitment also indicates an assimilationist view of the sort with which Lorraine Hansberry was unfairly charged is less than half true and ignores the larger objectives of Dickerson's efforts. He placed considerable emphasis on rights of property and home ownership for black Americans, but these aspirations did not preclude either an active commitment to the African American poor or a willingness to fight with uncompromising conviction for their cause. The failure of *Hansberry v. Lee* to defeat racially restrictive covenants on constitutional grounds (which would have to wait until the landmark decision in *Shelley v. Kraemer* in 1948) did not diminish its importance to working black families in Chicago who were hemmed in from all sides and prevented by law from expanding into the adjoining all-white Woodlawn neighborhood. The decision in *Hansberry v. Lee* opened this residential area to African Americans once and for all and constituted the first real victory against a restrictive covenant in Chicago. Lorraine Hansberry's account of her experiences during *Hansberry v. Lee*, however fictionalized, provides a unique opportunity to reevaluate Dickerson's achievements in light of the controversy the play was capable of generating.

The friction between middle-class integrationist aspirations and the preservation of African American identity is given a clear voice in *A Raisin in the Sun* through Beneatha Younger's vociferous enthusiasm for African culture and the patient yet disdainful response this elicits in both Ruth and Lena (the other two women of the family). For them, moving to a white neighborhood represents the promise of a better life and an end to the grinding poverty of the Chicago ghetto, and any talk of African heritage or identity is treated as little more than a misplaced youthful enthusiasm.

In the play the Youngers receive a life insurance payment of ten thousand dollars after the death of the family patriarch and paternal grandfather. The family—which includes Walter; his wife, Ruth; their small son, Travis; Walter's teenage sister, Beneatha; and their mother, Lena—live in a cramped kitchenette apartment typical of black neighborhoods on the South Side of Chicago at that time. Walter, who works as a chauffeur, wants to use the money to start a business, and his sister, Beneatha, needs tuition to attend medical school. But Mama Lena (the beneficiary of the policy) uses half of the money to make a down payment on a house for the family in an all-white neighborhood. She then entrusts the remainder to Walter for his business and for Beneatha's education. The family is then approached by Karl Lindner, a white man representing the neighborhood association where they plan to move. At first he insinuates and eventually admits that as African Americans they are not welcome, and then he offers to buy back the house at a profit to the Youngers. Walter, in the meantime, has lost all the remaining money in a crooked business deal and favors accepting Lindner's offer. At the last minute and after much painful deliberation, the family rejects the neighborhood association's offer and prepares to move into their new home, ready to face whatever comes. At the end of the play, though, we discover that Beneatha's African boyfriend, Asagai, whom she met at college, has proposed marriage and that she plans to go to Africa with him. Having resolved their differences and excited over the prospect of a new life in a better neighborhood, the family members are packing the last of their belongings, and we are left with a mother-daughter dialogue in which Lena objects to Beneatha's plans and urges her to stay in the United States and marry a man with money.

Far from ignoring the contentious issue of African American identity and the consequences of assimilationism, Hansberry addresses this directly in a conversation left hanging at the end of the play. An apprehension that was beginning to plague the civil rights movement at the onset of the 1960s becomes, in Hansberry's dialogue, an unresolved issue for the Younger family itself. Is a loss of African American identity implied by the move to a white neighborhood? Is it possible to enter the larger society while maintaining one's ethnic and cultural uniqueness? Does universalism imply the defeat of particularity, and is the uniqueness of black experience effaced by the wish to become and to be treated as middle-class Americans? Lorraine Hansberry's play situates her experience within the framework of such troubling questions as these and defies its audience to resolve them neatly.

PERHAPS THE BEST way to evaluate the issue of *Hansberry v. Lee* is to look directly to the effect it had on the Chicago South Side neighborhoods adjoining Hyde Park. White residents in these areas reacted to the decision in two stages. For more than a decade there was panic accompanied by attempts to shore up racially restrictive covenants through violence. Then, beginning in the 1950s, in Hyde Park–Kenwood and southeast Chicago, a successful movement began to achieve a stable interracial community (which will be discussed in a later chapter).

For the immediate reaction we can draw upon a slim volume published by the Fisk University Press in 1947.[25] Concerning the panic and defensive reactions to the *Hansberry* decision in southeast Chicago, the authors give a number of specific instances, such as:

The Oakland-Kenwood Property Owners Association, one of Chicago's most vocal and powerful neighborhood groups, acclaimed in its report these accomplishments for the year 1943–44:

1. The eviction of undesirables—Negroes—from dwellings at 4608 Drexel Boulevard, 44th and University, Northwest corner of 47th Street and Woodlawn Avenue;

2. Successful opposition to a bill to nullify race restrictive agreements;

3. The initiation of suits to restrain sale to Negroes of four pieces of property between 39th and 40th Streets on Ellis and Oak Park Avenues and on Oakwood Boulevard;

4. The initiation of suits to restrain sale to Negroes of seven pieces of property between 36th and 42nd Streets on Ellis and Lake Park Avenues;

5. The renewal of interest in restrictive agreements through organization of block-by-block anti-Negro contracts.[26]

The Federation of Neighborhood Associations in Chicago, sharing offices with the Woodlawn Property Owners Association, published a twenty-six-page pamphlet in July 1944 dealing with restrictive covenants. The pamphlet gave justification for the use of such agreements and called for support on behalf of the 350,000 whites from Chicago in the armed forces who were presumably fighting to keep their neighborhoods racially segregated. The federation warned against having to greet the returning white soldier with the excuse: "You have won a good fight. We are going to give you a job to help pay for the victory. But, at the request of a very limited number of people hereabouts, we have altered your home and neighborhood conditions while you were away fighting for America. So sorry."[27] The Kenwood–Hyde Park Property Owners' Improvement Association devoted an entire section in its 1943 report to the justification of racial restrictions.

A report of the Chicago Commission Against Religious and Racial Discrimination indicates that the number of terrorist attacks on black homes in Chicago during a two-year period after *Hansberry v. Lee* almost doubled in comparison to the number of similar incidents occurring within a two-year period preceding the 1919 riot. From July 1, 1917, to July 27, 1919, there were twenty-four arson bombings against black homes in Chicago, while from May 1, 1944, to July 20, 1946, there were forty-six such acts of violence. These were without exception cases where black families rented or bought homes in white neighborhoods.[28]

Although the immediate violent aftermath of the *Hansberry* case could be construed as a setback in the fight for integration when viewed strictly in terms of the subsequent racist reaction, in the long run it was a necessary if painful step toward the final defeat of legal segregation in the United States.

In the spring of 1947, Dickerson bought a luxurious three-story building at 5027 South Drexel Boulevard. This is more than one block east and several blocks south of the previous racial dividing line. After extended litigation, Earl, Kathryn, and their daughter, Diane, took up residence in August 1949. They were the first African Americans to live in Hyde Park since the pre–World War I period. Judge William Sylvester White recalled an anecdote from the early 1950s: "I lived next door to Earl when he lived in a beautiful three-flat building, surrounded by a quarter of an acre of lawn, enclosed by an iron fence. One Sunday morning my father and I were returning from church and we saw a white man riding a lawn-mower cutting Dickerson's grass. My dad said, 'I never thought I'd live to see the day when a white man on Sunday would be cutting a Negro's lawn.'"[29]

Covenants Declared Unenforceable

The legal principle announced by the U.S. Supreme Court in the 1940 *Hansberry* case concerning the limits on class suits left considerable room for interpretation in the lower courts. After *Hansberry*, several state courts upheld racially restrictive covenants, and several others invalidated them. In December 1945 the Superior

Court of Los Angeles voided a covenant on a technicality, and one of the judges based his concurrence on the principle that it violated the Fourteenth Amendment. He wrote: "It is time that members of the Negro race are accorded, without reservation or evasion, the full rights guaranteed under the Fourteenth Amendment. Judges have been avoiding the real issue too long."[30]

Cases were approaching the U.S. Supreme Court that would force it to face the issue squarely. One was *Shelley v. Kraemer*. Kraemer, a white man, brought suit against Shelley, an African American, to enjoin his ownership and occupancy of a property in St. Louis on the ground that it was part of an area protected by a restrictive covenant. The Circuit Court of St. Louis held that the covenant was not effective because the requisite number of signatures had not been obtained. The Supreme Court of Missouri reversed the judgment, holding that the covenant was indeed effective and its enforcement violated no rights guaranteed Shelley by the U.S. Constitution. The case then went to the U.S. Supreme Court as *Shelley v. Kraemer*. A similar case, *Sipes v. McGhee*, went to the U.S. Supreme Court from Michigan at around the same time. The Supreme Court ordered writs of certiorari to the courts of both Missouri and Michigan and heard them together on January 15–16, 1948. Both were decided on May 3, 1948.

Although Dickerson was not directly involved in these cases, he worked closely with organizations that helped fight them. Thurgood Marshall and Loren Miller argued the case for Sipes, and on the brief with them were eleven other attorneys. Marshall was head of the NAACP Legal Defense Fund at that time, and all the other lawyers on the brief were also members of the Defense Fund. Four members of the National Lawyers Guild (NLG) were amici curiae (friends of the court) in the case, and Dickerson was then on the executive committee of the NLG. Three members of the National Bar Association (NBA) were also amici curiae—Dickerson, Richard E. Westbrooks, and Loring Moore. Dickerson was then completing his second year as president of the NBA.

But perhaps most important, in declaring the judicial enforcement of restrictive covenants unconstitutional in the combined cases of *Shelley* and *Sipes*, the U.S. Supreme Court cited two precedent cases: one was *Corrigan v. Buckley*, and the other was *Hansberry v. Lee*.

The decision of the U.S. Supreme Court in these cases is clear:

> Private agreements to exclude persons of designated race or color from the use or occupancy of real estate for residential purposes do not violate the Fourteenth Amendment; but it is violative of the equal protection clause of the Fourteenth Amendment for state courts to enforce them. . . .
>
> Such private agreements standing alone do not violate any rights guaranteed by the Fourteenth Amendment. . . .
>
> The actions of state courts and judicial officers in their official capacities are actions of the states within the meaning of the Fourteenth Amendment. . . .
>
> In granting judicial enforcement of such private agreements in these cases, the states acted to deny petitioners the equal protection of the laws, contrary to the Fourteenth Amendment.[31]

On the same day, May 3, 1948, in *Hurd v. Hodge* (334 U.S. 24), the U.S. Supreme Court also ruled that under the guarantee of due process in the Fifth Amendment, federal and state courts are prohibited from enforcing restrictive covenants.

These rulings did not end residential segregation, of course, nor did they readily open up existing housing to black residents. One study found that the availability of housing was still "subject to the realities of various other devices designed to prevent Negro entry."[32] Nevertheless, the enforcement of racially restrictive covenants by the state had been declared unconstitutional, and in this victory Earl Dickerson played a significant role.

Chapter Six

THE FIRST FAIR EMPLOYMENT
PRACTICES COMMITTEE

During the early years of World War II, African American workers profited from the defense effort even less than they had during
World War I. World War I began with a labor shortage, World War
II with a labor surplus of ten years' standing—and blacks made up
a large part of that surplus. A fourth (25.9 percent) of all black
males above fourteen years of age and over a tenth (12.2 percent)
of the females were "seeking work" in private industry. Most were
on relief, worked for the WPA, or were being supported by friends
or relatives. This was at least three times the unemployment rate
among the white population.[1]

As the defense program grew, the relative status of blacks in employment service placements in twenty selected defense industries
declined by 53 percent between October 1940 and April 1941.[2]
The president of North American Aviation Company expressed the
view of that industry when he said in the spring of 1941, "Regardless of their training as aircraft workers, we will not employ Negroes in North American plants. It is against company policy."[3] The
general organizer of Aeronautical Mechanics Local 751 of Seattle
expressed the views of most AFL and independent unions when he
said, "Organized labor has been called upon to make many sac-

rifices for defense and has made them gladly but this [the hiring of African Americans] is too much."[4] The U.S. Office of Education and state employment services cooperated with employers who discriminated against minority groups, particularly blacks,[5] and the training-within-industry programs sponsored by the Office of Production Management (OPM) discriminated increasingly.[6] Walter White, executive secretary of the NAACP, reported that the OPM refused to meet with any black delegation and that President Roosevelt had not responded to numerous requests to speak out against discriminatory hiring.[7]

African Americans supported defense against the Axis powers because they understood better than any other group the consequences of the racist policies of the Nazis and Fascists. Indeed, they fiercely resented the barriers against their full participation in the U.S. armed services. Although short of manpower, the army segregated black soldiers, the navy restricted black sailors to menial jobs, and the other branches excluded them altogether.

This situation provoked a nationwide protest and a threatened march on Washington, which brought about results that were to alter American society permanently. It broke the passive acceptance of the two established political parties among African Americans— the Republican until 1936 and the Democratic from then until 1941. It broke the black community's dependence on the leadership of white liberals and led to a questioning of the uncritical support for President Franklin D. Roosevelt, who had been more popular among blacks than any president since Abraham Lincoln. Mr. Roosevelt had to be pressured to give an executive order against discriminatory hiring, and Mrs. Roosevelt was then called upon to persuade African American leaders to cancel the scheduled protest march on Washington.

The protest also questioned the generally accepted belief, as expressed in 1896 by the U.S. Supreme Court in *Plessy v. Ferguson*, that "legislation is powerless to abolish . . . situations based on physical differences" and challenged the idea that African Americans were peripheral to American life. As one commentator suggested:

> One may even be so bold as to say, the opposition to the idea of a fair employment practice law, or support of it—and this is certainly true of the South—has been determined in large part by the prevailing conception of the place of the Negro in American economic life. In this sense, the rights of Negroes have been the touchstone for the rights of all minority groups in this country. The affirmation of their rights has meant the affirmation of the rights of all minority groups, indeed of all Americans.[8]

Earl Dickerson played a key role in ameliorating these circumstances during the war.[9] He was a member of the first Fair Employment Practices Committee (FEPC) and its acting chairman much of the time. He insisted that the committee hold public hearings and publicize its findings instead of simply conducting studies and giving reports. Because of his aggressiveness and his skill as a lawyer, he was the committee's most effective member in the public hearings. As acting chairman of the committee he forced Roosevelt's hand when the president's backing of the FEPC faltered. The ensuing public agitation pressured the president to create a second committee and give it strong support. Yet, because he crossed Roosevelt and defied the authority of the chairman of the War Manpower Commission, Dickerson was the only one of the four remaining members of the first committee not appointed to the second FEPC. Indeed, many thought that the main reason for the creation of the second committee was to get rid of Dickerson.

The catchphrase of the movement that finally pressured Roosevelt to establish the FEPC was "double victory"—victory for democracy abroad *through* victory for democracy at home. Despair drove the movement, and increasing anger at the betrayal of African American hopes fueled it. Those hopes had been kindled and then extinguished by the Emancipation Proclamation, by the Reconstruction, and by World War I with its slogan "Make the world safe for democracy." As World War II approached, white leaders, with President Roosevelt as their most eloquent spokesman, proclaimed even more fervently than they had during World War I that the survival of the democratic way of life was at stake and that the extension of democracy was their aim. Yet African American hopes were being frustrated once again.

The ignition of African American anger during this period can probably be traced to September 27, 1940. On that day President Roosevelt, Secretary of the Navy Frank Knox, and Secretary of War Robert P. Patterson met with Walter White of the NAACP, A. Philip Randolph of the Brotherhood of Sleeping Car Porters (BSCP), and T. Arnold Hill of the National Urban League. This was the first time black leaders had gained access to the highest government officials, and the meeting took place shortly after the Selective Service Act had been passed. It was toward the end of Roosevelt's reelection campaign against Wendell Willkie, and the African American delegation urged the president to integrate the armed forces as well as ensure fair employment in government agencies and defense industries. The president said he would consider their request and make a suitable reply. On October 9 the White House issued a statement saying that the policy of the War Department "is not to intermingle colored and white personnel in the same organization." White House Secretary Stephen Early explained that the segregation policy "was approved after Mr. Roosevelt had conferred with Walter White of the NAACP, two other Negroes, and Secretary of the Navy Frank Knox and Assistant Secretary of the Army Robert Patterson," implying, intentionally or not, that black leaders had surrendered. Almost simultaneously the U.S. Senate killed a federal anti-lynching bill.[10]

Earl Dickerson's activities in the pursuit of fair employment were of long standing in Illinois and, as his influence grew, throughout the country. On November 6, 1940, as president of the Chicago Urban League, he had called upon the national body "to mobilize countrywide agitation to move President Roosevelt to issue an executive order requiring equitable employment of black workers in government and defense industries." The *Chicago Sun* of April 17, 1941, reported:

> Alderman Earl B. Dickerson of Chicago, who is chairman of the war production committee of the National Negro Congress, conferred with War Production Chief Donald Nelson on proposals for increased use of Negro manpower in the war production program. The Dickerson plan calls for training 50,000 Negroes for war production industries in the next three months and other steps to take advantage of the vast pool of unemployed Negroes. One step would be to recommend that President Roosevelt appoint a Negro member on the proposed War Manpower Board.

The *Chicago Defender* of July 12, 1941, under a headline "Leaders Ask Roosevelt to Name Dickerson to New OPM Board," named those making the request as Miss Charlotte Carr of Hull House, Ira Williams of the Chicago NAACP, Albon L. Foster of the Chicago Urban League, Samuel Goldsmith of Chicago Jewish Charities, and Mrs. Irene McCoy Goins of the Chicago Council of Negro Organizations.

On January 15, 1941, A. Philip Randolph first made the suggestion that blacks organize a march on Washington to attain the integration of the armed services and fair employment in government agencies and war industries. The proposal grew from a goal of ten thousand to fifty thousand and finally to one hundred thousand; from a possible bluff that the president could ignore to a possibility that had to be taken seriously; from a threat that could be averted to a final showdown between black leaders and President Roosevelt.[11] Walter White recalled a meeting with FDR to discuss this problem: "The president turned to me and asked, 'Walter, how many people will *really* march?' I told him, 'No less than one hundred thousand.' The president looked me full in the eye for a long time in an obvious effort to find out whether I was bluffing or exaggerating. Eventually he appeared to believe I meant what I said. 'What do you want me to do?' he asked."

Randolph told the president that he wanted him to issue an unequivocal executive order to effectuate the speediest possible abolition of discrimination in war industries and the armed forces.[12]

On the day of the showdown, June 18, 1941, the president appointed a committee to draw up an agreement. As a result the president issued an order, on June 25, and Randolph called off the March scheduled for July 1.[13] (Many African Americans accused Randolph of a "sellout" because the executive order dealt only with discriminatory hiring and not with segregation in the armed forces. On the other hand, the only African American in Congress, Democrat Arthur W. Mitchell of the First Congressional District of Illinois, viewed Randolph as a real threat to the racial status quo and called him "the most dangerous Negro in America.")[14]

What would have happened if the president had not yielded and if black leaders had not accepted half a loaf? When asked this question in 1983, Dickerson, who himself was prepared to march, said simply, "The blacks would have taken to the streets."

EXECUTIVE ORDER 8802, issued on June 25, 1941, was the most important effort in the history of the United States up to that time to use federal authority to eliminate discrimination in employment and in union membership. The order declared it "the duty of employers and of labor organizations . . . to provide for the full and equitable participation of all workers in defense industries, without discrimination because of race, creed, or color, or national origin." It ordered all federal departments and agencies concerned with vocational and training programs for defense production to administer such programs without discrimination and all defense contracts thereafter negotiated by agencies of the federal government to include "a provision obligating the contractor not to discriminate because of race, creed, or national origin." The order established a committee, unsalaried, with a chairman and four members appointed to the OPM by the president. However, the committee was an independent body, responsible only to the president and dependent on his discretionary funds (two points that were later to become crucial). The committee was "to receive and investigate complaints of discrimination," redress valid grievances, and recommend measures required to implement the order to government agencies and to the president.[15]

Executive Order 8802 was enormously significant in that it was the first time since the Reconstruction period that the federal government had intervened on behalf of the rights of black Americans. This order, wittingly or not, laid the groundwork for equal employment statutes that subsequently became law in forty-six states.[16] It also laid the groundwork for the Federal Civil Rights Acts of 1957 and 1964.

By Executive Order 8823, issued on July 18, 1941, the president added a fifth member to the committee in addition to the chairman. The chairman was Mark Ethridge, publisher of the *Louisville Courier-Journal,* a moderate southerner. The other members were David Sarnoff, president of the Radio Corporation of America; William Green, president of the AFL; and Philip Murray, president of the CIO. (Because these two labor leaders could not attend the meetings, Roosevelt later appointed Frank Fenton as alternate to Green and John Brophy as alternate to Murray. Fenton resigned in December 1942 and was succeeded by Boris Shishkin.) The committee was then increased to six, and two new black members were appointed. One was Milton P. Webster, first vice president of the Brotherhood of Sleeping Car Porters, who was Randolph's surrogate. The other was Earl Dickerson, who was Walter White's choice.

One can only speculate why the two new black members were appointed. Randolph would surely have insisted on black appointees because the March on Washington was his brainchild, and restricting the protest to African Americans was his tactic.[17] There were also reasons that Walter White, executive secretary of the NAACP, would have wanted a black member who supported his views. While the NAACP supported the march, its policy had always been interracial, whereas the proposed march was closed to whites. Moreover, the NAACP had never been able to fire the imagination of the African American populace and was in danger of losing its primacy to a brand-new organization, the March on Washington Committee, which Randolph was already making into a continuing March on Washington movement.[18]

White recommended Dickerson because, as alderman of the Second Ward in the Chicago City Council, he had established himself as an uncompromising fighter for equal rights and opportunities. Also, as chairman of the Legal Redress Committee of the Chicago NAACP he had led the struggle against discrimination in many cases, including the celebrated victory over restrictive covenants in the U.S. Supreme Court's 1940 *Hansberry v. Lee* decision. He was also a director of the national NAACP and president of the Chicago Urban League and was well known not only by the board and staff of the national NAACP[19] and the National Urban League but also nationally through newspaper stories about his activities.

The Fair Employment Practices Committee, appointed in full on July 18, went right to work. The *New York Amsterdam News* of July 26, 1941, reported:

> Roosevelt's Fair Employment Practice Committee today held its first meeting and mapped its fight to end job bias. After meeting with William Knudsen and Sidney Hillman [joint heads of the Office of Production Management (OPM), under which the FEPC had been placed for administration], the committee agreed to meet every Monday noon in the Social Security Building.

The *St. Louis Call* of August 8 reported:

> The first official act of the President's recently created FEPC was to ask the chief executive to instruct all the Federal agencies and departments to abolish discrimination against Negroes seeking government work. The letter to the President was instigated by

committee member Earl B. Dickerson. The Joint declaration by the FEPC and the Council for Personnel Administration was signed by President Roosevelt.

On August 12, Lawrence W. Cramer, professor at the Harvard Law School, was employed by the committee as its executive secretary. Robert C. Weaver, an African American on the staff of the Labor Division of the Office of Production Management, headed the committee's staff.

The FEPC was in business,[20] but with a budget for the first year of only eighty thousand dollars[21]—too little for regional offices and personal investigation. Therefore, during several weeks of organizing and planning, the committee decided to hold a series of public hearings in each major section of the country in order to get the facts, to publicize and explain the existence and purpose of the committee, and, where possible, through direct negotiations and the pressure of public opinion, to resolve cases of discrimination established during the hearings.

In 1984 attorney Elmer Henderson said that the FEPC decided to hold public hearings at Dickerson's insistence. Henderson was chosen in November 1941 to direct activities in eight states, including Illinois. (He had headed the staff of the Illinois State Commission on the Condition of the Urban Colored Population from 1940 to 1941.) Henderson commented on Dickerson's role in the hearings:

> The other members of the FEPC were generally supportive of its objective, but most were passive. Earl put passion into it. The hearings were his idea. Otherwise the committee would have made a study and issued a report. But Earl said, "No. We must go around the country holding hearings, showing discrimination and how it impedes the war effort." His role in the FEPC was pretty much as it had been in the Illinois Commission. Because of the force of his personality and his ability to make his points so well, the committee did pretty much as he wanted it to. It was a rocky road. There were many differences of opinion.[22]

The pattern of the hearings was (1) the chairman would explain the executive order, (2) the committee would call upon prominent citizens in the region for information, and (3) the committee would question representatives of management or unions against which complaints of discrimination had been filed. These representatives had the right to counsel. Afterward, in executive session, the committee would decide on action in cases that had not been resolved in public. As the only lawyer on the committee, Dickerson regularly went to each city a day or two before the hearings to examine the witnesses charging discrimination.

Opening the Los Angeles hearing on October 20 and 21, 1941, the chairman, Mark Ethridge, stated that the proceedings were not to be considered a trial. However, the three subsequent hearings and one subcommittee hearing were conducted as though they were court proceedings, and even the Los Angeles hearing had aspects of a trial.[23] For example, at that hearing Dickerson asked the head of Lockheed-Vega Aircraft, who had testified that the corporation needed employees, "How many employees did you hire last month?"

The executive answered, "About forty-one thousand."

Knowing the number, Dickerson asked, "Of that forty-one thousand, how many Negroes?"

The executive replied, "Nine."

Dickerson pursued: "In what departments?"

"The custodial department."

"You mean they are janitors, don't you?"

"Yes," the embarrassed executive replied.

At the close of the session many young people, black and white, thronged around Dickerson. Extensive coverage was given to this exchange by the Los Angeles papers and by black papers nationally. The *Omaha Star* of October 31, 1941, ran a story headed "Dickerson's Action Praised; Hailed a Second Lincoln," with a subhead, "Proved Master Cross-Examining Company Officials."

At its first hearing the committee faced the question of how to prove the existence of discrimination. It worked out two sets of criteria, one for employers and the other for unions, which would be accepted as prima facie evidence of discrimination. Using these, after each hearing the committee issued directives to employers and unions found guilty of discrimination to "cease and desist" from specified activities. Here, taken from the committee's files, are four examples of fact patterns applied to employers: (1) the practice of "employing members of minority groups as laborers or in custodial work regardless of their particular skills" (Los Angeles hearings); (2) the hiring of employees "based upon the theory that religious beliefs are an indication of employment qualifications" (Chicago hearings); (3) the submission by an employer to public or private employment agencies of requirements for workers bearing racial or religious qualifications (New York hearings); and (4) the refusal to hire blacks unless certified by a labor union that discriminates against blacks in its certifications (Chicago hearings).[24] Here are three examples of the fact patterns applied to unions: (1) the refusal to admit blacks to membership or to permit them to work in any capacity as long as members of the union are not employed (Los Angeles hearings); (2) the barring from membership of blacks or other minority groups by exclusionary clauses in their constitutions, practice, custom, tradition, or other device (Chicago hearings); and (3) the opposition to employment of blacks except on condition that the employer arranges to have white and black workers in separate buildings (Birmingham hearings).[25]

The hearings, which took place in four cities, involved forty-nine industries, unions, and defense programs and revealed a widespread pattern of discrimination. Seventy-five percent of the cases of discrimination involved African Americans, 10 percent Jews, and 15 percent other minorities.[26] But the committee had no power to enforce its "directives." At most it could call on the federal contracting and regulatory agencies to punish the violators by intermediate sanctions such as cancellation of contracts or the denial of manpower and material priorities; or it could ultimately refer the case to the president for disposition. The government agencies were free to act or not to act, and, of course, the committee had no power over the president except possibly through public opinion.

The hearings in Chicago on January 19 and 20, 1942, were held in the chambers of the city council, where Dickerson was an alderman. Clementine Skinner attended them and later recalled: "After a minister invoked the blessing, Mayor Edward J. Kelly welcomed the committee and then started to leave. Earl said, 'Mr. Mayor, I think you should hear this. The audience knows the situation that is going to be revealed.' Red-faced, the mayor went back and sat down."[27] The Chicago findings led to directives to such large local plants as Buick Aviation, Studebaker, Majestic Radio, Stewart-Warner, and Hallicrafters Radio.[28]

The hearings in New York City on February 16 and 17, 1942, found unfair employment practices by employers and discriminatory policies by unions, as it had found in Los Angeles and Chicago, and also found the same vicious circle perpetuated by employers, unions, and government agencies: a member of a minority group could not get a job if he or she did not have the necessary training and was refused the necessary training for lack of proof that a job was waiting.[29] At the New York meeting the committee decided to hold a follow-up hearing in Chicago on charges of discriminatory policies by unions. A subcommittee composed of Dickerson, as chairman, Frank Fenton, and Milton P. Webster held a follow-up hearing in the chambers of the city council on April 11, 1942. These are documented through a press report in the *Chicago Bee* of April 12, 1942:

> A controversial, stormy session attended the FEPC subcommittee hearing in the City Hall chambers here Saturday, when Negro plumbers and steamfitters openly accused the AFL-affiliated Chicago Journeymen Plumbers Union, Local 310, and the Steamfitters Protective Association, Local 597, with discriminatory practices in agreeing to keep colored qualified workers out of unions. Vigorous denials by union officials and white contractors

to the charges precipitated a heated discussion, which ended in the subcommittee holding that unions were seeking "a purported agreement as an excuse for barring Negroes from membership in their organization."

Chairman Dickerson concluded: "It is my conviction that, while we must use all our efforts to make war against the Axis powers, it is important for us to carry on the one here at home, along with the other war. It would not do to wait until the war is won overseas, for that would push back the progress of the Negro for 20 years." In his opinion, concurred in by Mr. Webster, the chairman states he was not satisfied with the results obtained.[30]

In the council galleries at this subcommittee hearing was Lovelyn Evans. In 1983 she vividly recalled a dramatic moment:

I will *never* forget that meeting. The council chambers were packed. The FEPC was sitting in judgment. Earl Dickerson got up, unafraid, and asked us Negroes, "Do you have somebody who can speak for you so that the committee can understand the situation?" Mr. Dunlap said, "Yes, I can speak for the plumbers." He got up and told about the situation of the plumbers. They had their own union, but the white union wouldn't let them in. He had been coached by Edward Doty.[31] Then Mr. Dickerson said, "When you went to the union heads and presented your case, what did they say?" Dr. Dunlap said, "They denied that they discriminated against us." Mr. Dickerson asked, "Did you bring your complaint to this committee?" Mr. Dunlap said, "No, sir, we didn't. We wrote to President Roosevelt. Mr. Roosevelt wrote back saying, 'We stand for no discrimination on any job financed by the federal government.'" So Earl Dickerson interrogated Mr. Dunlap with his, I'll call it, "moxie," and he brought Mr. Dunlap out to give the pertinent facts about what happened to this particular skilled group as far as unions were concerned. Earl Dickerson said, "Mr. Dunlap, when you went back to the heads of the union and told them that the president had said there should be no discrimination, what was their response?" Mr. Dunlap said, "They told me, 'To hell with the president.'"

There was *pandemonium* in that place, *pandemonium!* Mr. Dickerson said, "Are you sure?" Mr. Dunlap said, "Yes. They said, 'To hell with the president!'" Then the head of one of the unions got up and said, "But we have just bought twenty-five thousand dollars' worth of war bonds. We're not un-American."

Mr. Dickerson interrogated this man about half an hour, and one of the union heads said, "You send Mr. Doty to me in the morning, and we'll fix this thing. We'll look into it and see if there is any discrimination."

Well, Mr. Doty got in touch with this particular union, and they mapped out a program. They had a big affair at the Parkway Ballroom when the mayor came out and the union heads came out, and that broke the discrimination in the trades council.

The men were very happy. The bricklayers got jobs, the carpenters, and all got jobs down there when they had that big powder plant at Jeffersonville. That was the first big job that I remember where they put skilled Negroes on.[32]

The supreme test of the first committee came when it held its meeting in the South, in Birmingham, on June 18 to 20, 1942. Mark Ethridge, a southerner, fearful for Dickerson's life, advised him not to go. Although Dickerson was light brown and Webster was coal black,[33] Ethridge judged that Dickerson was in greater danger because of his aggressive and skillful cross-examination. Dickerson replied to Ethridge's warning, "Read our charter. The committee has jurisdiction within the United States and its territories. Is Birmingham in the United States? I will be there." And so he was, accompanied from arrival to departure, including during the hearings, by a six-foot four-inch U.S. marshal assigned by the U.S. attorney general.[34]

In Birmingham there was a new chairman, Dr. Malcolm S. MacLean, the white president of Hampton Institute, a black college in Virginia. Ethridge had resigned as chairman but remained on the committee as a member. (Executive Order 9111, issued May 25, 1942, had increased the number of the committee to seven members, including MacLean, who was appointed chairman.)[35] After his explanatory introduction, MacLean, instead of calling upon prominent local citizens as the chairman had done in previous meetings, called on Mark Ethridge, a moderate white Kentuckian who was influential in the South. Ethridge said that the goal was to win the war, that the indulgence of racial prejudice harming the achievement of that objective was worse than black marketeering, that the committee had not come to create tensions, and that he defended the granting of civil rights and equal opportunities to blacks. But he also affirmed support for social segregation in the South. He said that the committee "has taken no position on social segregation," that "Executive Order 8802 is a war order and not a social document," that it did not require the elimination of social segregation, and that had it done so, he would have regarded it "against the general peace and welfare . . . in the Nazi dictatorial pattern rather than in the slower, more painful pattern of the democratic process." He denounced those black leaders who "have adopted the 'all-or-nothing attitude,'" who "have interpreted 8802 as a second Emancipation Proclamation and have magnified the import of its possibilities" (an obvious thrust at Randolph). Ethridge denied that the federal government could legislate segregation out of existence and proclaimed:

There is no power in the world—not even in all the mechanized armies of the earth, Allied and Axis—which could now force the Southern white people to the abandonment of the principle of social segregation. It is a cruel disillusionment, bearing the germs of strife and perhaps tragedy, for any of their leaders to tell them that they can expect it as the price of their participation in the war.

They would do better to learn and to tell plain truths to their people and to stimulate them into giving the evidence of self-discipline and the example of willingness to sacrifice which will shame the demagogic, and challenge the admiration of decent white people. . . .

The Southern white man can purchase his own security, his own happiness, and his own self-respect only in that measure in which he is willing to accord them to the Negro.[36]

Then followed three days of hearings during which Dickerson played his characteristic aggressive and skillful role. Immediately after the proceedings Dickerson released his reply to Ethridge in a public statement:

Mr. Ethridge's statement, in support of segregation in the South, in my opinion, violates both the letter and the spirit of the President's Executive Order 8802. It is inconsistent with our professed belief in the principle of democracy. It shows very definitely that the South is still more interested in "keeping the Negro in his place" than in winning the war for democracy. Instead of marshaling its forces for an all-out effort to beat the totalitarian powers, the South is still fighting the Civil War, which, history records, was won over seventy-five years ago at Appomattox.

The philosophy expressed by Mr. Ethridge, representing as it does the majority opinion of the white people of the South, is certainly not heartening to America's colored allies. It gives aid and comfort to the enemy, who have long been broadcasting to the world that America is not fighting this war for freedom.

If the function of the committee is to bring about full participation of all groups in the war effort, and I believe it is, then it must press vigorously toward this end. Because of the very nature of its creation, the Committee on Fair Employment Practice must be opposed to segregation and discrimination.

It cannot hedge on so-called delicate issues. It cannot make concessions to the South, which, after all, is still a part of the geographical boundaries of the United States. There should be no "pussyfooting" on segregation by members of the committee.[37]

Black leaders and newspapers throughout the country, except in the South, called for Ethridge to resign, which he did not do at that time. The committee finally accepted the position that segregation could be a cause for complaint to and action by the committee only if it resulted in discrimination and that segregation per se was not prohibited by the executive order.[38]

The Birmingham hearings were the high point of the first FEPC. The White House congratulated Chairman MacLean when he returned to Washington. Five days later the committee celebrated the first anniversary of 8802. It made plans, approved by the president, to increase its staff and establish twelve regional offices.

Then, without warning, on July 30, 1942, President Roosevelt transferred the FEPC "as an organizational entity" to the War Manpower Commission (WMC) under the direct supervision of Chairman Paul McNutt. No reason was given, but it should be remembered that the campaigning for the midterm elections to the House and Senate was well under way, and the Democratic Party had one of its major bases in the South, particularly in committees in Congress and their key chairmanships. Later events indicate that the purpose of the transfer was to restrict the FEPC's activities.[39]

The transfer to the War Manpower Commission changed two basic factors: the committee was no longer directly responsible to the president, and its budget was no longer within the president's emergency funds. His emergency funds were not under congressional control, but the WMC's were, and at that time Congress was severely cutting the WMC budget.

Outcries against the transfer by minority and liberal groups were so immediate and loud that on August 17, through Stephen Early, Roosevelt issued a statement that it was his "intention to strengthen, not to submerge, the Committee, and to reinvigorate, not to repeal Executive Order 8802."[40] The statement eased criticism. The committee began discussions with McNutt about integrating its activities with those of the War Manpower Commission.

The discussions were futile for three months, until the committee declared that it would not accept responsibility for failure to arrive at an agreement. An agreement was finally reached on October 26.[41]

The FEPC prepared for action on a budget of about $320,000. It announced that hearings would be held in Detroit in February 1943 and later in St. Louis, Cleveland, Philadelphia, and Baltimore. It scheduled hearings on complaints against specific railroads and unions for January 25 to 27, 1943. On December 1 the committee directed the Capital Transit Company, Washington, D.C., to bring its employment policies into line with Executive Order 8802 by December 5. (No hearings had been held with the company because it had refused to attend, but evidence of discrimination had been gathered and checked.) On December 5 the committee issued "cease and desist" directives to a company and union in Savannah, Georgia. Early in January it issued similar directives to four leading industrial concerns in the South.[42]

Despite these successes, all was not well with the committee, either internally or externally. The War Manpower Commission had not yet put into effect its October 26 agreement with the FEPC. Representative Martin Dies of Texas, chairman of the House Un-American Activities Committee, used the *Chicago Tribune* soon after the December 1 directive to the Capital Transit Company to accuse the committee of being a communist tool that sought "to raise racial issues in the Nation's capital." At about the same time, Representative John E. Rankin of Mississippi, on the floor of the House, also attributed the committee's Capital Transit directive to "alien" influences and warned it might lead to disorders in Washington.[43]

Earl Dickerson was intimately involved in all this. Soon after the Birmingham hearings, the FEPC unanimously elected him to serve as its acting chairman when Chairman MacLean was not present, and MacLean was absent much of the time in the fall of 1942 and that winter. Hence, Dickerson chaired the committee during crucial episodes from the summer of 1942 until the late spring of 1943. For three months he pushed the reluctant McNutt to get a working agreement between the War Manpower Commission and the FEPC. For another two months he pulled the heel-dragging McNutt to implement the October 26 agreement.[44]

During those five months Dickerson led the committee to take evidence, issue directives, and schedule hearings. The two hottest cases were the Capital Transit Company, scheduled for January 8, 1943, and the railroad companies and unions, scheduled for January 25 to 27, 1943. These two were potentially explosive because, on the evidence the committee had already gathered, the former would reveal gross discrimination in the nation's capital, and the latter would reveal equally gross discrimination throughout the nation's transportation system, particularly in the South.[45]

Unknown to the committee, these two dates could not have been more poorly timed from Roosevelt's point of view. January 8 was the day the president, in strictest secrecy, was planning to leave for Casablanca, French Morocco, to confer with Prime Minister Winston Churchill on war aims and strategies. January 27 was the day when the news of the ten-day conference at Casablanca— January 14 to 24—was released to the press.

With the Capital Transit hearings scheduled for the next day, White House Secretary Stephen Early called Dickerson, as acting chairman, to tell him that the president wanted them postponed. Dickerson told Early that he would postpone the hearings only if the president personally requested him to do so. Dickerson was summoned to the White House that same afternoon, and Roosevelt reiterated the request. Dickerson replied, "I will do so, Mr. President, because you ask me to, but when I leave here, I will tell the reporters why I am postponing them." And he did.

His announcement did not make much of a splash. Other events were dominating the attention of the press and public. The president's State of the Union address, given only two days before, was still being analyzed. The battles in North Africa were continuing, the German armies were retreating along the entire Russian front, and Japanese forces were withdrawing from Guadalcanal. Then on

January 11, 1943, McNutt, without consultation with the FEPC, "indefinitely postponed" the railroad hearings. He gave no reason. The *New York Times* reported on January 12, 1943: "The chairman of the War Manpower Commission was reported to have requested Lawrence Cramer, executive secretary of the FEPC, several days ago to postpone the scheduled hearings of his committee, but the explanation advanced was not satisfactory to the members, so Mr. Cramer declined the request. Therefore, Mr. McNutt took the responsibility in his own hands."

That action dealt a mortal blow to the first FEPC. It was in limbo until it was buried four and a half months later.

A few days after McNutt postponed the railroad hearings, he issued a statement claiming that he had done so in order to enable the FEPC to bring about full utilization of manpower in the railroad industry and asserted that the War Manpower Commission could "take care of the situation much better without using force."[46]

Before the end of January, MacLean resigned as chairman and member of the committee, and Ethridge and Sarnoff both resigned as members. Three attorneys whom the committee had retained to prepare for the railroad hearings also resigned: Harry Epstein, Harold A. Stevens, and Charles H. Houston. Houston, an African American and counsel for the NAACP, included in his letter of resignation a protest and a warning, concluding: "McNutt's action disappointed but does not discourage us. We shall work all the harder to rally the liberal forces of the country behind a program which works by principle and not by panic."[47]

Liberal whites along with African Americans and other minorities quickly rallied. So many delegations came to McNutt that he finally said he would not see any more. This effort quickly had an effect. On February 3, 1943, President Roosevelt announced that he had asked McNutt to call a conference of minority group leaders to reconsider the status of the FEPC and to discuss plans to widen its scope and strengthen its powers. The conference on February 19 included Attorney General Francis Biddle and twenty-four representatives of nineteen government departments and agencies in addition to many minority group representatives. The invited representatives made recommendations, but the government officials revealed no plans and no decisions were reached.[48]

The remaining four members of the FEPC also sent recommendations to McNutt in February: that the agency be returned to independent status; that it be given a budget adequate for a staff of at least 120 persons and twelve regional offices; and that, where no agreement could be reached with an offending party, the case be certified to the president. Moreover, on March 1 the committee, with Dickerson as acting chairman, wrote President Roosevelt accusing McNutt of failing to carry out the WMC-FEPC agreement of October 26, 1942.[49]

Nothing happened for several weeks. Then late in April 1943 the FEPC went into action. Dickerson announced that the committee would hold hearings in Detroit on May 24 and 25 and other hearings later in St. Louis, Cleveland, Philadelphia, and Baltimore. Dickerson explained that the committee had received word on February 4 that it would be reorganized. He also said:

> It was only natural for us to sit by for a while and see if it was going to affect the decisions we had made.
>
> But now so much time has passed—it's been two months almost to a day, now, since the big conference of agencies interested in the reorganization was held here—that we really don't know if there is going to be any reorganization.
>
> And it doesn't seem right for us to keep on sitting by and letting all the charges [of discriminatory practices] go by. We feel that enough time has passed for us to determine now to move forward vigorously.
>
> And if it is true that we are going to be reorganized, you will know as quickly as we will whether the decisions made by us today will be proper.[50]

Both the decision to schedule the hearings and Dickerson's announcement violated the rules of the WMC. Indeed, McNutt had censored Dickerson's announcement. That announcement was the penultimate act of the first FEPC. Its last action was the statement of the postponement, at the request of the White House, of the hearings scheduled for the Capital Transit Company and in the other five cities.

On May 27, 1943, President Roosevelt, by Executive Order 9346, created a new FEPC. The only member remaining who was not appointed to the second committee was Earl Dickerson. The White House gave a rationale for the membership of the second committee: it was designed to be "representative."[51]

Why Dickerson was not appointed to the second committee, as were Milton P. Webster, John Brophy, and Boris Shishkin—the other three remaining from the first committee—is open to interpretation. A plausible answer might be that he was not "representative" in such ways as were the other members of the second committee, and, after all, there were two blacks on the second committee; besides Webster there was P. B. Young, publisher of the *Norfolk (Virginia) Journal and Guide.* But another reason is also probable:

> Undoubtedly, his aggressive, if somewhat unorthodox, efforts to prevent the first committee's extinction, his granting of press interviews without prior permission from McNutt and, in the words of one newspaper [*Chicago Defender,* July 1, 1943], "his militant stand during" FEPC hearings, had much to do with his not being reappointed. His absence raised doubts in the minds of Negro leaders concerning the committee's competence and sincerity. The *Chicago Defender* editorialized: "Perhaps Dickerson was too insistent on the observance and application of the expressed provisions of the Executive Order 8802, and as a result the old Committee was abolished. Failure to reappoint him raises the question that it was the desire of the Administration to have a handpicked committee.[52]

Contrary to the doubts many people had at the time, the second committee proved to be competent and committed to its objectives, and President Roosevelt gave it strong support consistent with his primary goal—to win the war.[53]

The Philadelphia rapid transit case was the supreme test of the second FEPC's effectiveness and of the president's commitment to its objective. In November 1944, President Roosevelt ordered the army to enforce a directive to the Philadelphia Transportation Company and the Philadelphia Rapid Transit Employees Union, which had resulted in a strike that paralyzed the city. The army was prepared to operate the system, fire all resisting employees, and draft into the army all resisting employees who qualified for induction.[54] Both the strike and the discriminatory practices were ended, but bitterness remained. This coercive action throws a favorable light, in contrast, on the resolution of the Chicago transit case by peaceful means. That achievement was the result of a provision in an ordinance that Dickerson, as alderman, forced through the Chicago City Council on February 11, 1942—when he was also a member of the first FEPC.

Support of the FEPC continued even after Roosevelt's death on April 12, 1945. Representative Adolph Sabbath, Democrat from Illinois, told the House Rules Committee that "the very last request made by the late President Roosevelt on the day he died was that the Fair Employment Practice Committee be continued."[55]

But this voice from the grave was not heeded. Reactionaries in Congress finally eradicated the FEPC.[56] Specifically, Senator Theodore G. Bilbo of Mississippi killed it by filibuster.

HOW MUCH DID the FEPC increase minority hiring during the war? It certainly increased to some extent. One author concluded: "There is no doubt . . . that the executive order and FEPC's efforts contributed to increased Negro and other minority group employment."[57] But how much difference the committee made by itself cannot be assessed because of the many other factors involved. One was the incalculable but real change in the attitudes of employers and union members, modified, however slightly, by the first official federal policy stating that discriminatory employment practices were harmful to the nation. This change in attitudes was certainly enhanced by the committee's exposure through public hearings and the attendant publicity addressing the damage discrimination was doing to the war effort. However, economic necessity probably played the major part in opening up employment opportunities to blacks and other minorities during the war.[58] Experience during and since the war has shown that full employment is a necessary condition for FEPC laws to succeed.

More observable than the economic consequences were some of the long-term social effects of the FEPC. It was more than an agency opening up jobs to members of minority groups. It also brought hope to many African Americans and strengthened their waning belief in democracy and its possibilities. The FEPC quickened a change in the attitudes of Americans concerning the role that government could play in altering custom and mores and helped to change the organizational strategy and tactics of later civil rights advocates. The strategy would henceforth be based on decisive intervention by the federal, state, and local governments to promote fair treatment and equal opportunity, and the tactics would be based on continuous agitation and propaganda.

WHEN ASKED YEARS later about the substantive effect of the FEPC on discriminatory practices in hiring, Dickerson responded:

> I can't say that the FEPC itself achieved much. There was no statute to enforce its findings and directives. It was public opinion that moved some companies and agencies to employ more minority members. But even that wasn't enough. We of the first committee began agitation and propaganda in various states, such as Michigan, Illinois, and New York, to have state legislatures require fair employment practice. The other members of the committee and I went to the legislatures and into the pulpits and to many kinds of meetings and agitated for enforcing legislation. This helped lay the foundation for other activities toward that end.

These activities include federal and state fair employment practice legislation. Beginning in 1945, bills forbidding discriminatory practice were introduced in both houses of Congress during every session until the Civil Rights Act of 1964 was finally passed. Title VI of the 1964 act prohibits discrimination in projects receiving federal funds, while Title VII prohibits discrimination in employment more generally. Beginning in 1945 with New York and Wisconsin and followed by Massachusetts in 1946, the states began to adopt fair employment laws. By the turn of the twenty-first century, forty-six states and the District of Columbia had adopted statutes prohibiting discrimination in employment by government and private businesses.

THE BROADER SOCIAL and historical impact of the FEPC is illustrated in concrete human terms by the reminiscences of Mrs. Lovelyn Evans. These are offered at length as a case study of how democracy can sometimes be made to work.

> I became interested in the plight of Negro skilled tradesmen. I knew many carpenters, bricklayers, electricians, and so on. I heard about their hard times from their women. Negro skilled tradesmen were not let into the white unions. The only ones who had unions of their own were bricklayers and steamfitters, and these were not let into white unions, and their members were restricted to jobs by Negro employers. The bricklayers wanted to be let in on a full basis to all jobs that opened up. So I spearheaded the movement with them.
>
> And then Earl Dickerson was on the FEPC. We renewed our acquaintance. I gave him the picture. There were many big projects. Foreigners and other whites from all over the country were getting good jobs, but very, very few Negroes in Chicago.
>
> Charley Duke, a technician, was head of the Technological Society. That was an organization of Negro men who had joined together to promote their interests. Mr. Duke was working on a big project at the University of Chicago, and he had a lot to do with Negro bricklayers. He said to me, "These skilled tradesmen are

getting very despondent. All they get is manual jobs. If they don't get recognition, I'm afraid they'll do something desperate."

They called themselves the American Consolidated Trades Council—Negroes who were skilled tradesmen. I would go to some of their meetings. Edward Doty, a plumber, was a strong man. He didn't use violence but worked quietly. He and I kept in touch, working on the idea that someday the white unions would accept Negro plumbers.

One day I met with the Consolidated Trades Council. Everybody said to me, "Why are you interested? Your husband has a good job with the telephone company." I said, "You need assistance. You don't know how to go about it. Some of you are thinking about being violent. Let's do it the smart way. I know Earl Dickerson. And then there's Sidney Hillman. He's sympathetic. Earl says so."

Things came to a head with the Ida B. Wells housing project. Some of the skilled tradesmen and I were standing around. We saw all those big vehicles coming from Georgia and California with white men operating them, and the only Negroes working on this government project were laborers with low pay. Somebody said, "I'm going to blow this place up." I was frightened. I told Earl Dickerson. He said, "Try to keep them calm. I'll see what I can do. We'll take up the case when we have our hearings in the FEPC." And he did, as I told you.

A time came when some of the bricklayers came to me and said, "You know, they're building at the Great Lakes Naval Training Station. They're not hiring any Negro bricklayers." It was a challenge to me. At that time I was driving my own car. Every time I went to one of these places, I always took with me two corner men [bricklayers who bring two walls of brick into exact alignment]—the most skilled.

We went out to the Great Lakes Training Station. I said I wanted to see the superintendent in charge of the work and started to walk in. The naval guard had his bayonet fixed. He said, "Just a minute, madam." I said, "Put that thing down. I want to see the superintendent of the work that's going on." He said, "You can't." I said, "Who says so?" I had on my Civil Defense uniform; I was in the morale department. I said, "I have something very important to tell him." The guard said, "*You* have something important to tell him?" I said, "That's what I said." He said, "You can't see him." I said, "You want to bet?"

We went to the next town, and I called up the superintendent on the phone. I told him, "I'm representing Negro bricklayers. They can't get any work on your project because you are discriminating against them. They are not hiring any Negro bricklayers on your project." The superintendent said, "There isn't any discrimination here. You come here and see how many Negroes are working." I said, "Yes, but they are all working as common laborers. If you don't want Washington to come, you had better let me come and show you. I've got a copy of the president's order." (I always carried around a copy of 8802.) He said, "Where are you?" I said, "I'm in the next town. That dumb boy held a bayonet against me." He said, "You come back, madam. You'll be admitted."

We went back, and when I saw that young man, he was bowing and scraping. He said, "The superintendent will see you." I said, "Thank you." I went in and saw the superintendent and said, "Now here is Executive Order 8802 signed by the president. It's supposed to be in every toolhouse in the country." He said, "We're not discriminating," and he took me to show me how many Negroes were working. I said, "Yes, but I don't see any Negro skilled tradesmen here." He said, "None of them have come here, and this is important work. Do you know any qualified Negro bricklayers?" I said, "I have two in my car." So he said, "Bring them in, and I'll talk to them." I did. They were from Alabama. They were corner men—the best.

I had more fun laying out the superintendents of different big jobs, including Great Lakes and Melrose Park, and getting these men good jobs and keeping them from doing something they'd be sorry for. That's the reason Charley Duke and I worked together.

We would meet every week and advise the men. And it was Earl B. Dickerson, FEPC, who guided us to do the intelligent and right thing.

Every time the FEPC would meet, there was me and Mr. Polk, the steamfitter, sitting in the front seats. If it was in Washington, there we were sitting in the front seats. If it was in New York, there we would be sitting in the front seats. In New York the meeting was at that big lawyers group [the Bar Association]. Polk was there. He didn't care who he was talking to, and he couldn't pass for white, either.

Mr. Dickerson said that one day one of the other committee members said to him, "Dickerson, what the hell goes on here? Every place we meet, there are this woman and this man looking up at us to see what decisions we are going to make." Mr. Dickerson said, "Well, these people are pretty angry, and their families are suffering. All this government money is being spent and there is not supposed to be any discrimination, but things aren't being conducted that way. These people are just waiting to see that our committee takes up their case."

The climax was when Mr. Dickerson told us, "We're going to meet at David Sarnoff's house on Sunday afternoon.[59] We're going to take up these cases, and I'm going to bring them up. You send me a letter." I said to myself, "Oh, no." I told the bricklayers, the carpenters, the steamfitters, and all the other people who were interested: "Send a telegram to Earl Dickerson, FEPC, in care of David Sarnoff."

Earl said that the doorbell would ring, and there would be a telegram for Mr. Dickerson. The doorbell would ring, and there would be another telegram for Mr. Dickerson. Mr. Sarnoff said, "Dickerson, what the hell goes on here?" Earl said, "I don't know. I told you these people are all steamed up." Mr. Sarnoff said, "How did they know we were meeting here?" Earl said, "They knew it." Mr. Sarnoff said, "Well, we are going to get on with this thing and find out what all this scuttlebutt is and get it straightened out." That's what happened with that fine committee.

And that wonderful Sidney Hillman and the Citizens Committee here in Chicago,[60] headed by Dr. Clarence Payne[61] and Irene McCoy Goins,[62] of the colored women's organization. They said, "We'll meet in Washington because that's where Sidney Hillman is in charge of seeing that discrimination will be wiped out." We got our dimes together and stayed at the Y in Washington. I was head of the employment committee. E. Franklin Frazier[63] was head of some other committee. Mr. Polk and I worked together on the employment committee.

When we were talking about how we were going to try to see Mr. Hillman, some said, "Mr. Polk doesn't have a good command of the King's English." I said, "So what? He knows what he's talking about because he's one of the ones who are being ripped off. Mr. Polk is going to be on that delegation if I'm going to be on it. He can talk for the skilled tradesmen who are being given the shaft by the country." So Dr. Payne said, "All right, if you can get an appointment with Mr. Hillman, go ahead."

So I went to see Rob Taylor [Robert R. Taylor, as an entrée to Hillman].[64] I thought I had it made. I thought you always had to have an introduction to meet an important person. But Rob's secretary said, "I'm sorry, Mr. Taylor is out of the country. But you can go directly to Mr. Hillman."

We got in a cab and went directly to the office of Sidney Hillman. His secretary was sitting outside the door. I told her of my association and said, "Is there any way I can talk to Mr. Hillman about discrimination against Negro skilled tradesmen?" She said, "Oh, Mrs. Evans, Mr. Hillman has been trying hard for weeks to get the background of discrimination and the backlash of Negroes. He's heard so much about it, but he hasn't been able to get any information helpful to him." I said, "I have a gentleman here who belongs to the Consolidated Trades Council, and all the Negro skilled tradesmen belong to that." She said, "You wait right here."

Now, follow me. I'm sitting there talking to this secretary. The door opens, and out comes a little man with about half a dozen other men who looked like the backfield of Notre Dame. One of the big men said, "Sidney, we're expecting you in Pittsburgh tomorrow morning at nine." The little man said, "I'll be there." He shook hands with all these big men. I asked the secretary, "So that's Mr. Hillman?" She said, "Yes." When he started to go into his office, the secretary—this white secretary—said to him, "Mr. Hillman, here's a lady who I think has some important information for you."

Mr. Hillman asked me how I knew about the situation. Then he said, "You heard me tell those men that I will be in Pittsburgh tomorrow morning at nine. But I'll tell you what I'll do, Mrs. Evans. I'll have you talk to my first deputy. He will listen to your committee. My secretary will make an appointment." She made an appointment for the next morning.

I went back to the Y, and all the committees made reports—Mrs. Goins on education, somebody else on something else, and I said, "We have an appointment with Mr. Hillman's first deputy tomorrow morning at nine." Some of the big shots were going to take over. There was much elbowing about who would be on the committee to see Mr. Hillman's deputy. But I stood for myself and Mr. Polk.

The next morning we sat at a big long table with Mr. Hillman's first assistant. He had a stenotypist. He wanted to hear from Mr. Polk. The stenotypist took it all down. At the end Mr. Hillman's assistant said, "You don't know how grateful we are to you, Mrs. Evans, and you, Mr. Polk, and to your committee. You have given us and the FEPC the correct picture."

Maybe Mr. Polk didn't look right. Maybe he looked more like a Bushman than Rudolph Valentino. Maybe he didn't speak the King's English. But he knew what he was talking about.

I've still got a copy of Executive Order 8802. They were beautiful—white type on blue. I should keep it up here on the wall of this room.[65]

DICKERSON FAMILY COLLECTION

After his father's death in 1896, Dickerson (here about age eight) was raised by four women in Canton, Mississippi (counterclockwise from bottom left): his maternal grandmother, Eliza Garrett; his mother, Emma Garrett Fielding Dickerson; and his two half sisters, Gertrude Dickerson and Luella Fielding.

DICKERSON FAMILY COLLECTION

Dickerson and an unknown girl with his maternal grandmother, Eliza Garrett, circa 1900.

F.L.Williams '16   Harpole '16   Dickson '16   C.L.M.Cooper '15

W.J.Prince '15   G.C.Ellis '14   E.B.Dickerson '13   B.F.Kenner '15

DICKERSON FAMILY COLLECTION

The founders of the Beta chapter of the Kappa Alpha Psi fraternity at the University of Illinois at Urbana-Champaign received their charter on February 8, 1913.

DICKERSON FAMILY COLLECTION

Second Lieutenant Dickerson was commissioned in the fall of 1917.

COURTESY OF THE UNIVERSITY OF CHICAGO LAW SCHOOL

Dickerson (far right, second row from bottom) *was a member of the University of Chicago Law School graduating class of* 1920.

DICKERSON FAMILY COLLECTION

After being rejected by several Chicago law firms in 1920, Dickerson opened his own law office on January 3, 1921, at 184 West Washington Street in Chicago.

Dickerson as a young professional.

DICKERSON FAMILY COLLECTION

DICKERSON FAMILY COLLECTION

Earl and Kathryn Dickerson with John H. Johnson (left), *publisher of* Ebony *and* Jet *magazines. Dickerson helped Johnson get started by giving him an office at Supreme Liberty Life and by letting him use a list of policyholders from which Johnson sold advance subscriptions. Johnson later succeeded Dickerson as president of Supreme Life.*

DICKERSON FAMILY COLLECTION

Dickerson in his office at Supreme Liberty Life Insurance Company, where he served as general counsel, vice president, and president.

DICKERSON FAMILY COLLECTION

Dickerson (second from left) *with President Franklin D. Roosevelt at the White House. Dickerson was a member of FDR's first Fair Employment Practices Committee from 1941 to 1943.*

DICKERSON FAMILY COLLECTION

Dickerson with his wife, Kathryn; stepson, Rodger Wilson Jr.; and daughter, Diane.

DICKERSON FAMILY COLLECTION

Dickerson's wife, Kathryn.

DICKERSON FAMILY COLLECTION

Dickerson escorted his daughter, Diane, at her wedding in 1956.

DICKERSON FAMILY COLLECTION

President-elect John F. Kennedy nominated Dickerson as assistant secretary of commerce. Because of Dickerson's reputation as an agitator on the FEPC and in the National Lawyers Guild, the appointment was quickly dropped.

DICKERSON FAMILY COLLECTION

*Earl and Kathryn Dickerson entertained Eleanor Roosevelt
at their home at 5027 South Drexel Boulevard in Chicago.
Eleanor Roosevelt was on the national board of the
NAACP with Dickerson.*

As head of the Supreme Life Insurance Company, Chicago attorney Earl B. Dickerson keeps in touch with its many branch offices by flying. He flies American three or four times a month.

After 20 years of air travel, Mr. Dickerson is now on his second million miles. "I do so much flying, sometimes I think of an airplane as my other office."

Supreme Life operations cover 12 states and the District of Columbia. Mr. Dickerson says, "Unless I flew, I couldn't possibly visit our branch offices as often as I do."

EARL B. DICKERSON: HOW HE CHALKED UP HIS FIRST MILLION.

At New York's LaGuardia Airport, Earl Dickerson boards one of American Airlines' new 727 Astrojets on his way home to Chicago. He'll do an hour's work en route.

EARL B. DICKERSON started out in 1941. That's when he flew from Chicago to Washington, D.C. Since then, he's chalked up well over a million miles of flying.

As president and chief executive officer of the Supreme Life Insurance Company of America, he's one of the busiest men in the country. And only by flying can he meet his many business and civic commitments.

"I first flew American Airlines during the war, when President Roosevelt appointed me to the Fair Employment Practices Committee," he says. "In addition to almost weekly flights to Washington, I also flew all over the country investigating labor employment practices."

Today, Mr. Dickerson flies American Airlines three or four times a month.

His long career with Supreme Life Insurance started in 1921, when he graduated from the University of Chicago Law School. He also has served as assistant attorney general of the State of Illinois, assistant corporation counsel for the City of Chicago, city alderman, president of the Chicago Urban League, head of the National Bar Association, member of the boards of the NAACP, and the Cancer Prevention Society, and was one of the founders of Roosevelt University.

His many civic, educational and professional activities have taken him to all parts of the country. And since Supreme Life Insurance has branch offices in 38 cities—most of them served by American Airlines—he spends a lot of time flying with us.

"I've always found the people at American courteous and cooperative," he says. "I've really enjoyed my first million miles." So will you. **American Airlines**

Constantly on the go, he addresses Kappa Alpha Psi Fraternity at UCLA.

First class section of American Airlines Astrojet gives him privacy to catch up on work, get through the day's news, and enjoy an occasional coffee break.

The executive life is a demanding one. "If it weren't for flying, I'd never get home to spend time with my family," Mr. Dickerson says. Here he's seen in his Chicago home with his daughter and grandsons Mark, Stephen, and Joshua.

DICKERSON FAMILY COLLECTION

This advertisement featuring Dickerson as a frequent flier appeared in Ebony *magazine in October 1964. The ad highlights his many important roles that required travels to all parts of the country.*

Dickerson gave Martin Luther King Jr. a tour of Supreme Life's offices.

Sammy Davis Jr. visited Dickerson at his Supreme Life office on May 7, 1968.

DICKERSON FAMILY COLLECTION

DICKERSON FAMILY COLLECTION

Dickerson and Paul Robeson were close friends, and Robeson would often stay with the Dickersons when he was in Chicago.

COURTESY OF JOHNSON PUBLISHING COMPANY, INC.

*Dickerson was congratulated at the NAACP Legal
Defense Fund's early 1980s tribute to him by Secretary of
Transportation William T. Coleman, the principal speaker
at the dinner.*

COURTESY OF JOHNSON PUBLISHING COMPANY, INC

Dickerson overcome by emotion at the NAACP Legal Defense Fund testimonial, where he was honored as "the Master."

DICKERSON FAMILY COLLECTION

Dickerson with photographs of Martin Luther King Jr. and Malcolm X in the Supreme Liberty Life building.

DICKERSON FAMILY COLLECTION

Dickerson with Harold Washington, Chicago's first African American mayor.

COURTESY OF JOHNSON PUBLISHING COMPANY, INC.

At a meeting of the financial committee of Supreme Liberty Life Insurance
Company, Chairman and CEO John H. Johnson (center) *recalls the contributions
of Dickerson* (seated to his left). *Other top executives in attendance* (left to right)
*include Senior Vice Presidents Weathers Y. Sykes and Lloyd C. Wheeler, President
and COO Ray Irby, Senior Vice President S. Benton Robinson, and General
Counsel Harry H. C. Gibson. Dickerson was named honorary chairman in 1973.*

MELINDA C. MORRISSEY

Dickerson lounging at home at 4800 Chicago Beach Drive in 1984.

DICKERSON FAMILY COLLECTION

Dickerson enjoying drinks with two friends the night before his death in 1986.

Chapter Seven

CONSOLIDATING GAINS: LAWYER,
LEADER, AND ACTIVIST

After his term as alderman in Chicago from 1939 to 1943, Dickerson made two unsuccessful attempts to run for Congress (once as a Republican candidate and once as a member of Henry A. Wallace's Progressive Party) before retiring from politics altogether.

On May 22, 1943, the *New York Amsterdam News,* crediting the Associated Negro Press (ANP), reported:

> A "People's Movement for Independent Political Action," whose purpose is to rally Negro support behind issues and men regardless of party affiliation, has been launched under the direction of Attorney Earl B. Dickerson, acting chairman of the President's FEPC and former alderman of the Second Ward. Dickerson, acting chairman, explained that the movement would be promoted only in Illinois at first but might become national later.[1]

The *Chicago Sun* carried a story on December 5 headed "Second Ward GOP Out to Get Earl Dickerson on Its Side; Nomination for Congress Suggested as Inducement to Former Alderman." Dickerson did indeed run in the primary race as a Republican candidate for Congress from the First District. He explained that he had switched parties because by 1943 "the reactionaries have become dominant in the Democratic Party" and that "the best hope is in a strong and liberal Republican Party." He ran on a straight New Deal platform with a federal antilynching plank. He was supported by members of the People's Movement for Independent Political Action and also by the progressive faction of the Republican Party. His opponent was William E. King, who had been both state representative and state senator and was then Second Ward Republican committeeman. The *Chicago Daily News* endorsed Dickerson, but King defeated him in the April primary election. The incumbent Democrat, William L. Dawson, then defeated King in the November general election.

DICKERSON'S NEXT BID for a seat in Congress was also precipitated by a nonpartisan effort. He responded to a letter dated October 28, 1947, which read: "We invite you to meet with us and about 60 other national leaders to work out a *coordinated* program designed to win a major victory for Negro democratic rights in the coming session of the 80th Congress." The letter was signed by Paul Robeson, Hubert H. Delany (a judge of the New York City Court of Domestic Relations), John H. Johnson, and W. E. B. DuBois, among others.[2] This "coordinated program" later supported the new Progressive Party, which in 1948 nominated Henry A. Wallace for president and Senator Glen H. Taylor for vice president. Dickerson accepted an invitation from the Progressive Party to run on its ticket as a candidate for the seat from the Illinois First Congressional District. Although his candidacy failed once again, the high point of the campaign was October 15. Candidates Wallace, Taylor, and Dickerson held three rallies in Chicago, one of them in the First Congressional District. The *New York Times* of October 16 commented: "This was the first time in history that either a presidential or vice presidential candidate has ever spoken for a Negro candidate for office."

Harry Truman had forced Wallace to resign as secretary of commerce in September 1946 because of his open opposition to the president's foreign policy. The new Progressive Party had charged the Truman administration with responsibility for the cold war. Nevertheless, Wallace left the Progressive Party in 1950 after it repudiated his endorsement of the intervention by the United States and the United Nations in the Korean War. Dickerson stayed with the Progressive Party after Wallace's departure and was chairman of the Platform and Resolution Committee at its 1952 convention, held in Chicago June 26–29.[3] The preamble of the committee's statement summarized the platform: "Cease-Fire in Korea, Defend the Rights of Labor, Full and Equal Rights for the Negro People, Restore the Bill of Rights for All Americans, Abolish the Biggest Racket of All—the War Racket, the Key to Peace—Understanding and Cooperation Between the U.S. and the U.S.S.R."[4]

In 1984, Dickerson said:

> The Progressive Party was something we just had to have. There was no chance of winning, of course. But the progressive-liberal element of our country had to have a movement to show the importance of bringing the American people of age in dealing with public questions. The Progressive Party had an effect in many ways on the black people, who had been slaves to the Republican Party for decades and then slaves of the Democratic Party since 1936.

Integrating the Chicago Bar Association

In 1945, after leaving politics, Dickerson led the movement that broke the color barrier in the Chicago Bar Association (CBA). All applications by African American lawyers for membership in the CBA had been routinely rejected. No black lawyer had legally challenged this color barrier, and no white member of the CBA had spoken out against it publicly.

By the early 1940s a group of CBA members had begun to agitate to remove the race barrier. Among them were Charles Liebman, Elmer Gertz, Robert T. Drake, Frank McCulloch, and Leon M. Despres. Late in 1943 four African American attorneys applied for membership and were sponsored by respected members of the CBA. They were Dickerson; Archibald J. Carey Jr., who in addition to his law practice was pastor of the African American Methodist Episcopal Church; William Sylvester White, who had recently resigned as an assistant U.S. attorney to become a naval ensign; and Rufus Sampson Jr.[5] After nearly six months all were rejected. But for the first time these rejections were challenged. Superior Court Judge John P. McCoorty led a committee in drafting a letter to the CBA Board of Managers asking for reconsideration. The letter was not answered. The committee then sent a copy to every member of the association. Judge Russell Whitman, a former CBA president who had been one of Dickerson's sponsors, said, "This white supremacy stuff is exactly the kind of thing we are fighting against in Germany. . . . The Admissions Committee should be made to explain why it rejected these attorneys." Charles Liebman filed a suit in the circuit court to compel the association to open its records and put the issue to a vote by the full membership. The association's general counsel moved that the suit be dismissed because, as a voluntary, not-for-profit organization, the CBA was not subject to review by the courts. In mid-1945, before the circuit court could issue a ruling, J. Francis Dammann, an eminent corporate attorney, was elected president of the CBA. Elmer Gertz had written a letter appealing to him to bring about admission of blacks to the CBA as a memorial to Dammann's recently deceased sister who, as president of a fashionable Catholic girls' school in New York City, had been stolidly against racial discriminatory practices despite protests from some wealthy alumnae, parents, and students. Dammann, in response to Gertz, promised: "While I am president of our Association, Negroes will be admitted to membership on the same terms as whites." In a history of the CBA, the author said, "Dammann fulfilled his promise by giving the issue top priority, and at every opportunity pressed forcefully for a reversal of the association's stand. In November, 1945, Dickerson was admitted to membership, as were Irvin C. Mollison, Sidney A. Jones, Jr., and Loring B. Moore; and in their wake came Carey, White, and others."[6]

This official account, which gives credit predominantly to a group of white liberal lawyers, needs to be supplemented by an account of evasive measures taken by the CBA and the consequent pressures that a group of African American lawyers brought to bear. The CBA's evasive action was to seek out and admit a black lawyer whom the association's members could count on not to exercise his membership privileges and, above all, not to use the association's dining facilities. In the spring of 1945, Robert L. Taylor (not to be confused with Robert R. Taylor, the first black to serve as head of the Chicago Housing Authority) was admitted to the CBA under these tacit conditions. Taylor was assistant attorney for the Board of Election Commissioners and an authority on Illinois election laws.[7] In order to have token evidence against the suit charging racial discrimination, in the spring of 1945 the CBA sent a committee to Taylor with copies of the application form, induced him to sign, and secured the necessary endorsements. They then quickly admitted him to membership.

Refused admission by the CBA in 1943, Dickerson, Carey, White, and Sampson applied again in 1944. The CBA rule was that if an application had been approved, notice would be published in the association's *Bulletin* within thirty days. If an applicant was not accepted, he would have to wait a year before applying again. The thirty days following Dickerson's and his colleagues' applications passed without notice of acceptance. Late in 1944, a few days before the deadline for the year came, Charles Liebman took Dickerson to the office of Judge Russell Whitman, a former president of the CBA who was then nearly eighty years old. Whitman said, "Earl, I'm going to get you into the CBA if it's the last thing I do." He took Liebman and Dickerson to the offices of the CBA and asked the secretary, "Please show me the record of the association on the application of Earl Dickerson a year ago yesterday." The secretary consulted the records and answered that he had been rejected, as were the others who applied with him. Whitman asked for a new application form, had Dickerson fill it out, and endorsed it, saying, "Take this to Judge Otto Kerner Sr. for another endorsement."

Kerner was then a judge of the U.S. Circuit Court of Appeals. Dickerson had served for seven years as assistant attorney general under Kerner and was astonished when Kerner, faced with the application and told what Whitman had said, exclaimed, "Earl, I would do anything to help you. You were trusted and a good man in my office. But the members of the CBA have been friends of mine for years and have endorsed me as I moved forward to this position. I wouldn't want to enter into any controversy in this connection, and therefore I can't sign."

Disappointed but undaunted, Dickerson went to several other respected members of the CBA, received their endorsements, and submitted his application before the year's deadline. He encouraged Mollison, Jones, and Moore to reapply also. In due course Dickerson was called for examination before the CBA's thirty-five-member Board of Managers. Its chairman was Floyd Thompson, former chief justice of the Illinois Supreme Court. His first question was "Are you a communist?" To this Dickerson replied:

> As I understand communists, particularly in Russia, they don't mind being dominated by a few men at the top. Also the communist state takes over all private property. The test is this: in practicing law I have accumulated a few funds and pieces of property; if any one of you were to undertake to deprive me of that property, you would find out whether I am a communist. Of course I am not a communist. Does that satisfy you?[8]

The committee seemed satisfied on this point, but additional questions and answers went on for more than two hours.

The next day Dickerson was told by a fellow lawyer who had attended the meeting: "You made a good impression yesterday." Dickerson replied, "I'm sure I will not be admitted." To this the lawyer responded, "You'll be surprised. I was on the committee, and we stayed several hours discussing you. By an overwhelming vote you were taken in as a member." Mollison (whom President Truman had just appointed to the U.S. Customs Court of New York City), Jones, and Moore, and soon afterward Carey and White, were also admitted at this time.

Unlike Robert L. Taylor, who abided by the tacit understanding of his sponsors, Dickerson quickly claimed all privileges of membership. Less than a week after Dickerson's admission, Norman Manley, the prime minister of Jamaica, came to Chicago to speak to a West Indian group in the city. One of the group was Bindley Cyrus, a native of Barbados and a close friend of Dickerson's. Dickerson invited Cyrus and Manley to lunch at the CBA.

> When we went into the dining room, you should have seen the faces of the white lawyers there. They looked at us as though we had come from the stars. They looked at each other and punched one another, as though to say, "Look who's here!" That was my debut as a member of the CBA. After that, with my offices in the city and constantly clearing titles in the courts, I made it a practice to have lunch in the CBA once or twice a week.

Challenging the Coalition of Judges

No African American had served in the municipal court until Albert B. George was elected in 1924. But although ward committeemen could make nominations for the municipal court, the circuit and superior courts' jurisdictions were countywide, and committeemen had to share the power of nomination with delegates from outlying towns where African Americans were not represented. In 1947 the Democratic and Republican parties made a "sweetheart" arrangement through which they secured and protected their judgeships on the superior court by means of a Coalition ticket determining the twenty-one candidates they would support.

Earl Dickerson, Sidney Jones Jr., and Richard Westbrooks, all eminent black lawyers, formed and promoted an interracial ticket to oppose the Coalition ticket for the elections of November 1947. They named it the Progressive Party ticket because it was associated with the national Progressive Citizens of America, which would support the nomination of Henry Wallace for the presidency in the following year. In a whirlwind drive the Progressive Party ticket obtained 130,000 signatures on petitions to nominate twenty-one qualified candidates for the superior court. Dickerson, Jones, and Westbrooks were three of the twenty-one. Dickerson and Jones received endorsement from the Chicago chapter of the National Lawyers Guild, and the Cook County Bar Association backed the entire Progressive ticket. The *Chicago Tribune* of October 20, 1947, reported that the Chicago Bar Association had endorsed fourteen candidates on the Coalition ticket and three on the Progressive ticket: Dickerson, Jones, and Homer F. Carey, a white professor of law at Northwestern University. The CBA said of Dickerson: "He is a lawyer of broad experience and excellent character. He is alert, diligent, and industrious. He is qualified for office." In its lead editorial on October 31, the *Chicago Daily News* endorsed Carey and Dickerson on the Progressive ticket, and on the same day the *Chicago Sun* endorsed Dickerson, Jones, and Carey.

On November 4 the entire Coalition ticket of twenty-one was elected, but the lowest-ranking Coalition candidate received 334,000 votes while Carey received 313,000 and Dickerson 216,750. This demonstration of organizational ability and electoral support moved both political parties to include black candidates on their judicial tickets for the countywide courts in subsequent elections. Finally, in 1950, Wendell E. Green, a Democrat—Dickerson's classmate at the University of Chicago Law School and former law partner—was the first black to be elected to the Circuit Court of Cook County.[9]

Leading the National Bar Association and the National Lawyers Guild

The National Bar Association (NBA) was organized in 1925 in response to the policy of the American Bar Association (ABA) to exclude black attorneys from membership no matter how well qualified. After many years of serving on the committees and in the offices of the NBA, Dickerson was elected president at the national convention in Cleveland on December 8, 1945, and was reelected in Detroit on December 1, 1946.

The title of his inaugural address to the NBA in 1945 was "Separate but Equal and Mob Violence Must Go," and in February 1947, Dickerson proclaimed the week of April 6 to 12 of that year as "National Bar Association Week," with the theme "Second-Class Citizenship and Mob Violence Must Go."

In his address upon reelection in Detroit, Dickerson offered an analysis of American constitutional history beginning with the drafting of the U.S. Constitution and ending with an anticipation of the 1954 decision in *Brown v. Board of Education of Topeka:* "The Supreme Court of the United States has never ruled on the legality of segregation in tax-supported schools. The precise question, whether a State can by legislation enforce a separation of the races, has never been brought to court."[10] Dickerson's two years as president ended on December 6, 1947, by which time the NBA had achieved full recognition as a significant force in the legal profession. The official host of the NBA convention that year was the Washington, D.C., Bar Association, and among the guests present were Associate Justices Robert H. Jackson and Wiley B. Rutledge and Attorney General Tom F. Clark.

DICKERSON WAS PRESIDENT of the National Lawyers Guild from October 14, 1951, to November 21, 1954; he was the first African American to be elected president of this national lawyers association.[11] Unfortunately, Dickerson's presidency also coincided with the rise of McCarthyism in American politics, and the National Lawyers Guild soon came under attack by McCarthy's supporters.

In a speech to the American Bar Association, which convened in Boston on August 27, 1953, U.S. Attorney General Herbert Brownell Jr. announced that he would place the National Lawyers Guild on his list of "subversive organizations." He did this before any hearing had been held, contending that the National Lawyers Guild was "a communist-dominated and -controlled organization" and that he was "now prepared to make this determination public."[12]

Brownell purported to be acting under authority of Executive Order 10450 issued by President Harry Truman in 1947. In this order the president assigned the attorney general to maintain a list of organizations designated as subversive in order to alert various government agencies that such groups were "permeated with Communists and fellow travelers" and to take this into account in determining security risks. The guild and several other liberal organizations protested against this order on the grounds that "subversive" and "fellow traveler" were not defined and that the order permitted security decisions to turn upon the political prejudices of the incumbent attorney general.

That the executive order permitted personal bias is indicated by the facts. Between 1947 and 1953 three U.S. attorneys general preceding Brownell, with the same information available to them, had not targeted the National Lawyers Guild. On the contrary, between 1946 and 1953 four associate justices of the U.S. Supreme Court had commended the activities of the guild; they were Stanley Reed and Wiley Rutledge in 1946, Harold E. Burton in 1949, and Hugo Black in 1953. Moreover, the guild had been designated by the U.S. government as a consultant to the U.S. delegation that launched the United Nations in 1945, and in 1946 the guild, at the invitation of Justice Robert Jackson, chief U.S. prosecutor, had sent observers to the Nuremberg trials.[13]

One must therefore question why Attorney General Brownell tried to destroy the guild. The most probable answer is that President Dwight Eisenhower sought to appease Senator Joseph McCarthy and refused to support the case of *Brown v. Board of Education of Topeka,* which challenged racial segregation in the public schools.[14] (The *Brown* case was before the Supreme Court in 1953, and both the guild and the National Bar Association supported the NAACP Legal Defense Fund in its fight against the *Plessy v. Ferguson* doctrine of "separate but equal.") Dickerson saw the full significance of Brownell's attack and told the guild:

Mr. Brownell's attack on the Guild, if successful, would serve a three-fold objective: First, it would serve to disparage the FDR heritage and many lawyers connected with its development; second, it would serve to disparage that organization that is best equipped to expose the un-American and unconstitutional character of the current assault upon freedom and Mr. Brownell's program to subvert the Constitution; and third, it would inevitably serve to discourage lawyers even more than they are now from performing their solemn and imperative duty to provide legal defense for *all* accused persons.[15]

Dickerson moved quickly after Brownell's speech, and on August 27, 1953, declared publicly that the attorney general's charges were without foundation. In his words, the guild's record would "demonstrate to the Bar and the American people that as an independent, liberal bar association it is acting in the best traditions of American democracy and that those who are determined to silence it have abandoned that tradition."

On September 16 the guild, in a letter signed by Dickerson as president, filed a notice of contest in response to the attorney general's announcement that he proposed to designate the guild as a "subversive" organization.[16] In this notice the guild denied the charge and protested "any charge or insinuation that it was anything but an independent association of attorneys dedicated to the welfare of the American people and the bar. Its policies and actions are entirely a matter of public record." The guild then moved to its attack in four statements (which were to be the foundation of the guild's case in the subsequent court proceedings): (1) the attorney general is without constitutional power to make any listing such as he proposes; (2) no proper standards are set up in the president's executive order; (3) the procedures established by the attorney general deny due process; and (4) the attorney general has prejudged the issue.[17]

In these statements the guild was defending the independence of the American bar and the basic civil rights and liberties of the American people. On November 30, 1953, the guild sought a temporary injunction against Brownell's blacklisting from the U.S. Court for the District of Columbia, but on December 23, 1953, the court denied the injunction. The guild then filed an appeal with the U.S. Court of Appeals for the District of Columbia, and on May 4, 1954, the court ordered Attorney General Brownell to cease taking further steps to place the guild on his list pending a full and complete hearing in the district court.

One of the main points to be decided in this hearing was whether the attorney general had prejudged the issue. This involved the guild in trying to prove that the Department of Justice and the FBI had questioned attorneys employed or seeking employment in the federal government concerning their membership in the guild. On September 17, 1958, Brownell dismissed his proceedings, and the 1958 convention of the National Lawyers Guild was deemed a victory convention.

Leading the Chicago Urban League

The Chicago Urban League was an interracial organization in a city where rampant discrimination and segregation had created a solidarity and unity of purpose among blacks. The objectives of the Chicago Urban League were to reduce discrimination and segregation and to direct the energies of African Americans, aggravated by racial antagonism, into constructive channels. But these could not be achieved in a city whose white leadership refused to grant equal opportunities to an African American population, which was steadily increasing in numbers and just as steadily raising its aspirations and demands.

Earl Dickerson was president of the Chicago Urban League from 1939 until mid-1955 (except for the years 1948 and 1949 when he served as a director).[18] Throughout this sixteen-year period the city was wracked by violence against African Americans, including a number of riots that could easily have exploded into large-scale racial warfare comparable to that of 1919.

During Dickerson's years as president, the Chicago Urban League maintained reasonable working relations with both the black and the white communities, but these were tenuous at best. The league was always strapped for money and sometimes in arrears. Earl and Kathryn Dickerson personally raised substantial support, and holding the league together was no small accomplishment. At this time there was both a conservative and a progressive wing on the board, with Dickerson heading the progressives. But due largely to his leadership the conservatives remained a "loyal opposition."[19]

Under Dickerson's presidency the league weathered a crisis that resulted in the shake-up of its top staff.[20] In 1947 the executive director, Albon L. Foster, was fired, and Sidney Williams took his place. Williams had previously been a militant director of the St. Louis and Cleveland chapters of the league, and although Dickerson proposed and sponsored his candidacy, the decision to hire him was made by the board as a whole.

Williams's administration from 1947 to 1955 is referred to by Arvarh Strickland as a "Time of Troubles."[21] Feeling that a change in the executive position called for a change also in the presidency of the board, Dickerson resigned in 1947. After much difficulty the board agreed to offer a three-year presidency to Rabbi Louis Binstock, who accepted but then resigned after one year. Eldridge Bancroft Pierce, a former president and the elder statesman of the league, then accepted the office, but he, too, resigned after a year. Unable to agree on an acceptable conservative candidate, the board turned again to Dickerson; he reluctantly accepted in 1950, regarding himself as "caretaker" until a man "untouched by past forces" could step in.[22] But no such successor was found until 1955.

During this "Time of Troubles" much blame was laid upon Williams for his militancy. Dickerson's own militancy was another factor in the declining support for the league, but the main trouble lay in the city's racial division and in the Chicago league's lack of a clear-cut definition of policies and procedures.

Dickerson and Williams agreed on basic issues, but their circumstances were different: Williams was vulnerable in ways that Dickerson was not. Between 1945 and 1954 there were at least nine riots in Chicago, several of which were not reported in the white press.[23] Two of the most vicious were the Peoria Street riot and one of the several riots in Cicero. The Peoria Street riot took place between November 10 and 15, 1949, and Sidney Williams told the league board that he was not going to "fiddle while the city burned," as the Detroit league had done in 1943.[24] Therefore, on his own initiative, he called a meeting of black leaders for November 16. He then called for a second, larger meeting on November 19. At that meeting the Committee to End Mob Violence was formed, and Williams was chosen chairman. At a subsequent meeting the committee criticized Mayor Martin H. Kennelly and the Chicago Police Department and considered a resolution demanding the impeachment of both the mayor and the chief of police. The committee was subsequently labeled communist by a number of white newspapers, and, in fact, several communists were present at the meeting that day. As a result, a number of important groups and individuals resolved to withhold support for the league as long as Williams remained in office.

Dickerson also responded to the Peoria Street riot, and by January 1950, as president of the Chicago chapter of the National Lawyers Guild, he was leading a threefold program against the instigators of the riot, the perpetrators of the violence, and the police who had cooperated with the rioters.[25] Dickerson, who was both independent financially and backed by a professional association, did not receive the level of criticism directed toward Williams.

The Cicero riots of 1951 began in June when municipal police beat an African American war veteran named Harvey Clark Jr., who was moving into a house in that suburb. When Clark returned in July, the police joined a mob of four thousand who broke windows and started fires. Governor Adlai Stevenson declared martial law and sent in the state militia to restore order.[26]

On November 25, 1951, at the Chicago Coliseum, Dickerson addressed a huge "rally for justice" of the Chicago and Cook County Citizens Committee, which he had formed and of which he was cochairman, and he said:

Many have told us, publicly and privately, that they will consider going along with us if we would "screen out" this person or that. Sorry—we can't oblige them. We welcome the aid and assistance of anyone or any organization—and we still invite all who subscribe to our program to join us—but as Negroes we will not be dictated to, and we insist on the right to choose our own friends and associates.

I cannot be concerned with a man's political beliefs—but what does concern me is whether or not his criticisms are true. I don't care where he stands in the social register or the stock market—or on what side of the political fence, left or right. But I do care where he stands when the bricks are flying and when the bombs explode about my home.[27]

He then put forward the committee's program. It included punishment for the inciters and perpetrators; the outlawing of the White Circle League (a white supremacist organization) and the jailing of its leaders; the defeat at the polls of the county sheriff, the state's attorney, and Mayor Kennelly; and the calling out of federal troops to protect the homes of black families who move into restricted white areas.

Yet another incident involved Trumbull Park, a public housing project where racial disturbances occurred between August 4, 1953, and June 30, 1955. Elizabeth Wood, executive secretary of the Chicago Housing Authority (CHA), insisted on carrying out the authority's policy of open housing. John L. Yancey, the only African American on the CHA board, led a successful effort to reverse her policy, to demote her, and finally to force her resignation. Both Dickerson and Sidney Williams denounced Yancey and supported Wood. Nelson C. Jackson, director of community services for the National Urban League, criticized both men for involving "the Urban League in an internal conflict between the Housing Authority Director and the Housing Authority Commission without giving the board an opportunity to debate and vote on the issue."[28]

Faced with these various crises, as well as with dwindling income from other sources, the Chicago Urban League was increasingly dependent on an annual allocation from the Community Fund to which social welfare agencies looked for a percentage of their budgets. But the fund was troubled by the league's internal disarray and was itself imperiled by its support of the league, claiming losses of three hundred thousand dollars a year in public contributions because of the Urban League's participation. In October the fund made its 1955 grant to the league conditional upon a study of the "philosophy, purpose, and function of the Chicago Urban League." The National Urban League sent Nelson C. Jackson and two other staff members to conduct the study. Submitted in May, the report recommended a complete reorganization,[29] and in response conservatives on the board elected Dr. Nathaniel O. Calloway, a black physician, as president. Dickerson's "caretaker" period thereby came to an end, as did, at his request, his membership on the board.[30]

Under Calloway the league board began a thorough and careful reorganization. It closed the league temporarily as of July 15, 1955. All staff members, including Williams, were dismissed without prejudice and with severance pay. The search for a new director was begun, and the "new" league opened in January 1956. Edwin C. (Bill) Berry became its executive secretary. In a history of the Urban League, the author concluded that the "'new' Urban League has made significant contributions to the efforts being made [to facilitate the entrance of African Americans into the mainstream]; but without the 'old' Urban League, there would have been no 'new' Urban League."[31]

To this we might add that without Dickerson there would have been no "old" league upon which to build the "new." A column in the *Pittsburgh Courier Magazine Section* of July 30, 1955, written immediately after the shake-up, had this to say:

> Earl Dickerson is an individual who might rightly be called "controversial." In Chicago sooner or later your informant will tell you he is okay, and you'll be told in such a way that you don't dare disagree. For the first time I got a good look at him, a tall,

handsome, *café-au-lait* man with an easy smile and—of all things—a dimple.

I was rather surprised to hear Dickerson speak of "the great progress the Negro has made under our system of government," and later to speak of "Communist aggression in Korea."

I never discovered why Chicago Negroes were so staunchly militant and defensive about their hero. Even his critics or detractors will concede only that: "Well, maybe he is a little left, but . . ." and then follows a string of defense, crediting him with everything good, civil-rightswise, and devastating any argument you can devise—if you still have the courage to do so.

On the Board of the National NAACP

Dickerson was elected to the national board of the NAACP in 1941 and remained a member until the end of 1971. In 1934, after a bitter dispute over policy, authority, and budget, particularly with executive secretary Walter White, W. E. B. DuBois left the NAACP to chair the department of sociology at Atlanta University. However, in 1944 the NAACP and DuBois once again needed each other. The NAACP was then being forced to take a more militant stand, and DuBois had recently left Atlanta University under duress.[32] The president, chairman, and executive secretary of the NAACP jointly invited him to return, but DuBois was prickly and suspicious. Dickerson—his admirer since boyhood—helped ease the way for DuBois to assume the post of director of special research for the NAACP in September 1944.

In 1945, DuBois, representing the NAACP, sent statements and appeals to the delegations founding the United Nations in San Francisco on behalf of blacks in both the United States and in Africa. Two years later, on October 19, the NAACP sent a petition to each of the fifty-seven delegates in the General Assembly of the United Nations for consideration. It was entitled "An Appeal to the World" and was prepared for the NAACP under the editorial supervision of DuBois. In the introduction DuBois wrote: "Discrimination practiced in the United States against her own citizens and to a large extent in contravention to her own laws cannot be persisted in without infringing upon the rights of the people of the world, and especially upon the ideals and work of the United Nations." Five chapters follow DuBois's introduction—one each by Earl B. Dickerson; Milton Konvitz, director of research at Cornell University School of Industrial Relations; William R. Ming Jr., associate professor at the University of Chicago Law School; Leslie Perry, legal representative of the NAACP, Washington, D.C., chapter; and Rayford W. Logan, professor of history at Howard University. Dickerson's chapter 2, "The Denial of Legal Rights to American Negroes from 1787 to 1914," surveys those 127 years, buttressed by citations of forty-six court decisions.

On October 31, 1947, the *New York Herald-Tribune* reported that DuBois told reporters he had received twelve replies from U.N. delegates pledging sympathetic attention. The petition was formally filed with the Commission on Human Rights of the Economic and Social Council. This commission, at its Paris meeting in 1947, tabled the petition on the motion of Eleanor Roosevelt and Jonathan Daniels of the U.S. delegation. Their argument was that the status of African Americans should remain a domestic matter. The United States had supported the policies of several European nations with colonies in Africa, and, in return, no European member delegate would vote to consider the petition concerning the status of African Americans in the United States.[33]

Mrs. Roosevelt was also a member of the national board of the NAACP at this time, and her dual role was an embarrassment both to herself and to the organization. When the Soviet delegate proposed that the U.N. commission consider the NAACP petition, the commission rejected the motion by a vote of 11 to 1. Thus the petition was a casualty of the cold war. Mrs. Roosevelt told DuBois that she had been compelled several times to answer attacks on the United States for its racial practices by pointing out that other nations had similar problems. She also told him that if the matter were to be discussed in the General Assembly, she and her colleagues would have to defend the United States and that taking such a position would be so distasteful that she would feel compelled to resign from the U.S. delegation.[34]

A PARALLEL STRUGGLE to advance human rights was also taking place within the United States at this time. In 1946, President Harry S. Truman was evolving a bold and comprehensive civil rights program—one that defied powerful southern interests in the Democratic Party and which was to be a major reason for the succession of the "Dixiecrats," whose nominee for the presidency in 1948 was Senator Strom Thurmond of South Carolina. In his State of the Union address to Congress on January 6, 1947, Truman announced the establishment of the President's Committee on Civil Rights. When he received the committee's report, *To Secure These Rights*, on October 29, 1947, Truman explained: "I created this committee with a feeling of urgency. No sooner were we finished with the war when racial and religious intolerance began to appear and threaten the very things we had just fought for."[35]

For the document to be approved by the Senate, the fifteen members of the President's Committee first had to be approved by the Senate Judiciary Committee. Before Truman announced the creation of the committee, James A. Cobb[36] told Dickerson that the president was considering him as a member. Cobb later told Dickerson that his name had not been submitted because the southern members of the Senate Judiciary Committee would not approve his appointment. His work on Roosevelt's first FEPC—particularly his performance in Birmingham—had not been forgotten. In his stead Truman named, and the Senate approved, Mrs. Sadie T. Alexander, secretary of the National Bar Association.

TENSIONS WERE ALSO increasing within the leadership of the black community at this time. By 1954, Black Muslims in the United States numbered in the tens of thousands. The NAACP, whose policy was integrationist, and the Black Muslims, who pursued a separatist agenda, were by this time criticizing each other publicly. The NAACP board appointed Dickerson and A. Philip Randolph to seek a discussion with the Black Muslim leader, Elijah Muhammed, in order to find some common ground. To this end Randolph and Malcolm X went to Chicago and met with Dickerson in his office at the Supreme Liberty Life Insurance Company. The group was then taken by limousine to Elijah Muhammed's Nation of Islam's headquarters on Chicago's South Side, and with Randolph on Elijah Muhammed's right, Dickerson on his left, and Malcolm X facing Elijah, the four discussed their differences over lunch. "We were royally treated," Dickerson recalled. "The attendants were dressed in uniforms and wore white gloves. It was a very satisfactory event. I think it quieted down the public controversy."

W. E. B. DuBois and Paul Robeson

W. E. B. DuBois and Paul Robeson had long been militant fighters for equal rights and freedom, and Dickerson had relationships with both of them that developed into strong friendships. Dickerson had known Eslanda Good (who later married Paul Robeson) when they were students at the University of Illinois. He later met Robeson at a party in New York City in 1923, and when Robeson arrived in Chicago in 1937 seeking aid for the Loyalists in the Spanish civil war, Dickerson joined him in that support. In 1944 when Robeson was playing Othello in Chicago, Earl and Kathryn gave a party in his honor at their home at 3842 South Parkway. Among several African American notables present were Etta Moten, who was then playing Bess in *Porgy and Bess;* her husband, Claude Barnett; and Duke Ellington, who was playing in Chicago at that time. This party was jovial. But at a previous event an argument broke out between Dickerson and Ellington. Dickerson accused Ellington of not doing enough to advance the African American cause. Ellington responded that his contribution was music, which opens doors, but Dickerson contended that this was simply not enough and that Ellington should take a more active and vocal position on civil rights.[37]

DuBois's *The Souls of Black Folk,* published in 1903, was a book that had early awakened Dickerson's youthful mind. Dickerson read DuBois's writings in the NAACP's *The Crisis* and elsewhere and took every opportunity to hear the eloquent scholar in person. In 1944, Dickerson helped persuade DuBois to return to the staff of the NAACP, and from then until December 31, 1948, when DuBois's position with the NAACP came to an end, the two had frequent contact, including their collaboration in the NAACP's "Appeal to the World."

By the late 1940s both Robeson and DuBois were in considerable trouble with the U.S. government because of their militant advocacies, some of them collaborations. One such effort was through the Council of African Affairs, which DuBois and Max Yergan had founded in 1937. Early in 1948 the U.S. attorney general put the council on the list of "subversive" organizations. At about the same time Yergan issued a statement attacking communism. In a fierce internal struggle, Yergan was ousted and Robeson remained as chairman. After the NAACP fired DuBois, effective December 31, 1948, he became vice chairman of the council.

At the World Peace Conference, held in Paris in April 1949, Robeson made a speech in which he said, "The black folk of America will never fight against the Soviet Union." *The Crisis* of May 1949 attacked Robeson for this statement and characterized the Council on African Affairs as "long ago labeled a Communist-front organization by the Department of Justice." The *Negro Digest* of March 1950 carried a debate on the propriety of Robeson's statement, with DuBois defending and Walter White, executive secretary of the NAACP, attacking Robeson's view.[38]

Early in 1950, Earl and Kathryn Dickerson visited the Robesons in England, and Eslanda held a party for them in the Robeson home. Later in 1950 the U.S. State Department temporarily denied Robeson a passport on the grounds that he had refused to sign an affidavit stating that he was not and never had been a member of the

Communist Party.[39] Between 1950 and 1958 the Dickersons and the Robesons remained in close contact. Dickerson, as a prominent alumnus of the University of Chicago Law School, sponsored a concert for Paul in Mandel Hall at a time when Robeson was being denied the opportunity to perform elsewhere.

Paul Robeson was continually persecuted and harassed, and he was denied the opportunity to pursue his artistic career and to earn his living. The situation was worsened when in 1952 he was awarded and accepted the Stalin Peace Prize. Many threats were made on his life.[40] Dickerson recalled that the "support of Paul Robeson by blacks in this country, roughly from about 1936 on, was a rare phenomenon. I would say that from 1949 on, support by prominent blacks was almost nonexistent. I think that in the black community there was no one quite so prominent as Earl Dickerson as a supporter of Paul Robeson. Another, of course, was W. E. B. DuBois."[41] As efforts were intensified to destroy him, Robeson called on the black middle class to remain neutral if they could not support his radical prescriptions for an end to racial oppression and his right to remain friendly toward the Soviet Union. But neutrality was unsafe ground. Their abandonment of Robeson was almost total.[42]

During this time the U.S. government was prosecuting W. E. B. DuBois, who headed the Peace Information Center in New York City from April 3 to October 12, 1950. The center had been involved in the Stockholm World Peace Appeal, which was proposed to outlaw the use of the atomic bomb in war and had been signed by many prominent people in the international community. This proposal was given special cogency by the outbreak of the Korean War on June 25, 1950, and on August 11, 1950, the U.S. Department of Justice informed the Peace Information Center that in order to comply with the McCarran Act, its officers had to register as "agents of a foreign government." DuBois and others refused to do so. On February 1, 1951, he and others were indicted as unregistered foreign agents. After several postponements the trial was held from November 2 to November 19, 1951 (with a three-day recess for Armistice Day). On November 20, immediately after the prosecution had made its summation, Judge Matthews F. McGuire directed the jury to acquit all the defendants.[43]

DuBois and his wife, Shirley Graham DuBois, made a number of trips across the country denouncing the McCarran Act and raising money to pay sizable legal fees. Dickerson was active in his support of DuBois and was a sponsor of a testimonial dinner honoring DuBois on his eighty-third birthday, February 23, 1951, at the Essex House in New York City. When DuBois and his wife went to Chicago after the trial, they were guests of the Dickersons for ten days, and during this visit Dickerson drove DuBois to Gary, Indiana, to study the steel mills and the steelworkers there, who were of special interest to DuBois as a sociologist.

IN AUGUST 1949, Earl, Kathryn, and Diane Dickerson moved into a luxurious three-story house at 5027 South Drexel that had a half acre of trees and a lawn surrounded by an iron fence. This property, purchased from white owners, was in an area previously protected by a racially restrictive housing covenant. Kathryn's son, Rodger Wilson, lived with them until he entered the U.S. Army in 1942. He returned for a year after the war and then left to pursue a career as an artist. Diane enrolled in Mills College in Oakland, California, after graduating from Francis W. Parker School in the spring of 1952.

Before Diane left for college, she and her boyfriend, Nelson F. Brown, planned a farewell dinner at the Empire Room of the Palmer House, and Nelson's father made reservations. When they arrived, though, the maître d'hôtel told them there were no reservations and refused to seat them even though the dining room was nearly empty. When white couples who had not made reservations came and were seated, both Diane and Nelson called their fathers. Nelson's father, Sydney Y. Brown, came immediately to the hotel. He was a lawyer with the firm of Brown, Cyrus, and Brown. For his part, Dickerson called Jesse Mann, who also worked at Brown, Cyrus, and Brown, and said, "Get going on a damage suit under the Illinois Civil Rights Act." The suit for one thousand dollars was leveled against the Conrad Hilton Hotels, Inc., operators of the Palmer House. Dickerson, Jesse Mann, and Sidney A. Jones Jr. represented Diane and Nelson. After several hearings the jury awarded the couple a hundred dollars in damages, but this lesser amount did nothing to tarnish the victory. *Jet* magazine of June 27, 1953, reported: "The suit is believed to be the first of its kind won against a large hotel chain in this country."

To celebrate, Dickerson made reservations for a table close to the floor show at the Empire Room. The party was made up of Earl and Kathryn Dickerson, Diane Dickerson and Nelson Brown Jr., Mr. and Mrs. Sydney Brown, Mr. and Mrs. Jesse Mann, Mr. and Mrs. Sidney Jones, and Judge Herman E. Moore of the U.S. District Court of the Virgin Islands and his wife. The Dickersons, accompanied by the Moores, were the first to arrive. The same maître d'hôtel who had previously refused to seat Diane and Nelson now tried to put their party in the balcony. Diane recalled, "My father just raised hell. He said: 'We've just sued you and won. We'll have to sue you again. This is our table, and this is where we will sit.' And that is where we sat. We had a wonderful evening. It was great fun."[44] When the party was leaving, Dickerson delivered another admonition to the acquiescent but unrepentant maître d'hôtel. The Palmer House also was unrepentant, and Dickerson was forced to garnish one of the Palmer House accounts after it ignored the court order to pay the hundred dollars in damages. To the Palmer House, as for Dickerson, it was the "principle" and not the dollars that mattered.

Before this episode Dickerson was already quietly breaking color barriers in other major hotels around the country. In 1945, while traveling by train to New York City from Washington, D.C., where the National Lawyers Guild had held a convention, he told another member of the guild, a white lawyer, that he would like to stay at the Waldorf-Astoria. His companion said: "Let me know when. I'm a counsel for that hotel." The Dickersons went to New York City after he had been elected president of the National Bar Association in Cleveland on December 8, 1945, and reservations were made. They were given a sixth-floor suite that was often rented by Bing

Crosby, and the *New York Amsterdam News* carried a photograph and story of the Dickersons in the suite with the comment: "We have not known of any other Negroes to be served in the Waldorf-Astoria."[45] That evening Dickerson had as his guest in the Waldorf-Astoria dining room another African American, William Pickens, director of the NAACP's division of branches. Thereafter the Waldorf-Astoria was Dickerson's regular "home away from home" in New York City, and other blacks were soon given rooms and dining service at the hotel. Dickerson similarly broke the color barrier at the Mayflower Hotel in Washington, D.C.

The Original Forty Club

One of the few social organizations to which Dickerson belonged was the Original Forty Club, founded in 1915. The requirements for membership, by recommendation and pending approval by the group, were to have "good moral character and a legitimate occupation."[46] When the organization sought incorporation in 1920, it discovered that a group of LaSalle Street brokers already owned the name Forty Club, and so the name was changed to the Original Forty Club. Its membership grew over the years from half a dozen to a limit of forty at incorporation and to over eighty by 1984. The club meets to this day on the last Saturday of every month except during the summer "for fellowship, food, and forensics." The list of past and present members of the club reads like a who's who of the Chicago black community. Dickerson became a member in 1925. Another of the club's members was Dr. Leonidas Berry, who introduced gastrointestinal endoscopy into the practice of medicine in Chicago and who made improvements in the endoscope. He once correctly diagnosed Dickerson's persistent distress as the result of polyps on the lining of his stomach. After Dickerson had recovered from their removal, Dr. Berry introduced him as "exhibit A" in a presentation to the Chicago Medical Association, which at the time had denied him membership because of race.[47]

Chapter Eight

THE SUPREME LIFE INSURANCE
COMPANY

The first white insurance company to hire blacks was Royal Life, organized in 1912. It had a district office on the South Side of Chicago that was staffed entirely by African Americans, and nearly every black life insurance company organized in Chicago after World War I was founded by former Royal Life employees. One of these was Frank L. Gillespie, founder of the Supreme Liberty Life Insurance Company.[1]

Gillespie, born in Arkansas in 1887, graduated from high school in Little Rock and attended the Boston Conservatory of Music, hoping to make a career as a violinist. After severely injuring his fingers, though, he went to Chicago in 1900 and worked successively as a private secretary, a telephone operator, and an agent for Oscar De Priest's real estate company. He served an apprenticeship in the Royal Life Insurance Company, joining in 1916, and also worked for the Public Life Insurance Company, another white firm, which sold industrial life policies to African Americans. Ambitious, he laid plans to establish a black-controlled firm,[2] gathered together several prominent businessmen, and received articles of incorporation for the Liberty Life Insurance Company on June 3, 1919. Another incorporator was Midian O. Bousfield, born on August 22, 1885, in Tipton, Missouri. In 1889 his modestly prosperous parents moved to Kansas City, Kansas. Young Bousfield received a bachelor of arts from the University of Kansas in 1907 and an M.D. from Northwestern University's Medical School in 1909. After a year in Brazil he organized black railroad workers into the Railway Benevolent Association and attracted the attention of Gillespie, who hired him as Liberty's medical director.[3]

Earl Dickerson did volunteer work for Liberty Life before he was officially named general counsel and director in December 1920. At this time the company was still short forty-six thousand dollars of the necessary hundred thousand in capital plus five thousand in surplus that had to be deposited with the Illinois Department of Insurance by June 3, 1921. Gillespie exhorted the incorporators and stockholders to buy and sell more stock. Dickerson wrote advertisements and brochures, and on Sundays he regularly went to black churches and spoke before their congregations to promote the company.[4] One of his favorite biblical quotations was Mordecai's question to Queen Esther: "Who knoweth whether thou art come to the kingdom for such a time as this?"

Before the company was licensed to do business, Dickerson served without pay, but he was acquiring experience, knowledge, and contacts that would be invaluable to his future work. As he said, "I came to know all the agencies and organizations that were seeking to improve the character, raise the sights, and train the skills of young black people. I came to develop my already established interests in such organizations as the Chicago Urban League and the Chicago branch of the NAACP."[5]

Liberty Life needed offices, but before space could be rented, De Priest, who had once employed Gillespie, persuaded him to buy a building in which De Priest had his political headquarters. Gillespie went to Dickerson to arrange the purchase, intending to use money from the sale of stock that was being accumulated to meet the state's requirements for capital and surplus. Dickerson refused, warning Gillespie that this move would be illegal and that "if you do this, you'll go to the pen."

Liberty finally rented offices on the second floor of a building located at 3501 Grand Avenue (now King Drive), and Dicker-son handled the lease, which was signed on May 1, 1921, at three hundred dollars a month for three years. Alexander Flowers, who opened the Roosevelt State Bank on the first floor, had constructed the building earlier that year.

On June 1, 1921, Gillespie, George W. Holt, the treasurer, and Dickerson drove from Chicago to Springfield carrying $110,000 in first mortgages to the Illinois Department of Insurance—two days before the expiration date to qualify for a license to sell insurance. The trip took twelve hours because of several mechanical problems, including flat tires. The officers arrived at the Department of Insurance at 4:00 P.M.—one hour before closing time. Once licensed, Liberty Life Insurance Company became the first African American legal reserve life insurance company in the North.

At first the company sold only ordinary life policies,[6] but in the summer of 1921 Liberty Life issued a brochure entitled "A Golden Opportunity," which stated its purposes: to provide the insurance protection denied by white companies, to provide white collar and executive employment,[7] and to furnish a source of mortgages and loans to African Americans. The brochure also stated that "the whole future of the Race"[8] lay in the development of black busi-nesses to serve their own markets. Despite the race riots of 1919 and the relatively short recession after the war, African Americans continued to migrate to the North in large numbers, particularly to Chicago. They needed employment, which was scarce, and capital, which did not exist from white sources. Liberty Life Insurance Company thereby served a unique purpose.

From June 1921, when Liberty was first licensed, until 1942, when Dickerson became the loan and mortgage officer, he was paid $99.99 a month. This precise sum was set because his work was part-time, and the state insurance code required that any salary of $100 or more a month to an officer must be approved by the board of directors. Dickerson had other sources of income from his pri-vate law practice, which was growing slowly but steadily, as well as from his salaries as assistant corporation counsel of the city of Chicago (1923–27), assistant attorney general of Illinois (1933–39), and alderman (1939–43).

In 1924, Liberty bought the building at 3501 Grand Avenue from Flowers for a quarter of a million dollars, and by the spring of 1925 the company appeared to be on the verge of profitable operations. But on May 1, 1925, Frank Gillespie died.[9] That day was a Thursday. On the previous Sunday, Dickerson had visited him in his home. Gasping for breath, Gillespie addressed him angrily: "You didn't let me do what I wanted to do!" referring to the proposed purchase of the building from De Priest in 1921. Dickerson answered, "If I had, you wouldn't be here. You'd be in the penitentiary." Gillespie had been a great salesman and was also something of a practical joker (Dickerson related that Gillespie once "sold" one of the lions in front of the Art Institute to a man from the South), but it is clear from this episode that his judgment was not always good and that he relied on Dickerson's legal guidance to help make Liberty Life a success.

After Gillespie's death, Dr. Midian O. Bousfield, who had been an incorporator, medical director, and vice president, was elected president of Liberty Life. Dickerson's most remarkable accomplishment for the company during this period was to help save Liberty from being taken over by Jesse Binga, who had established the Binga State Bank in 1908 and was one of the wealthiest black men in the city. Bluff, rough, and tough, he had no interest in racial ideology but was interested exclusively in acquiring money and power.

According to Dickerson, Bousfield did not give much attention to Liberty Life's business, and its secretary, W. Ellis Stewart, and Dickerson conducted most of its affairs. Bousfield knew Binga personally and would often try to persuade him to invest in Liberty's stock. He sponsored Binga's election as chairman of the board of directors, and Binga quickly sent his accountants to study the company's situation. In one important respect this was not good. Liberty had a contract with an agency known as the Liberty Underwriters Company, which had undertaken to produce policies on commission and was using Liberty Life's money to carry on its own business. Binga wanted to control Liberty Life.[10] He went to the State Department of Insurance and told its officers that the relationship with Liberty Underwriters was bleeding Liberty Life, and he successfully requested that the department force the cancellation of the contract. In addition, Binga began to interfere with the affairs of company officers—the secretary and the medical director in particular—in an attempt to take charge. A sharp conflict soon developed between Binga on the one side and Stewart and Dickerson on the other.

Liberty's officers had authority to increase the company's stock by five thousand shares, and Dickerson used this strategy to oust Binga. As Dickerson said,

> We were in the process of selling stock to the public. We knew that if we got the additional capital and the proxies of the additional stockholders, we could get rid of Binga. We arranged the underwriting of the purchase of the stock with Alexander Flowers, president of the Roosevelt State Bank, undertaking to pay him back when the stock was sold. Flowers advanced the money. We got enough money through David Manson, one of our directors who had a big account with the Foreman National Bank (now the American National Bank), to buy 75 percent of the stock in cash. With the cash in the bank, the State Department of Insurance certified that the stock was subject to our call. That put us in charge again. When the time came for elections, we got enough proxies to put Binga out.

By the late 1920s Jesse Binga had become a vassal of Samuel Insull, the utilities magnate whose empire began to collapse when the "bubble burst." The Binga State Bank became the first in Chicago to fall in the wake of the stock market crash of 1929. The collapse of Binga's bank in 1930 "ended a chapter in the history of Negro enterprise,"[11] and "within a month, every bank in Black Metropolis was closed."[12] But Liberty Life Insurance Company survived.

The First Merger

In the late 1920s, the Liberty Life Insurance Company, the Supreme Life and Casualty Company of Columbus, Ohio, and Northeastern Life Insurance Company of Newark, New Jersey, were all pinched by their limited operations. Their presidents—Midian O. Bousfield, Truman K. Gibson, and Harry H. Pace, respectively—were close friends and members of Boule, a business and professional fraternity. Bousfield convinced Gibson and Pace at a Boule meeting that the three companies should merge, and it was agreed that Liberty should take the initiative. Bousfield then persuaded Stewart and Dickerson and asked Dickerson to draw up a proposal.

Dickerson drew up the terms of a proposed merger, which provided for the shareholders of the two other companies to accept a new issue of twenty thousand shares of Liberty stock at par value (ten dollars a share) in exchange for their original stock.[13] The twenty-nine directors of the three companies met in Chicago. They agreed to the merger and to the election of Pace as president and chief executive officer, Gibson as chairman of the board and director of production, Bousfield as first vice president and medical director, Stewart as secretary, and Dickerson as general counsel. Dickerson went to the departments of insurance of the three states and received approval. The stockholders agreed to the proposal on June 5, 1929, and the merger was completed.

The combined assets of the new company, Supreme Liberty Life Insurance Company of Chicago, increased to $1,458,000, up from Liberty's $832,000; its ordinary insurance in force was increased to $16,629,000 from Liberty's $10,401,000; and its industrial insurance in force was increased to $7,393,000 from Liberty's $1,964,000.[14] Dickerson handled all the legal transactions, for which he received a fee of $1,000. John H. Johnson, later chairman and chief executive officer of Supreme, commented in 1984: "The three companies were saved by the merger. Earl Dickerson handled all the legal matters, for which there were no clear precedents. Nobody has challenged the legal papers involved in the creation of the new company."[15]

Even with greater capital, new ranking officers, and a strong emphasis on industrial policies, Supreme Liberty did not make impressive gains—this despite relatively favorable conditions, such as the continued migration of blacks to the North, higher income, and the substantial growth of black-owned businesses. Supreme Liberty was not in particularly good shape, therefore, when the depression struck with full force in the early 1930s.[16]

Invention of the Policy Lien

Insurance companies throughout the country were in trouble during the depression, and African American companies were especially hard-hit. Two of the largest black insurance companies failed.[17] The Illinois Life Insurance Company, a large white firm, also failed, and this moved the Illinois Department of Insurance to begin an examination in 1934 of all insurance firms in the state. State auditors reduced the value of Supreme Liberty's real estate from $743,000 to less than $380,000.[18] The company had a large percentage of its assets in mortgages on real estate owned by African Americans, and foreclosures would have been disadvantageous because the properties were expensive to maintain.

In early 1934, Mr. Clausen, head of the Chicago attorney general's office, went to Dickerson, who as assistant attorney general was assigned to bring action in Chicago to liquidate insurance companies that the State Department of Insurance had declared insolvent. Clausen showed Dickerson a list of companies against which action was to be taken. Knowing that Dickerson was general counsel of Supreme Liberty, he put his finger on that name in the list. Dickerson immediately telephoned Harry H. Pace and W. Ellis Stewart and asked them to call a meeting of the Supreme Liberty executive committee the next day. At 5:00 P.M. Dickerson left his office as assistant attorney general and went to his private office to think through the problem. He stayed there until about four o'clock the next morning, and during this time it occurred to him that the case was like a creditor bankruptcy. He developed the idea that if enough policyholders with cash value claims on the company would sign over liens on those claims to the company, Supreme Liberty could list them as assets instead of debits and could be declared solvent.[19]

The next morning Dickerson looked over the first draft of what became known as the policy lien with the company's actuary, Mr. Glover. Glover said, "I don't know any company that has done this, but it sounds like a good idea." Dickerson showed the executive committee the order to liquidate Supreme Liberty, explained his idea, and presented the draft of the policy lien. Dickerson related what happened this way:

> One member said, "It's telling the policyholders too much. It will scare them." I said, "That's the heart of the whole thing. If they don't assign the lien to us, they will lose everything. This is the only chance they have to save their policies and their cash values." We wrote out the policyholders' acceptance and our conditions to repay the liens. The board adopted the instrument.
>
> Then I went to Attorney General Otto Kerner Sr. "What do you think of this, Judge?" He said, "It sounds pretty good. Take it to Palmer." Ernest Palmer was commissioner of insurance.
>
> We went down to Springfield the next day or two—Mr. Pace, Mr. Gibson, Stewart, and I. I called up Governor Henry Horner, whom I knew. Horner called Palmer and said, "Give Dickerson an audience." Palmer did so and turned the matter over to the assistant attorney general in charge of such matters, Mr. Kadek. In a few days Kadek wrote a long opinion that the policy lien was not sound and should not be accepted.
>
> I went back to Attorney General Kerner and asked him if I could file a mandamus proceeding [an order issued by a court to an official or a corporation to perform a duty required by statute]

in the Illinois Supreme Court ordering Ernest Palmer to recognize the lien and transfer the liabilities to assets, provided that we could get enough policyholders to sign the lien to keep us solvent. Kerner said, "You can't do that. You are one of my assistants." "Will you oppose it?" "No, but you'll have to get somebody else to file the suit." "Whom do you recommend?" "I recommend Floyd Thompson." Thompson had been chief justice of the Illinois Supreme Court and then retired to private practice.

We engaged Thompson. He filed a suit. Some of the other officers and I went down to hear the presentation. The Illinois Supreme Court upheld us by a vote of 5 to 2 and ordered Palmer to accept the lien as valid.[20]

Although liens had been commonly used to reduce an insurance company's obligations when reinsuring liquidated companies, this was the first time they were used on the cash value of insurance policies in order to keep a company from being liquidated.

Dickerson and other officers went on the road all over the country to visit policyholders. They asked them to sign over only 50 percent of their cash values and persuaded enough of them to transfer about five hundred thousand dollars from liabilities to assets. Other insurance companies subsequently used the policy lien to save themselves, and in 1937 a change in the Illinois Insurance Code voided such instruments. But Supreme Liberty was already out of danger by that time. The company had retired all the liens by 1937 and in the meantime had paid death benefits in full on all policies, including those that still had liens.[21]

By representing both Supreme Liberty and the state of Illinois, Dickerson's actions involved a clear conflict of interest. Although Dickerson was a social progressive and a political idealist, we should not forget that he was also a businessman and a pragmatist by nature; when he felt it necessary, he would willingly finesse legal and ethical issues in pursuit of what he believed to be the greater good. That he understood Supreme Liberty to have a larger social goal within the black community certainly played a role in his decision, as, no doubt, did his self-interest as a capable lawyer and businessman. The creative and resourceful manner in which Dickerson was able to juggle his various responsibilities as both an outspoken civil rights advocate and an African American professional and business leader is perhaps one of the most interesting and revealing aspects of his character. For Dickerson these sometimes divergent roles routinely coalesced in his professional activities so that his business and financial achievements, on the one hand, and his accomplishments in pursuit of civil rights, on the other, would come to represent one and the same thing: the overcoming of racial discrimination and poverty in America. That he felt himself to be an embodiment of these struggles is obvious, and he consequently believed that he could harness his idealism and moral outrage in the service of pragmatic business goals and, equally, that his pragmatic business goals would contribute directly to the realization of a better life not only for himself but for all African Americans.

THIS IS PERHAPS a good place to pause and raise two questions about Earl Dickerson. The first is, How was he able to do so many things simultaneously? From 1942 to 1955, when he was a full-time employee of Supreme Liberty, he was also alderman from 1939 to 1943; a member of President Roosevelt's FEPC from mid-1941 to mid-1943; president of the National Bar Association from 1945 to 1947; president of the National Lawyers Guild from 1951 to 1954; president of the Chicago Urban League most of the time between 1939 and 1955; and a member of the national board of the NAACP from 1941 on. The second question is, How was Dickerson able to build up a substantial personal fortune, which he used to support causes he believed in such as Parkway Management Company?

The many people who worked with Dickerson over the years provide a collective answer to the first question. Dickerson had enormous energy and was always alert to able young men and women who could help him do the many things he wanted to accomplish. John H. Johnson (president of Johnson Publishing Company and chairman of the board and chief executive officer of Supreme) is a good example, and there were innumerable others along the way. Johnson said, "Working under Earl Dickerson was a great training ground. He found, picked, encouraged, and developed bright young men and women. Many of the young people he brought in are holding important positions today because of the training they had and the associations they made with Supreme and Earl Dickerson."[22]

Dickerson had great skill in both "firing up" idealistic young African Americans and in delegating responsibilities to them, which would achieve his goals while also successfully furthering their careers.

The answer to the second question is simply that Dickerson possessed unusual business acumen and recognized opportunities to buy and sell properties and invest his capital wisely. Such opportunities, but not always good judgment, came with the territory. As general counsel for Liberty Life and Supreme Liberty from 1921 to 1955, he had to examine and judge the soundness of the company's mortgages, loans, and mergers. As vice president in charge of mortgages and investments beginning in 1942, he broadened his experience and deepened his knowledge and, consequently, was always alert to opportunities for private gain.

SUPREME LIFE BECAME increasingly profitable after 1938. In 1941 it paid its first dividend—thirty cents per share.[23] And while the company was succeeding in its business objectives, it was succeeding in its social mission as well, particularly through its involvement in the *Hansberry v. Lee* case of 1940.

In 1942, upon the death of one of Supreme's general officers, Dickerson was asked to head the investments and mortgage department, with the title of vice president. His salary was raised to eight thousand dollars—the same as those of Secretary Stewart and Agency Director J. G. Ish.

In 1934, Ish had introduced a sales program called mass production that resulted in a rapid expansion of the company's industrial holdings, but it had high administrative costs. In addition, because the pay of the agents was low, Supreme Liberty lost many of its best sales personnel to other firms, including white firms that were competing for the African American market after 1941, a time when African American incomes were rising and life expectancy was lengthening.[24]

The gradual rise of a black middle class raised the question of how black insurance companies could enter the mainstream of American economic life in the future. Stewart called this objective the "economic detour." Before 1920 the incomes and life expectancies of blacks were so much lower than those of whites that the African American insurance market was not attractive to white companies. After 1930 these differences became increasingly less pronounced, and the competition for the African American market grew sharply. The economic detour consequently got narrower and bumpier between 1930 and 1950, as the following figures show.[25]

Expectancy in Years of Life at Birth by Race and Sex for Chicago, 1930–1950

YEAR	WHITE POPULATION		NONWHITE POPULATION	
	Male	*Female*	*Male*	*Female*
1930	57.8	61.7	42.5	46.7
1940	62.6	67.2	51.0	56.3
1950	64.7	70.8	58.2	63.5

From this table it can be calculated that in 1930 the difference in life expectancies between whites and nonwhites[26] (averaging male and female) was 15.15 years. By 1950 that difference had narrowed to 6.9 years.

HARRY H. PACE died in 1943, and Truman K. Gibson became president of Supreme Liberty. His administration made no major changes until 1954, but Supreme Liberty continued to grow and pay dividends, although at a lower rate than the black life insurance industry as a whole.[27]

During this period Dickerson undertook an unusually risky enterprise—the White City Homes Project, which although shared by other officers of Supreme Liberty was essentially a private venture. White City was a thirteen-acre area between Sixty-third and Sixty-sixth Streets, directly south of the Washington Park area that had been opened up to African Americans after Dickerson's victory in the *Hansberry* case. The site was previously occupied by the White City Amusement Park[28] and had been cleared with the intention of developing housing in the area. This plan was eventually given up, and in 1942 a man named Journé White went to Dickerson with a proposal. Dickerson related the following:

> White, a promoter who had recently come from California, said that he wanted to develop a housing project on the cleared site of White City. He had expert architects to plan the housing; it was necessary to sell the properties from the blueprints to raise the funds essential to buy the site, and he wanted my help. Out of that conversation, and after some investigation, came the organization of Parkway Management Company, of which I was president. I invited two men at Supreme Liberty—Theodore Jones and Truman Gibson Jr.—to be officers as well.
>
> The first objective of Parkway Management Company was to hire persons on commission to sell the lots and the proposed buildings from the architects' blueprints in order to raise the money to buy the land. We hired agents. We had a certain deadline to meet, or the owner of the property would cancel our agreement and sell to another group. As the deadline approached, we were short by twenty thousand dollars, which we had to raise by the next day. My response was to raise half of the money personally. I borrowed the ten thousand dollars from a bank. Many an evening, when the sale of the properties was slow, I regretted that I had borrowed the ten thousand because I feared I would never

get it back. But I *did* get it back. I recall with satisfaction that I played a part—a *considerable* part—in raising the funds to get the project under way.[29]

The *Pittsburgh Courier* of June 28, 1946, reported that the transfer of White City Homes had been made to Parkway Management Company, of which Dickerson was president. The *Chicago Sun-Times* stated on June 18, 1950, that the Federal Housing Authority had approved the construction of "the largest mutual-owners housing development for Negroes in the country," on the site of the old White City Amusement Park. Approval followed the formal closing of a $6,179,000 mortgage transaction. The project was being built by Parkway Gardens Homes, whose board chairman was Earl B. Dickerson. According to the June 28 *Pittsburgh Courier:* "Of the 35 buildings, 24 will be three-story walk-ups and 11 will be eight-story structures. The purchasers of the mutual-owner certificates will pay $2,500 each—with monthly payments from $65 to $85. Some 330 of the 964 certificates have already been subscribed for."[30]

Dickerson's Presidency

By 1954, Supreme Liberty was forced to face the fact that while it continued to increase its volume of business and to be profitable, it was on a downgrade. After 1950 the black insurance industry grew less rapidly than the national industry, and Supreme Liberty grew less than the average black insurance company as a whole.[31] Supreme Liberty had several peculiar handicaps. One was the shortcoming of its sales force. Another was its administrative structure, which had been designed for a much smaller firm. A third handicap was that the company still followed what had been called the mass production policy. Although putting more emphasis on ordinary life policies (in keeping with the trend in the entire industry), it still aimed at the quantity of its policies rather than their quality. The company paid its sales agents poorly and gave them little training.

Their turnover was high, production was low, and the rate of lapses in policies was the greatest in the black insurance industry. In sum, income was declining and operating expenses were rising.[32]

In April 1954 the company promoted Dickerson to executive vice president, and the board soon adopted his recommendation to employ a business engineering firm to study the company's principles, methods, and processes and to make recommendations for improvement.

In the summer of 1955, President Truman K. Gibson called Dickerson into his office and offered him the presidency on the following conditions: that he, Gibson, continue as chief executive officer, that his elder son be officer in charge of investments, and that his younger son be general counsel. Dickerson replied: "I'm not that much interested. If I'm to be president, I am to be the chief executive officer also. I wouldn't mind your son being general counsel— I could help with that. But all the other key positions would be filled on merit alone." When Dickerson started to walk out, Gibson called him back.

The board of directors of Supreme Liberty unanimously elected Dickerson president and chief executive officer on October 4, 1955. (His salary was seventeen thousand dollars a year.) African American newspapers all over the country carried the story, as did all the Chicago dailies. Dickerson was officially installed on October 19, and at a luncheon that day in the Morrison Hotel, more than one hundred white business and financial professionals, black business and organizational leaders, and heads of interracial and civic agencies honored him. In his address Dickerson said, "The word 'Negro' is no longer needed in business names. I urge all colored businesses and organizations to take in all members of the community. If it's community action, it is not a colored action." The *Philadelphia Tribune* of November 19, 1955, reported a speech he made before a group of black leaders at a dinner in his honor:

> The implications of the U.S. Supreme Court decision in the *Brown
> v. Topeka Board of Education* case, outlawing segregation in the

nation's public schools, will ultimately extend to all so-called Negro businesses. It may be 25 years from now, it may be longer, because things like this move slowly—but ultimately the stream of free enterprise is going to be so vigorous in an integrated society that all businesses will be engulfed.

From the first day of his term Dickerson aimed to merge the African American economic "detour" with the main highway of American life. On March 31, 1956, he engaged the George S. May Company, a business engineering firm, to begin a review and analysis of Supreme Liberty's management. On April 3 he appointed a management team within the company and gave officials and departments a program of assignments and goals. The general goal was to sell more insurance at less cost. A manual of instructions was prepared and distributed. On June 30, Dickerson reported to the stockholders: "This year we are under a strict budget system installed with the advice of the George S. May Company. At June 30 we are meeting our budget goals, which are to provide a substantial profit over 1955."[33]

Dickerson immediately changed Supreme Liberty's emphasis from industrial to ordinary life policies and from quantity to quality. He improved the selection, training, and pay of agents. He appointed a new agency director (J. G. Ish had died), and on his motions various other changes were made. In 1956, Supreme Liberty elected three new members to its board. One was Mrs. Cora Stewart, widow of W. Ellis Stewart. The others were Frank Summers, an attorney in East St. Louis, and John H. Johnson. Johnson was elected chairman of the board. (Truman K. Gibson became honorary chairman.) The company opened new offices in San Francisco and Los Angeles, increased its capital stock, and applied for licenses to operate in two new states.

During this time the home office building was remodeled, at the cost of more than four thousand dollars. Work began in mid-March 1956 and was completed by mid-August. From August 16 to 19 the company celebrated the remodeling and also the thirty-fifth anniversary of its operations. This remodeling brought Supreme Liberty's home office into harmony with the huge, shining, interracial Lake Meadows residential and shopping development directly across Thirty-fifth Street to the north on South Parkway.

Edward Gillespie, who under Dickerson was vice president and director of public relations, explained the importance of the remodeling of the home office: "From the Chicago Council on Foreign Relations we had been getting visitors from many countries. I would squire them around. We kept this up for a number of years, but it was embarrassing. The building was not spick-and-span. The carpets were worn, and so on. Finally we dropped the program of visits. But with the building remodeled, we were presentable."[34]

Early in 1957, Supreme Liberty entered into an arrangement with the U.S. State Department to be on a list of sites in Chicago to show foreign visitors.

Dickerson's main goal during this period was to increase the company's rate of growth so that it could compete in the new social environment—the rising economic status of middle-class blacks and the increasing bid for the black market by white firms. On April 3, 1960, the stockholders approved Dickerson's proposal to change the name to Supreme Life Insurance Company of America. "It is simpler and more accurately describes our goals of strength, scope, and excellence," he said.

The most spectacular achievement of Dickerson's administration was a series of seven acquisitions of other African American firms. Between 1956 and 1961, Supreme absorbed Friendship Mutual Life Insurance Company and the Beneficial Life Insurance Society, both of Detroit; the Dunbar Life Insurance Company of Cleveland; the Federal Life Insurance Company of Washington, D.C.; and the Domestic Life Insurance Company of Louisville, Kentucky. (Two more companies were acquired after 1961.) According to the company, "The direct purchase of Domestic Life for $1,800,000 was the largest single business transaction in the history of Negro-owned insurance companies to that time."[35] Supreme Life was now operating in twelve states: Illinois, Missouri, Kansas, California, Kentucky, Tennessee, Michigan, Indiana, Ohio, West Virginia, Pennsylvania, and Maryland (and the District of Columbia).

Dickerson was guided by a vision that to many seemed then and still seems quixotic: to make Supreme Life an instrument of racial integration. He expressed this ambition in an interview he gave to a reporter in late 1961. The interview took place in Dickerson's office, from which they could see, the reporter wrote,

> a virtual sub-city of gleaming steel, glass, and concrete stretching northward toward the Chicago Loop . . . the famed Lake Meadows residential and shopping development. . . .
>
> The successful development is dramatic proof of a point Dickerson has argued for decades . . . that racial integration will work if given even a minimum of official sanction and support. But of infinite more import to businessman Dickerson . . . is the fact that the money-coining project is owned by another insurance company—big, rich New York Life. . . .
>
> The achievement of New York Life Insurance Company . . . [holds] for Dickerson a monumental challenge. As president of Supreme he has set the company's sights on the kind of development represented by Lake Meadows and he is more than a little impatient to produce similar results.[36]

Dickerson projected this vision to the entire African American insurance industry. On July 20, 1964, he gave the keynote address to the National Insurance Association's Forty-fourth Annual Convention in Philadelphia. He told his audience that American blacks were making satisfactory adjustments to social changes but not to economic changes and that the black life insurance industry was growing but was still very small compared to the white industry. He added:

> We must begin to regard competition as a friend, and not as foe. . . . There can be no doubt that competition has been directly responsible for the many improvements we have made. . . .

The law of the land says: "Desegregate!" Let us take the law of the land literally; let us desegregate. Let us reach far beyond the Negro market and claim a fair share of the nation's economy that is rightfully ours. . . . If our white competitors no longer recognize color as a barrier in matters of business, why should we?[37]

As president of Supreme Life, Dickerson practiced what he preached. On November 22, 1957, he was elected to the board of directors of the South Side Bank and Trust Company, located at Cottage Grove Avenue and Forty-seventh Street. The *Chicago Defender* of November 30 reported: "Dickerson becomes the first Negro to be elected to the board of any white banking institution in Chicago. The South Side Bank and Trust Company, on the other hand, becomes the first commercial bank in Chicago to integrate its board." That bank ran a half-page advertisement in the *Chicago Daily News* on January 28, 1958, carrying "A Message to My Community, by Earl B. Dickerson":

I have been asked by many of you as to what motivated my acceptance of this position. This is my answer.

1. The bank is strong financially.
2. It has assured me that it will concern itself with the problems of mortgage loans in our community.
3. It was the only bank with a Negro officer. . . .
4. It appeared to me that as a member of the policy-making committee, I could best serve my friends and the community with the progressive and friendly South Side Bank and Trust Company.

My choice has proven wise and fruitful to the community because the South Side Bank and Trust Company has already done the following:

a. Purchased a $4,500,000 group insurance contract from Supreme Liberty Life Insurance Company. This is the largest group insurance contract ever sold to a member of the National Insurance Association.

b. Provided counsel and financial guidance to many groups in our community in resolving their financial problems.

On July 7, 1964, Dickerson reported to the board that Supreme Life had become the first black-owned and -operated company to be added to the National Association of Security Dealers Ask and Bid quotations on its over-the-counter (OTC) listings in major financial journals. Dickerson said, "This makes an investment in Supreme a living force in the economic life of our country, bringing to the holders of such stock economic power readily available to them. It is a further step of the company to enter into the mainstream of the economic life of America."[38]

Alvin Boutté, chairman and chief executive officer of the Independence Bank of Chicago, said in 1983: "Being on the OTC isn't unusual for Negro businesses today, but in those days it was a marvelous feat."[39]

The best example of vigorous promotion during Dickerson's administration was the company's role in the feting of Nigeria's ambassador to the United States. Nigeria received its independence on October 1, 1960, and its first ambassador to this country, Julius Momo Udochi, visited Chicago from August 15 to 17, 1961. He was given the royal treatment. Dickerson attended to the ambassador during much of his stay and had a dinner for him and others in his home at 5027 South Drexel Boulevard in Hyde Park. The climax of the visit was a banquet for about nine hundred people, given by Supreme Life, both in honor of the ambassador and in celebration of the fortieth anniversary of the company's founding. The banquet took place at the McCormick Exposition Hall—the first ever in that vast place, which was not completely finished. "Those three days put Supreme on the map in Chicago," Edward S. Gillespie reminisced.[40]

How did Dickerson's policy of integrating the staff in the offices and in the field work out? He said, "We tried hard. We brought in whites in the home office and a few elsewhere. In California we brought in some Hispanics. But it did not succeed. The conception of race, black and white, was too strong. There was jealousy on both sides. Also the board did not back me up. Finally the policy fell to the ground."[41] Edward Gillespie added: "One reason was that at long last white companies had begun to realize that the best way to get rid of black companies was to hire away our best people. We trained them up to a point; the white companies would spot them and hire them away. They would not hire the white people hired by Supreme."[42]

How did the policy of trying to enter the market of white policyholders work out? According to Dickerson, it did so "only with those persons or organizations that supplied us with goods and services. We would press them to take policies. Lawyers, data experts, and such took out a considerable number of policies. We spread the idea. We enlisted black policyholders to push Supreme among their friends and associates. We had some success. It should be a continuing policy."[43] And while Supreme's attempts to get off the economic detour had only limited success, its service to the black community was immeasurably great: "Not many years ago a black could not get a loan except from Supreme or Chicago Metropolitan [a smaller black insurance company]. In many instances Supreme was the only place to go in the late 1940s and during the 1950s."[44]

Alvin Boutté offered the following:

> My brother-in-law came to Chicago about 1958. He had a degree in actuarial science. In those days there was no place for such a degree held by a black. Earl Dickerson gave him a job.
>
> Earl was a mortgage lender when there were no others for blacks. Supreme was the only source of capital our people had.
>
> We in Independence Bank got into the banking business after the Civil Rights Act of 1964. Blacks hadn't been successful in the banking business since the Reconstruction period. (There was Jesse Binga, of course.) None of us knew what we were doing because we had not been permitted to be in the business world. Earl gave us strong encouragement and good business advice, and he was a great source of raising capital for us.

Many, many people out here were able to buy properties and to start businesses because of mortgages taken by Supreme.[45]

In 1970, Dickerson told his board that he wanted to retire. Supreme Liberty appointed a search committee, and the position was offered to the executive of the Atlanta Life Insurance Company in charge of the Nashville, Tennessee, office at a salary of $36,831. (Dickerson was then being paid $32,500.) This offer was at first accepted but then declined. As a consequence, the board asked Dickerson to stay, and he agreed to do so for a year at the salary that had been offered to his replacement.

On April 14, 1971, Dickerson was finally able to retire as president and chief executive officer, a position he had filled for fifteen and a half years. John H. Johnson succeeded him in both capacities, and on the occasion of his retirement, Dickerson said to the board:

> Without a doubt the greatest thrill of my fifty-year association with the Company was to recommend this publishing genius, John H. Johnson, as President and Chief Executive Officer of Supreme Life Insurance Company of America.
>
> I now dream the dream that the new men of our management ... will always hear and heed the echoes of those pioneering stalwarts who have preceded them: men such as Gillespie, Pace, Gibson, Bousfield, Stewart, Holt, Bentley, and all the others who firmly believed that words without action are the assassins of idealism—the killers of the dream.[46]

The following table shows the growth of Supreme from the end of the year Dickerson assumed the presidency to the end of the year he retired as president.[47]

	1955	1971
Insurance (business) in force	$121,244,656	$197,363,000
Income	4,584,018	9,828,185
Assets	17,000,000+	37,872,386
Capital and surplus	2,500,000+	1,436,386

Upon retiring as president of Supreme Life, Dickerson continued to serve as chairman of the board until January 1973. From then until January 19, 1977, he continued as director, but in late 1976 he informed Johnson that he would not stand for reelection to the board. He did want to continue his association with the company, however, and in conformance with the company's bylaws he automatically became an emeritus member of the board of directors, honorary chairman of the board, and financial consultant. When he retired as president on April 14, 1971, Dickerson began his remarks with a quotation from the Old Testament: "Your old men shall dream dreams and your young men shall see visions." In June 1919 when he walked briskly into the office of Frank Gillespie, he was a young man who saw visions. By the time of his retirement in 1971, with many of these visions realized, he found that he had become an old man who could only dream dreams about what remained to be done.

Chapter Nine

THE LATER YEARS: NATIONAL GADFLY AND COMMUNITY ACTIVIST

From October 1955, when he was elected president of Supreme Liberty Life Insurance Company, until his death on September 1, 1986, Earl Dickerson remained active in the civil rights movement and played a number of important roles. Of these the most far-reaching were his contribution to the Illinois Fair Employment Practices Act of 1961, his continuing efforts to integrate Chicago's South Side, his enduring association with the NAACP, and his contributions to the black revolution of the 1960s.[1]

The Illinois Fair Employment Practices Act of 1961

When Dickerson was a member of FDR's Fair Employment Practices Committee, he and his colleagues worked hard to persuade the legislatures of several states to enact fair employment practice (FEP) laws, and these efforts did not end when he left the FEPC in 1943. In 1945, Chicago was the first city to adopt an FEP ordinance, but it had no provision for enforcement.[2] In the following year the mayor's Commission on Race Relations stressed that a state statute was needed. The Democratic-controlled Illinois House passed FEP bills in every two-year session from 1947 through 1959, but the Republican-controlled Senate invariably voted them down.[3] Dickerson testified in favor of these bills on several occasions, and by 1961 the "new" Chicago Urban League had achieved enough clarity of purpose and enough financial strength to give effective support to the bill introduced that year. Both houses passed the bill, and Governor Otto Kerner Jr. signed it into law in June 1961. That law established an enforcing commission of five members—two from each party unpaid and a nonpartisan chairman paid twelve thousand dollars a year.

On September 19, Governor Kerner named Earl Dickerson and Ralph Helstein (president of the United Packing House, Food, and Allied Workers Union) as the Democratic members and Charles W. Gray (director of industrial relations for Bell and Howell Company) as chairman.[4]

These appointments were subject to confirmation by the Senate, and even before the meeting of the special session of the Illinois General Assembly, Senator Paul Broyle indicated that the Republicans would investigate Dickerson's and Helstein's backgrounds. Broyle, a staunch anticommunist, had been the author of a law requiring all state-paid employees to swear that they had no intention of overthrowing the U.S. government.

By the end of October, seven of the most prominent leaders in Chicago telegraphed Governor Kerner supporting his appointees; among these was Charles Percy, who at the time was chairman of the board of Bell and Howell Company and later became a U.S. senator.[5] Dickerson characteristically threw gasoline on the mounting flames by stating in the *Chicago Daily News* of October 31, 1961: "The attack is a smokescreen. They don't want a Negro on the commission who would stand up and fight for Negro rights. They want a compromising, gradualist Negro." On the previous day Dickerson and Helstein and their wives had driven to Springfield for a session with the governor and several Democratic members of the Senate executive committee to prepare for the hearings. Ralph Helstein recalled these hearings:

> Senator [Donald J.] O'Brien grilled Earl mercilessly. Earl answered politely, serenely, and sometimes with amazement. I became convinced that O'Brien was not here to help and that he would perform the same way the next day. Finally I said, "I don't see any point in continuing this." Afterward I told Marshall Korshak, our senator, "I don't think there has been any preparation for confirmation. The Democratic Party will fall on its face tomorrow."
>
> Kathryn, Earl, Rachel, and I had dinner together that evening. He and I agreed that if we were not assured that the Democratic senators would be solidly behind us, we would not appear. I called Korshak and said, "You tell somebody that if by seven tomorrow morning we are not informed that we will have unanimous support from the Democrats, the two of us will not appear, and we will call a press conference and tell the reporters why." Korshak said, "You can't do that." I said, "Either or."
>
> Korshak called us the next morning before seven. He said, "I've had an unpleasant night. The governor has talked to every Democratic senator on the executive committee, and you'll have a unanimous Democratic vote."[6] I said, "We'll be there."
>
> When we went into the executive committee room, I saw taped on its walls copies of lists of organizations that Earl then belonged to or had belonged to.
>
> First the committee voted to recommend that the Senate approve the nominations of Gray, the chairman, and the two Republican nominees. Then they turned on Earl. These primitives treated him primitively. The questions they asked—mean, nasty, insinuating! There was no overt racial slur, but it was implied. Earl answered politely and rationally. "Were you on this committee?" "Yes. That was when Russia and China were our allies." "Justify what you did on the FEPC!" "That's not under your jurisdiction. I was under President Roosevelt's orders, and I am not free to discuss it." This went on for two or three hours.[7]

The executive committee, along straight party lines, voted 11 to 8 to recommend that the Senate not confirm Dickerson's appointment. Two Republican senators voted "Present." The *Chicago Sun-Times* of November 1, 1961, reported that W. Russell Arrington of Evanston, one of the two who had voted "Present," told Dickerson: "I don't think they have made a case against you, but an opposition to you has grown that could perhaps destroy your effectiveness." After the hearings a reporter asked Charles W. Gray, who had received the favorable vote, what he thought of the examination of Dickerson. He replied, "It was a travesty," and the Chicago newspapers quoted him the next day. They also quoted a statement by Dickerson that read in part:

> As president of a multi-million-dollar insurance company, which I have helped to build, I am unequivocally dedicated to capitalism. But I do not believe that big business has the right to run roughshod over little people.
>
> I believe that anyone who discriminates against another on the grounds of religion, country of origin, or race is not only downright undemocratic, but he is also an enemy of the United States because he is actually weakening his country's ability to know its full potential.

During the rest of the week the Chicago daily newspapers carried stories with quotes defending Dickerson and expressing outrage at his rejection—all except the *Chicago Tribune*, which meticulously quoted the charges made by the hostile Republican senators. On Saturday, November 4, in the *Chicago Daily News*, Charles Nicodemus wrote: "Most of the material on Dickerson was furnished by such groups as the Illinois Manufacturers Association, which has long been an arch-foe of the FEPC." On November 6 the Senate executive committee voted to reconsider its recommendation of Gray to determine whether he had in fact said that Dickerson's examination had been a "travesty."

The next day the committee questioned Ralph Helstein. Because he had fought against communist influence in his union since 1946, the Republicans focused on his relationship with the Highlander Folk School in Tennessee whose workshops on community action had been attended by Martin Luther King Jr., Rosa Parks, and other black "agitators."[8] The Republican members of the committee passed around newspaper clippings with photographs showing racially mixed dancing and swimming at Highlander. According to Helstein, "I didn't have the same trouble Earl had because he is a gentleman and I am not, and I know how to deal with men who are not gentlemen. They voted not to recommend me, too, on straight party lines, except for Senator Arrington who abstained. I still think they would have been hard put to reject me, but they didn't want to reject only a Negro."[9]

On November 15 the executive committee reexamined Gray, who confirmed that he had called the examination of Dickerson a "travesty" and refused to retract the description. Nevertheless, the committee voted 17 to 6 again to recommend that he be confirmed. That same day the full Senate, without discussion, voted to confirm Gray and the two Republican nominees and not to confirm Dickerson and Helstein. On December 27, Governor Kerner nominated two other Democratic members for the commission—an official of Illinois Bell Telephone Company and James Kemp, a representative of the Building Service Employees Union. In terms of public relations, Kemp served double duty: he was an African American and an officer of a labor union. Those nominations were confirmed.

Looking back, Elmer Gertz remarked: "Once we got an FEP law in Illinois, its opponents seemed to be doing two things: to exclude really militant fighters from the commission and to starve it financially."[10]

EARLIER THAT YEAR Dickerson received an even greater political rebuff. During Senator John F. Kennedy's campaign for the presidency in 1960, he had appointed Dickerson as a member of a national business and professional men's committee. When Kennedy, as president-elect, was forming his cabinet, he proposed to his brother Robert that Dickerson be appointed assistant secretary of commerce. But Congressman William L. Dawson worked against the appointment. In addition, Kennedy received papers hostile to his "radical" performances on the FEPC and with the National Lawyers Guild during the McCarthy period. Dawson convinced the chairman of the Senate Judiciary Committee that Dickerson's nomination would be "too hot to handle." So the president-elect withdrew Dickerson from consideration.[11] Judge William Sylvester White recalled: "When I looked at Dawson and Dickerson, I thought it unfortunate that they could not talk in the kitchen and come to an agreement: Dawson to do things on the inside and Dickerson to raise hell on the outside, thereby giving Dawson a basis for doing more on the inside—playing different roles toward the same end."[12]

St. Clair Drake and Horace Cayton describe this tactic explicitly in their book *Black Metropolis:*

> Paradoxically enough, [gains] have come not from a monolithic unity but from a diversity of competing leaders stimulating each other to win gains for the Negro people. There has been a kind of informal and even unplanned division of labor with "accepted" leaders negotiating and pleading for the Negro, while "radicals" turned on the heat. A shrewd leader can always remind the white folks that he's trying to control the unruly masses but he doesn't know whether he can continue to do so if some concessions aren't made right away. This—coupled with the Negro vote, desired by both major parties—is an effective minority tactic.[13]

Working for Integration in Southeast Chicago

The Chicago Commission on Race Relations in its report on the causes of the 1919 riot found that four types of neighborhoods had developed: (1) mixed, unadjusted, (2) mixed, adjusted, (3) congested, and (4) entirely white or African American. The commission's recommendations were aimed at increasing the "mixed, adjusted" neighborhoods and decreasing the other three types. Unfortunately, things didn't work out that way. The "black metropolis" became ever more congested and gradually expanded despite continual resistance from whites. By 1925 the favored method of resistance—bombings—had ceased, at least for the time being, because a more effective method had been developed: the racially restrictive housing covenant. By 1937 the black population had expanded southward, leaving only one square mile, the Washington Park area, as a "white island" protected by restrictive covenants. But in 1940 the U.S. Supreme Court in *Hansberry v. Lee* ruled that the covenant in Woodlawn was not enforceable, and in 1948 the high court ruled that no racially restrictive covenant was enforceable. Panic quickly struck in white neighborhoods south of Forty-seventh Street and east of Washington Park.

This panic was fed by knowledge of trends documented in Otis and Beverly Duncan's *The Negro Population of Chicago: A Study of Residential Succession*. In this study the authors claimed that whites were displaced by African Americans through a process of four successive stages: (1) "penetration," (2) "invasion," (3) "consolidation," and (4) "piling up." (This last stage becomes a prelude to the extension of the process into adjacent areas.) The authors wrote: "There is no implication that the sequence, once begun, necessarily continues to completion. . . . As a matter of definition, there is nothing to preclude the halting or even reversal of the cycle of succession. However, the use of the stage scheme would be hard to justify except that this is unlikely to happen."[14]

But this is exactly what *did* happen in the Hyde Park–Kenwood area, bounded by Cottage Grove on the west, Forty-seventh Street on the north, and Sixty-third Street on the south. This area, exclusively white since before Earl Dickerson entered the University of Chicago Laboratory Schools in 1907, had by 1949 already been "penetrated" by blacks. (The Dickerson family was the first, moving in that year to 5027 South Drexel Boulevard.) According to the Duncans' stages, Hyde Park–Kenwood would soon be "invaded" and then "consolidated" by blacks. But Drake and Cayton describe what in fact happened: "Here, for the first time, a group of white people in Midwest Metropolis made a deliberate attempt to create 'interracial neighborhoods with high community standards,' that is, to accept Negroes as neighbors on the basis of their social class position rather than [exclude them or flee from them] on the basis of race."[15]

Dickerson, who had been the foremost figure in breaking racially restrictive covenants in Chicago, was a leader in this effort. He did so in several ways.

Dickerson became a member of a committee chaired by Henry Heald, then president of the Illinois Institute of Technology, to persuade policy makers in the major institutions on the South Side to stay where they were and to cooperate in building interracial neighborhoods.[16] This committee approached institutions such as the University of Chicago, George Williams College, Mercy Hospital, and Michael Reese Hospital. These pivotal institutions had already considered moving out of the area. The committee pointed to an alternative. On December 12, 1949, twelve representatives of fifty civic and religious organizations signed the first policy statement of the Hyde Park–Kenwood Community Conference with the goal of creating a "stabilized, integrated community of high standards."[17] By that time the movement was well under way for the erection by the New York Life Insurance Company of a group of high-rise, interracial apartment buildings on the site of demolished slums. (This became Lake Meadows, where white and African American middle-class residents lived side by side and shared supermarkets and schools.)

The major institutions in the area responded in various ways. In 1962, George Williams College decided to move to the suburbs. Michael Reese Hospital in early 1960 erected Prairie Shores, a development similar to Lake Meadows. The University of Chicago, on May 19, 1952, led in the founding of the South East Chicago Commission. Eventually the Hyde Park–Kenwood Community Conference and the South East Chicago Commission cooperated in implementing a comprehensive plan for the entire lakeside area from Forty-seventh Street to Sixty-third Street and from Cottage Grove to Lake Michigan.[18]

Dickerson was a charter member of the Hyde Park–Kenwood Community Conference and a board member of the South East Chicago Commission from its inception. Paul Berger, who was on the board of the South East Chicago Commission with Dickerson, remarked: "Julian Levi [the University of Chicago executive who chaired the commission] was protecting the university and the surrounding environment, and he wasn't interested in getting help on policy. But he would ask, 'Can you help with X, Y, and Z?' That's where Earl played an important part."[19]

The redevelopment of Hyde Park–Kenwood resulted in the massive clearing and redevelopment of inferior properties. Dickerson thought this was necessary but insisted that people displaced by these changes should also be given an opportunity to acquire low-cost public housing, and he did all he could to achieve that end. His efforts were a continuation of efforts that began when, as alderman, he successfully opposed state legislation giving the city the power of eminent domain until it also included a provision prohibiting racial discrimination in the new housing to be developed.

Another way in which Dickerson supported the stabilizing and improvement of interracial neighborhoods was through the Drexel Boulevard Block Organization. The *Chicago Defender* of April 19, 1958, reported that, as chairman of the planning committee of the Block Organization, Dickerson "sent a letter to all residents of Drexel Boulevard, expressing his pleasure at the urban renewal plans for Hyde Park–Kenwood and urging their support through the Hyde Park–Kenwood Conference."

Dickerson was also an original board member of the Hyde Park Savings and Loan Association, incorporated in 1963. On this topic Paul Berger, one of the founders of the Hyde Park Savings and Loan Association, said:

> Our Savings and Loan was the first, and for a time the only, white financial institution whose prime purpose was to be a catalyst in the community, to find those areas where there are problems, to

try to do something about them. We wanted to have an interracial board of directors. We wanted to get the most "militant" black who also had business experience, both to sell the bank and to meet the issues. The first person who popped into my head was Earl B. Dickerson. When I asked him to be on the board, he said, "I'm getting off a lot of things, but I'll give it a try." He spent ten years with us. Earl was a very big help. He had the drive, the finesse, the knowledge of how to get things done. I could always go to him when I was discouraged and ask, "What are we going to do?" He was always able to help by saying, "This is what we are going to do," and he would do it.[20]

Dickerson's Role in the Black Revolution

Throughout the turbulent events that came to be known as the Black Revolution, Dickerson kept steadily pushing toward the complete public integration of the races, considering the questions of private assimilation or voluntary separatism matters of personal choice.

In July 1963, Dickerson headed the Chicago Exposition of the Centennial of the Emancipation Proclamation, and on August 28 he took part in the March on Washington for Freedom and Jobs.[21] The March was led by A. Philip Randolph, then vice president of the AFL-CIO, and was attended by more than two hundred thousand people, both black and white, from every part of the country. When they assembled in the mall before the memorial to the man who a century earlier had signed the Emancipation Proclamation, Randolph and Dickerson stood before them, flanking a man of the new order who rose to proclaim, "I have a dream today." The March for Freedom and Jobs was organized to secure passage of the civil rights bill then being fiercely debated in Congress. In February 1964 the House passed the bill, 290 to 130, and in June the Senate, voting cloture for the first time in its history, passed the bill, 73 to 27. The Civil Rights Act of 1964 was the most far-reaching and comprehensive law in support of racial equality that Congress had ever passed. Its Title VII gave special satisfaction to Earl Dickerson. The legislative history of Title VII shows that it was modeled on the National Labor Relations Act (NLRA, the Wagner Act of 1935). Dickerson may have been the first person to formulate the basic analogy between protection from discrimination in employment on the grounds of union membership and protection on the grounds of race, creed, or color. In 1984, attorney Ruth Weyand wrote: "I believe that Earl's role in helping draft the first-ever-in-the-world law requiring employment without regard to race discrimination is the true beginning of the whole body of law not only in the United States but also in other countries which mandate equal employment opportunities."[22]

In 1941, Ruth Weyand was in the enforcement section of the National Labor Relations Board, which administered the NLRA. In the spring of that year Dickerson phoned her saying that he had been working on the language of a bill paralleling the National Labor Relations Act that would give minority groups protection against discrimination because of race equal to the protection that the NLRA gave to applicants and workers against discrimination because of union affiliation. She wrote that when Dickerson was on the FEPC, he repeatedly called her to work with him to prepare memoranda, opinions, and rulings to achieve such protection. "We spent hours drawing drafts of bills applicable to race discrimination."[23]

A biographer of Martin Luther King described his Chicago efforts:

> After the campaign in Birmingham, Alabama, Martin Luther King Jr. decided to take the struggle for Negro freedom nationwide. He and his aides looked around for a "Birmingham in the North" in which to launch a direct-action campaign against slums. He chose Chicago. Al Raby of the Coordinating Council of Community Organizations (CCCO)—a coalition of thirty-four civil rights, religious, and civic groups—communicated to King that the CCCO was engaged in a fierce struggle against de facto

segregation in the public schools and was trying to oust the superintendent, Benjamin C. Willis.[24]

Dickerson was at the forefront of that struggle. Lerone Bennett Jr. remembered him in this role: "In the front line leading tens of thousands against Willis. That said a lot more than only money could say. It was not unusual for sensitive black businessmen to give money to CCCO behind the scene. But Dickerson came out in the open and marched. I recall him at the head of a swarm of people— erect, head up, marching against the board of education."[25]

BEFORE KING CAME to Chicago on July 23, 1965, Raby approached Dickerson. As Dickerson related:

> Al Raby sought me out to lead a committee to raise funds to help King's program. I got a list of black businessmen, fifty to seventy-five, and then I invited them to a cocktail evening in this room. Raby stated the case. I made a plea for contributions. We got about fifty of the men to subscribe one hundred dollars a month for a year. I started the subscription off. That was successful.
>
> In the second year we made a renewal. About twenty-five of the same men, including myself, pledged a monthly contribution of a hundred dollars. Al Raby, whatever he was doing at the time, always talked to me about it, and I cooperated very actively.

Civil rights organizer Bill Berry also recalled these events:

> That first year many of the same people who pledged and paid were available in addition for money to meet special needs.
>
> What I remember about the second year is that we had a group of younger business and professional men who said, "Why can't we get in on it? We can't afford a hundred dollars a month yet, but we can afford fifty a month." And they pledged and paid.
>
> All that money was very important when Martin came to Chicago. He spent twenty-three months here, and this became his main base of operations all over the country. Our support and Earl's continued throughout.

I think that not only was Earl a part of the Black Revolution, but in many ways he was one of its fathers. What he had started years ago, we were building on. . . .[26]

Dickerson said that Black Revolution "was a tremendous thing. I participated in every part of it because I wanted our country to have a policy of integration rather than separation. But for that we'd be in a terrible state at the moment."[27]

Many older leaders, such as Dickerson, and many younger ones, such as Berry, did not share the goals of those who advocated black secessionism and the rejection of whites as allies in the civil rights struggle.

This was also the period during which the term "black" came to replace the term "Negro" in accepted usage. Judge James B. Parsons humorously commented, "I was born a colored, I grew up a Negro, and now I'm a black."[28] Elmer Gertz recalled that

Earl was amused and amazed by the gradual process of Negroes becoming blacks. He said once, "I'm a Negro. I don't understand this 'black' business." All the vocabulary of the young activists of the late 1960s and early 1970s—Earl never shared that. He didn't look on being a Negro as demeaning in any sense.[29]

Dickerson did not quibble long over words, but he did insist on being clear about their meanings. To him, as to Bill Berry, "black power" meant a process by which blacks, aided by their white friends, do everything they can to achieve a parity of power—"black's rightful power, not that rightfully belonging to somebody else."[30]

Dickerson put special emphasis, though not exclusive, on economic power—"without which political and social power cannot be fully realized," and on July 20, 1964, he told the convention of the National Insurance Association: "The sooner we realize that financial power, like all forms, yields only to power and act accordingly, the sooner we will attain our goals. Let our struggle for excellence be our contribution to the Negro revolt."[31]

Dickerson on the National Board of the NAACP

Dickerson was a member of the national board of the NAACP for thirty years, but he did not stand for reelection in 1971. Instead, he was named a director emeritus, which he remained until his death. Of his role between 1955 and 1971, one episode is illustrative. John F. Davis, who had been on the national NAACP board during the 1960s, wrote a piece in the *New York Amsterdam News* of June 26, 1984, commemorating Dickerson's ninety-third birthday: "I still remember the first time I heard Earl speak at a meeting of the NAACP national board. They were considering a resolution of censure of one of their members who had given a speech calling for the resignation of Roy Wilkins as executive secretary. The resolution was believed by most members to be certain to pass. . . . When Earl finished speaking, the resolution was finished."

U.S. District Judge Jack E. Tanner of Tacoma, Washington, an African American elected to the national board of the NAACP in 1963, had given a speech in California early in 1964 calling for Wilkins's resignation, the retirement of the chairman of its board, the election of a black president, and the replacement of most of the board by younger people. He was one of three members of the board known as the "Young Turks." At the April 1964 board meeting, the Old Guard demanded that he apologize for the speech, but he refused to do so. Judge Tanner later wrote:

> My "trial" began immediately. It was the "Young Turks" challenging the "Old Guard." Into the affray stepped Earl Dickerson. He described the injustices he had suffered because he was a black and believed in freedom of speech and justice for all mankind. He equated his experience to the proceedings against me. The "Old Guard" could muster only one vote in favor of censure.
>
> Earl and I met again in July of this year in New Orleans at the national convention of the NAACP. We were also celebrating the twentieth anniversary of the "Young Turks." Despite his age, he is still a "Young Turk."[32]

The *New Orleans Times-Picayune* of July 13, 1983, featured a story on Dickerson at the seventy-fourth annual convention, entitled "NAACP Veteran Keeps on Fighting." It stated: "Dickerson sees a new agenda for the NAACP. He sees it moving away from previous methods to a more sophisticated manner of dealing with the issues. 'The thrust of the future must be to make the May 17, 1954, decision in *Brown versus Topeka* work. The law is on the books. The role must now be to implement it, so that all vestiges of discrimination will be removed.' "

Private Affairs

After 1955, Dickerson made several trips abroad. One notable tour was for two months in the summer of 1957, during which Earl and Kathryn visited Tokyo, Hong Kong, Singapore, Indonesia, India, Pakistan, Turkey, southern Russia, Spain, Italy, and France. Another was in the spring of 1958 when they made a "goodwill" tour of the Caribbean Islands, as well as Central and South America, returning some of the visits that citizens of those countries had made to Supreme Life Insurance Company. Dickerson's other trips included one to Egypt, Sudan, Ethiopia, and Kenya and another to Scandinavia, Eastern Europe, and the Soviet Union.

On their visit in the Caribbean, the Dickersons spent a week in Barbados, Trinidad, Tobago, and Jamaica to celebrate the West Indies Federation.[33] Sir Norman Manley, prime minister of Jamaica, feted the Dickersons. He had been one of the guests whom Dickerson entertained in the previously all-white dining room of the Chicago Bar Association when he was admitted in 1945.

These experiences reinforced in Dickerson a perspective "not limited to the precincts of my time and place," he said. "My experiences have made me fully *un citoyen du monde*—a citizen of the world. In India I read on a monument to Mahatma Gandhi one of his sentences, 'Let the window of your mind be open so that the civilizations of the world may flow through it.' "

On two of his travels Dickerson had reunions with his longtime friends and fellow warriors W. E. B. DuBois and Paul Robeson.

In 1961 DuBois was again in trouble with the U.S. government. The U.S. Supreme Court upheld the constitutionality of the McCarran Act, under which DuBois had been tried but acquitted in 1951. DuBois was horrified and angered. The decision threatened his plan to go to Ghana at the invitation of President Kwame Nkrumah[34] to live there and to edit the *Encyclopedia Africana*. On October 1, 1961, DuBois wrote to Gus Hall, chairman of the American Communist Party, applying for membership. That same month he and his wife, Shirley Graham, went into voluntary exile in Ghana.[35]

Nkrumah and DuBois held a seminar, "World Without a Bomb," in 1962, which Dickerson attended and later commented that "Dr. DuBois gave the keynote address, although he was not well. He sent a big Russian limousine with a chauffeur to take me from the hotel to dinner at his home. I spent a week in Ghana."

In 1958, Paul Robeson, having received a passport that had been denied him for eight years, moved to London, where Dickerson visited him. Robeson returned to the United States in 1963 but made several trips abroad, even though he was not well, and received medical treatment in East Berlin in 1965. That year Dickerson attended the International Peace Conference in Helsinki, Finland, which was also attended by Jean-Paul Sartre and Bertrand Russell, among others. On his way to Helsinki, Dickerson visited Budapest, Moscow, and Leningrad and stopped in East Berlin to see Robeson.

Later that year, Robeson, ill in body and bitter in mind, retired to live with his sister in Philadelphia. During his last years Robeson wanted to stay in touch with only a few people,[36] and Dickerson was one of those. Robeson died on January 23, 1976, and on August 10 of that year the Kappa Alpha Psi fraternity gave its first Humanitarian Award to Robeson posthumously. Presenting the award, Dickerson said:

The sacrifice of all his personal interests to the interests of his people was not at the time appreciated. Indeed, not a few of his own people, as DuBois has written, joined in hounding him. It is a very happy occasion that some of us who failed him in the past now come to recognize what we owe him.

America could not deal with a man of Robeson's stature. After all the glory he had won, he remarked, "I am never for one moment unaware that I live in a land of Jim Crow. The realization that I am a Negro in a land of Jim Crow does not leave me. Nor do I think it can, even for a moment." That stand, more than any other, led to his being the victim of the greatest persecution campaign in American history.

In 1963 the Dickersons sold their property at 5027 South Drexel Boulevard and moved into a high-rise apartment building at 4800 Chicago Beach Drive, overlooking Lake Michigan and with an uninterrupted view of the Chicago skyline to the north. In 1975, Kathryn Dickerson was diagnosed with Alzheimer's disease, and after a period in the hospital and care at home, she was confined to a nursing home, where she died on March 6, 1980. She and Earl had been married for nearly fifty years.

The building at 4800 Chicago Beach Drive became a condominium effective January 1, 1980, and that month Dickerson purchased his apartment. "I thought about renting a place for myself when I knew that Kathryn would not be able to return. But memories compelled me to buy and stay. I'm happy I did. I live here with constructive memories of her every day. I can see her now, sitting in that chair, with her lovely, graceful legs."

In a feature story titled "Active Oldsters," *Ebony* magazine included a picture of Dickerson making a speech. After describing his role with Supreme Life Insurance Company, the text continued:

He's an avid reader, who, five days a week, spends about 10 hours a day in his library. "I like to keep in touch with what's going on around me," he says. "That, plus the reading and my support of community organizations, keeps my life from being so dull." During the past three years Dickerson, a much-sought-after speaker, has accepted more than 100 speaking engagements. "I just enjoy being around people," he says.[37]

In his last years Dickerson enjoyed the company of friends, old and new. He enjoyed the companionship of his daughter, Diane Montgomery, and her husband, Charles, and their three children, Stephen Brown, Joshua Cohen, and Judith Cohen. He also kept in touch with the fading remnants of his old family life from Canton, Mississippi. Every Sunday he would have a telephone conversation with his sole remaining cousin, Hettye Garrett Gary, the daughter of "Uncle Ben," in Memphis, until she died in 1983, after which he kept in touch with her daughter, Bennie Williams, in Memphis. Earl Dickerson died on September 1, 1986. He was ninety-five years old.

Chapter Ten

ASSESSING A LIFE AND A MAN

Previous chapters have followed the dictum *Res ipsa loquitur*— "The thing speaks for itself"—but this chapter inquires more directly: What sort of a man was Earl Burrus Dickerson? What were his key concerns and motivations? What will be his place in history? By relying primarily on the observations of those who knew Dickerson best, in both his public and private life, the present discussion will hopefully shed light on an important, complex, and often overlooked figure in the struggle for racial justice in the twentieth century. Earl Dickerson's public life was a sometimes paradoxical composite of three roles: the successful businessman, the history-making lawyer, and the social activist.

The Successful Businessman

As general counsel for Supreme Liberty Life Insurance Company from December 1920 until October 1955, Dickerson's legal ingenuity and business skills saved the company on several occasions. These accomplishments were crucial to the survival of the company, and Dickerson's achievements as its president from 1955 to 1971 have already been documented. But, as suggested earlier, Supreme

Life was a business with a social mission to improve the quality of life for African Americans. Paul Berger, who organized the Hyde Park Savings and Loan Association and who persuaded Dickerson to serve on its board, said of him: "Earl's greatest accomplishment—and it was a phenomenal one—was the building of Supreme Life. He recognized early that for the achievement by blacks, or anybody, of any degree of real freedom, they had to have some degree of economic freedom."[1]

Dickerson stated Supreme Life's mission best when he relinquished the presidency to become chairman of the board on April 4, 1971:

> What we attempted to provide was a significant break in what [Gunnar] Myrdal has characterized as the "process of circular causality." Being denied the right to compete for jobs on anything approaching an equal basis, the black man was unable to furnish businessmen of his own race with a viable market or a source of capital. Coincident with this factor, the circle was thereby closed with a continuation of poverty, reduced mortality, diminished educational opportunity, and finally a tragic loss of incentives.[2]

Dickerson saw clearly that the black insurance industry must leave the economic detour and merge into the main thoroughfare of American business and that the way to do this was through financial strength and excellence of service.

Although Dickerson understood that challenging and changing the law was key to improving life for African Americans and that segregation could not be tolerated in any form, he also understood that formal, legal civil rights had to be accompanied by the creation of real and concrete economic opportunities and that black Americans had been largely excluded from the economic life of the country. For Dickerson racism was not solely a legal and social problem; it was also, and equally, an economic problem. As an officer of Supreme Life he sought to help create an economic base for the black community.

Dickerson saw the struggle for civil rights as a two-pronged process: the strengthening of legal rights and the securing of economic opportunity. Legal reform had to be accompanied by the creation of wealth, and this could only happen through education and the freedom to compete in the open marketplace. Dickerson combined his skills as a lawyer and a businessman to achieve these ends.

The History-Making Lawyer

As a lawyer, Dickerson is best known for his successful challenge in the U.S. Supreme Court to a racially restrictive covenant on Chicago's South Side. The Court's 1940 decision in *Hansberry v. Lee* helped set the stage for the landmark 1948 Supreme Court decision prohibiting judicial enforcement of racially restrictive covenants.

In addition, Dickerson repeatedly took on the roles of pioneer and activist within the legal profession. He broke the color barriers of both the Illinois State Bar Association and the Chicago Bar Association. He led the National Bar Association, the preeminent minority bar association, in the 1940s. Dickerson also led the activist National Lawyers Guild during the McCarthy era of the 1950s—a time when the attorney general labeled the guild a subversive organization and tried to destroy it.

The Social Activist

As an activist Dickerson fought for the basic principles of American democracy, and never on rigid ideological grounds. As an alderman he fought for jobs during the Chicago traction negotiations as well as for decent housing and education. His efforts as acting chairman of the FEPC were directed at securing jobs and economic opportunities for blacks, and the *Hansberry v. Lee* case sought access for blacks to housing and home ownership.

Dickerson once said: "Of all those in the long line of dreamers who have sought the ultimately just society, none had to seek alien sources for moral authority. They had only to say to the American people, in remembrance fulfill the greatest promise in your first statement as a nation: 'All men are created equal.'"[3] In asserting these principles and in his criticism of the country's failure to implement them, Dickerson was without fear. Attorney Jonathan A. Rothstein, Midwest regional vice president of the National Lawyers Guild, wrote: "Dickerson's courage is perhaps best exemplified by the prominent role he assumed as National President of the Guild during the 1950s; a difficult period in the organization's life."[4] Dickerson fought not just for blacks but for all individuals and groups who were oppressed or threatened, and he fought these battles throughout his public life. For example, shortly after he was seated as alderman, he spoke at a rally of eight thousand people in the Chicago Coliseum welcoming Tom Mooney to Chicago after his release from prison.[5] Mooney had been convicted on perjured evidence as a participant in the bomb killings at the San Francisco Preparedness Day Parade in 1916. His sentence of death was commuted to life imprisonment. In January 1939, Governor Culbert Olson of California pardoned him unconditionally.

Dickerson also struggled against the system of state-imposed segregation, starting long before 1954 when the U.S. Supreme Court eroded the legal justifications for segregation in *Brown v. Board of Education*. Yet Dickerson consistently argued that although the segregation of, or discrimination against, any minority on the basis of creed or color is unconstitutional, the choice between assimilation and separatism must always remain one of personal freedom. Only by protecting the freedom of individuals would the distinctiveness of the African American community and its unique contributions to the larger society be sustained. He once mused, "Perhaps someday there will be neither black nor white, but, alas! only gray."

DICKERSON'S OVERLAPPING EFFORTS to be an activist, a successful businessman, and a history-making lawyer shaped the course of his professional life—both his successes and his failures. Edwin "Bill" Berry, a longtime executive secretary of the Chicago Urban League, said: "Earl proved that it is possible to do all the things he did, to be fought by the mainstream, to be bucked and hurt at every turn, and still to be a success on the basis of monetary achievements."[6] Tom Lewis, chairman of the board of Interbroadcasting Stations, said: "His greatest legacy is one of the social responsibilities of black corporate executives and of lawyers and of their leadership. They are not following just because of him, but because he put so many of them in their place and helped them to survive and advance."[7]

Dickerson used his economic freedom to give support to organizations that sought to promote what he believed in and to help needy and deserving individuals. When, on May 17, 1981, the University of Illinois Alumni Association gave him its highest award, it cited him as "that rare phenomenon, a 'have' with a burning passion for the 'have-nots.'" On December 21, 1984, he established the Earl B. Dickerson Endowment Fund at the University of Chicago Law School to "benefit a student recipient each year who would exemplify strong moral character and who is committed to projects in the law that seek to improve the social climate of our land."

Dickerson served one term as Democratic alderman of the Second Ward in the Chicago City Council. Being an alderman in Chicago is often a rung to higher office, but Dickerson was not permitted to climb that ladder. He sought a political career, and the reason he wanted it was the reason he did not get it. He wanted to serve the public interest according to his own vision, not to build up his political power. Weathers Y. Sykes, a friend and admirer who recalled as a boy hearing Dickerson speak publicly, said: "He was not charismatic. He did not scream on street corners. He would strike at the heart of issues without studied appeals to the mass media or theatrical appeals to the crowd. He didn't try to make journalistic hay. He worked at a deeper level. He was not a self-promoter. Those methods hurt him politically. He did things on principle, not personality."[8]

Dickerson faced continuous difficulty in politics largely because he was not a natural politician. People have said that even in defeat Dickerson won by leaving a legacy of independence and that he was a good loser. Yet his disdain for compromise quickly forced the door to political office closed. It is possible that he could have achieved a great deal as a U.S. congressman, but this was not to be.

Yet, despite his failure to achieve higher political office, Dickerson was able to find other means to fight for social justice, principally as a lawyer and businessman. This flexibility was well served by his diverse professional roles and competencies in the service of the African American community, and he quickly became a model for aspiring young black professionals. John H. Johnson, who worked for Dickerson during his term as alderman in Chicago, has been previously quoted as saying that Dickerson attracted and inspired able young people by putting them in a position to help him, by giving them the freedom to act, by holding them accountable, and consequently by helping them develop. Dickerson became a model and mentor to a whole generation of young black professionals and activists in Chicago who were able to observe his uncompromising commitment to freedom and equality at close quarters. Many of them were also active in helping him fight for African American communities both in Chicago and nationwide.

Attorney Elmer Henderson, a member of the Illinois State Commission on the Condition of the Urban Colored Population in 1940, said: "I wanted to be a part of what Earl was doing. I attribute my interest in the law directly to him, and also whatever success I have had. Many, many people like myself have been greatly influenced by his character, personality, and what he has done."[9]

Judge Odas Nicholson of the Circuit Court of Cook County said:

"I worked for Earl many years. He drove me as he drove himself. Whatever I am is directly attributable to him. But it was hard discipline."[10]

Dr. Quentin Young, a leader in public health care policy, founder of the Chicago-based Health and Medicine Policy Research Group, and a host of *Public Affairs* on Chicago Public Radio, related:

> My father was a contractor. He did projects for Earl Dickerson. They became personal friends. It was unusual in the 1930s for a white and a Negro to become personal friends. They became social friends—house guests and dinner guests in a casual way. At the table Earl would—not pontificate, that isn't the word—but hold forth. He was the most impressive man I met in those days. I was just emerging into the world of ideas. I think he related to me in conversation as an adult would to a bright child. I believe that my subsequent interest in [the civil rights movement] was really conditioned by that.
>
> I think Harold Washington's naming him honorary chairman of his campaign for the mayoralty is relevant. Washington introduced Dickerson as "the kind of man I want to be when I grow up." Washington does indeed look to Mr. Dickerson as a model. I have felt that when I was with the two."[11]

After he was inaugurated in April 1983, one of Mayor Washington's first official acts was to proclaim May 1 "Earl B. Dickerson Day." When asked what relationship he had with Washington before his successful 1983 campaign, Dickerson replied: "None at all, I knew his father and about his son, but I did not know the son personally." Such was Dickerson's reputation among a younger generation of activists and civil rights leaders.

Bill Berry said: "Earl was one of my heroes since I entered the Urban League movement in 1937. I think he knew early on that I regarded him as a role model. And that was true of him—more than anybody else in public life. I don't think I have loved any man the way I love him, with affection and admiration, with the one exception of Martin Luther King."[12]

Lerone Bennett Jr., a social historian and the executive editor of *Ebony* magazine for more than forty years, said:

> I grew up in Jackson, Mississippi. In the 1940s I read the *Chicago Defender*. Dickerson's name was constantly in that weekly. I could see the light in the distance. Through the *Defender* and the *Pittsburgh Courier* his influence extended not only throughout Chicago and Pittsburgh but throughout the whole country. How important those journals were to us young blacks growing up in Mississippi, Alabama, and Georgia! And through them he had an influence on people he has never heard of. His militancy on the FEPC—his taking on a liberal white southern editor, Mark Ethridge, in the very pit of southern racism, Birmingham, Alabama! This unknown, fearless black man from Chicago raising all that hell! And young boys and girls read about him throughout the South.

Sterling Stuckey, biographer of Paul Robeson, commented:

> My family moved in the summer of 1945 from Memphis to Chicago, where my mother had a brother living and working as a union organizer. It was from him that I first heard of Earl Dickerson. I was still in grammar school at the time. My uncle spoke of Earl Dickerson with such reverence. He appeared to me as a kind of legend in 1945. This was during his most active years, but he seemed to me, like most legends, remote, partly because of my age and partly because of the awe in which my uncle approached the mere mention of his name.[13]

The Reverend Kenneth Smith, former president of the Chicago Theological Seminary, said:

> When I was on the Chicago Board of Education, appointed by Mayor Jane Byrne, I used to tell my troubles to Earl Dickerson. He would say, "Your salary is paid by the congregation of the

Church of the Good Shepherd. Stick to your principles." I did so, and the mayor appointed a new board.

I don't know any other person who has touched so many lives as he has. I count it one of the greatest things that have ever happened to me, getting to know Earl Dickerson.[14]

Alvin Boutté, cofounder of the Independence Bank of Chicago and former CEO of Indecorp, the largest African American–owned financial institution in the United States, offered the following comments:

Out here [at Independence Bank of Chicago] Earl Dickerson is a father figure, as he is to most black businessmen, because he operated successfully in an era when there was very little opportunity. Another thing is the kind of leadership he provided and the kind of image he has left all of us. He was involved in literally everything that was of political, economic, and social significance. I wanted to grow up and be like him.

He did something else. He kept the black leadership always striving for higher goals. Even though the time was not with us, he forced us to imagine and prepare for a better situation.[15]

Dickerson expected the struggle for freedom and equality in America to be a protracted battle with broad social and economic implications that could not be won through legal reform alone. Better education and greater economic opportunity would not follow automatically from changes in the law—a quite prophetic observation.

Judge William Sylvester White, who applied with Dickerson for membership in the Chicago Bar Association in 1943, said:

By his own example and what he demanded of others, he had a sense of excellence. And what impressed me even more was the fact that he had the wherewithal to do things first-class.

You will probably talk to people who will tell you he has inspired them to be audacious, to strike out away from the beaten path. And indeed I did that. But even as a young man in my twenties I was very conscious of what he had to back it up with.[16]

Despite Dickerson's long-standing reputation in the African American community, by the 1960s many militant young African Americans had become contemptuous of the civil rights leaders who had preceded them, and most whites were fearful of what these young black activists were demanding. The increasingly combative stance of the Black Panther and the Black Muslim movements, among others, was not conducive to the legal reformist agenda of older civil rights activists. The assassinations of Martin Luther King Jr., Malcolm X, and Chicago Black Panther leader Fred Hampton; police crackdowns leading to the arrests of radical leaders such as Huey Newton, Eldridge Cleaver, and Bobby Seale; as well as the race riots that hit major cities throughout the United States led to an atmosphere of mistrust and violence that tended to polarize the civil rights movement. Ultimately, however, Dickerson's accomplishments enabled him to bridge ideological and generational gaps. As historian Lerone Bennett Jr. said:

> The honors he has received! That is a thing that has to be explained. Through these honors and recognitions of the man and his accomplishments, he has become an influence upon the generations that have followed Al Raby and Martin King. Now you see all these testimonials to Earl Dickerson. Young people who had never met him, but who have been influenced by somebody who knows him, come to know about him. They come up to meet him. And it just goes on and on.[17]

The quality of Dickerson's mind can be discerned in his public utterances. Dr. Kenneth Smith remarked:

> He can discuss the philosophical aspects of religion and theology with the best. He reads Paul Tillich and went to some of his lectures at the University of Chicago. He made a speech on the day we [the Church of the Good Shepherd] broke ground for our rebuilding. He spoke on the responsibility of the church to the

world. The president of our church was there. Afterward he said to me, "Kenneth, who is this man?"[18]

Sterling Stuckey said the following about Earl Dickerson:

> As a public figure he was concerned, not exclusively with black affairs, but with all national and international affairs also. It seems to me that what distinguishes him from other successful black businessmen is the sweep of his view. What strikes me as unusual about him as a successful businessman is his intellectual side: his almost constant application of much of the best thought of the past to the present situation, his treating knowledge not as an abstraction nor as an adornment, but as something to clarify an issue or to illustrate a principle or to drive home a point. He is all the time borrowing from the Greeks or Latins one moment and from the French another. He is at home with business people and lawyers, of course, but also with scholars and poets.[19]

Although Dickerson left formal teaching in the spring of 1915 when he resigned as principal in Vincennes, Indiana, to enter the University of Chicago Law School, he remained an inveterate teacher. One of his many "classrooms" was the Kappa Alpha Psi fraternity. Black fraternities were very important to ambitious young African American men from 1911, when Kappa Alpha Psi was first chartered, until segregation began to loosen. Their significance during the early years of the twentieth century can be shown by the fact that in 1911 *Crisis,* the NAACP monthly magazine edited by W. E. B. DuBois, printed a picture of the founders of Kappa Alpha Psi at Indiana University and under it the fraternity's motto: "I will make ready and maybe my chance will come."[20] Dickerson introduced the larger world to that fraternity and that fraternity to the larger world by persuading Robert S. Abbott, owner and publisher of the *Chicago Defender,* to join the first alumni chapter in 1919 and by arranging a meeting of the national officers with President Coolidge in 1926. In his banquet address to Kappa Alpha Psi at its sixty-sixth annual convention in Washington, D.C., on August 8, 1985, Dickerson said:

We should regard the mind as an instrument for learning, not as a storehouse for knowledge. The difference is that between process and product. Products decay and become obsolete. Process continues, restores, constructs, and advances. The stress should be upon learning to learn—on self-initiated learning, on self-directed learning, on the proper methods of inquiry, on learning how to find out.

He urged the undergraduate chapters, the alumni chapters, and the national fraternity itself to hold "periodic continuing educational experiences on vital issues, including strategies and tactics for action."[21]

People have used the words "aristocratic," "meticulous," "conscientious," "scrupulous," "elegant," and "fastidious" to describe Dickerson. Some of these words connote both the moral and the aesthetic, and both qualities were often combined in his thought and character. Dickerson's insistence on excellence included attention to decorum, civility, courtesy, and decency. His old-fashioned manners sometimes—as in the hearings before the Illinois Senate committee that rejected his nomination for the FEPC—drove whites into rages through the shock that any black man so polite could cling so stubbornly to what he believes. But at other times his courtesy would give way to defiance. Of Dickerson one can say what Samuel Johnson wrote of Richard Savage: "He did not suffer his esteem of himself to depend upon anything sacred in the voice of the people who were inclined to censure him." According to Sterling Stuckey: "There is a certain autonomy of spirit about Mr. Dickerson. He could not have been both a successful businessman and an effective radical without a great self-confidence, without this freedom of spirit, without that awareness that in a certain sense complete freedom comes from within. He has that quality to an unusual degree."[22]

An illustration of Dickerson's complex, perhaps paradoxical, nature is the fact that on his office wall he had a picture of Martin Luther King Jr. and Malcolm X side by side in a montage. Etta Moten Barnett, wife of Claude Barnett, Dickerson's fraternity brother and longtime friend, observed: "Earl is a paradox only in one sense. He is a capitalist, not a socialist. He wants everyone to have a fair chance, and he wants everyone to work for what he gets. He'll give money to causes and to a person. He'll give a person advice. He is not at all simple. Some of the things he does and believes in I don't think people who are ideologues can understand. He follows not ideologies but principles."[23]

Dickerson could be a difficult and irascible man to work with and was at times very demanding of those around him. Judge Odas Nicholson, who worked for Dickerson in several capacities from 1942 to 1973, gave a glimpse into their relationship:

He was a slave driver. He drove himself, too. He expected us to keep up. We tried. He was likeable even when you wanted to choke him. He had a commanding presence. Young women would sometimes burst into tears.

The first day I worked for him he was an alderman. He came into the office in the late afternoon. He dictated twenty-eight letters. I had them all done by the next day. He read them over. He asked, "How many p's in 'apartment'?" I said, "One, of course." He said, "Then why do you have two?" That was his only comment. No compliment—*that one error*!

Another time in 1942, when he was acting chairman of the FEPC, he had a report to get in. It was very long. I typed like mad. It was a hot Saturday. There was a fan going in the window. Throwing back the carriage, I stuck my finger in the fan. I went down to the drugstore, got bandages, stanched the bleeding, and finished the report. I have a crooked finger to this day. A finger in the fan and those two p's!

But he complimented me indirectly to other people. Once he said to me, "One thing about you, you may be cantankerous, but you are bright."

He tried to discourage me from becoming a lawyer. He said, "It's tough for a man. It would be too tough for you, a frail southern colored girl." But he would give me bonuses at Christmastime. And when I went into private practice, he threw a lot of valuable work my way.[24]

Dickerson was also capable of explosive anger when he felt slighted or insulted, particularly if this was perceived to have racial overtones. Attorney Robert McDougal, who with Dickerson was a founder of the Chicago Committee of the NAACP Legal Defense Fund, recalled:

> There was a meeting of the Chicago Legal Defense Fund at the Conrad Hilton. I had worked quite a bit with Henry McGhee, who was then president of the Hyde Park Co-op and was later Chicago's postmaster. While he and Earl didn't look at all alike, when Henry came along with Kathryn Dickerson, I greeted him, "Hi, Earl!" Earl got as mad as the dickens. He said to me, "You can't tell one nigger from another! We all look the same to you!" Diane was so embarrassed, she said, "Daddy! That's no way to talk!" Later I apologized, after he had time to collect himself. From then on we were good friends.[25]

But Dickerson's anger could have a mischievous quality and a sense of irony as well. On several occasions he sued restaurants and hotels for turning him or his family away because they were black. After winning a small legal award from the Palmer House in Chicago, he returned and used the money to throw a party for himself and his friends.

Yet when Dickerson saw basic issues at stake, he never rejected an ally. He said at a mass protest meeting in Cicero: "I do not discriminate against a person because of the color of his skin or the color of his politics." His many quarrels seem to have been, at least on his part, purely ideological and not to be taken personally, although others sometimes did treat them as personal affronts and nurtured animus against him—the most notable being the politician William L. Dawson. But no bitterness on Dickerson's part seemed to remain. He had a cultivated capacity, like Mithradates, to be immune to the poisons of resentment.

AT THE BEGINNING of this book it was suggested that Dickerson's life fits the pattern of what University of Chicago sociologist Allison Davis has referred to as "the reality-oriented leader," one who is "relatively objective about the nature both of himself and of society, driven chiefly by affiliative rather than destructive feelings toward others, and controlled inwardly by principles which the culture regards as leading to its highest goals." "I have always been trying to give life to the Constitution, to give it vigor, to make it tell the truth," he said in one interview. "The kind of life I have tried to live from every standpoint is to give life to and assure the continuing progress and development of the institutions and people I consider worthwhile," he said in another. His whole life was devoted to gaining freedom and equality for African Americans, not simply because they were black like himself, but because they were the most oppressed people in America.

The Reverend Kenneth Smith recalled that Dickerson once called him and said, "You should preach a sermon on Mordecai's question to Queen Esther: 'Who knoweth whether thou hath come to the kingdom for such a time as this?'" Smith did so. This had been the text of many a lay sermon Dickerson delivered to black congregations as a young man, and for him its meaning was clear: "Do not forget your origins; use your talents and position to serve your people."

On June 22, 1983, Supreme Life Insurance Company observed Dickerson's ninety-second birthday. To the company he wrote: "I salute each of you and thank you for joining me this day in extending our plea for immortality, not alone of the company, but of the men and women who set in action the 'squib' for immortality more than sixty-four years ago." A "squib"—or lighted fuse—is a figure of speech sometimes used in tort cases dealing with a sequence of actions: Who is responsible? Who was the proximate cause? Who was the original cause? Dickerson seemed content with the hope that, at the very least, some of what he had set in motion would be a squib for good in the world.

In *The Jerusalem Bible*, the book of Esther includes a passage not found in the King James Version: a prayer that Mordecai offered after he had helped save his people. One stanza in that prayer is an apt ending for this story of Earl Dickerson's life:

> What I did, I did,
> rather than place the glory of a man
> above the glory of God;
> and I will not bow down to any
> but to you, Lord,
> and in so refusing I will not act in pride.

NOTES

Introduction

1. Interview and correspondence with Robert Colescott and Jandava Cattron, October 2003.

Chapter One

1. Davis, pp. 8–9. This University of Chicago psychologist and social anthropologist, who was a close friend of Dickerson's, distinguishes three chief types of leaders "with respect to the manner in which they handled their own aggressions: (1) sadistic, (2) masochistic, or (3) affiliative" (p. 7).

2. The personal information in this chapter is based upon seven interviews with Dickerson: September 7, September 22, September 28, October 5, and December 22, 1983; January 4, 1984; and September 25, 1985.

3. The personal accounts of Dickerson's years in Mississippi in this chapter are based on eleven interviews with him: on July 18, September 7, September 14, September 28, October 5, October 21, November 11, December 2, and December 7, 1983; on January 20, 1984; and on September 25, 1985.

4. Buckmaster, p. 9.

5. Free blacks in Mississippi reached their greatest number in 1840, when the census listed 1,336. They declined steadily in numbers until 1860, when the census listed 775. Wharton, p. 12. With emancipation, of course, the legal distinction between *free* blacks and *freed* blacks disappeared.

6. The Mississippi Reconstruction legislature in 1871 established Alcorn College, the legal counterpart for blacks of the state university for whites in Oxford. In 1872, Alcorn had 117 students. Wharton, p. 253.

7. Letter from Ruth Weyand, January 22, 1984.

8. James Weldon Johnson said that *The Souls of Black Folk* "had a greater effect upon and within the Negro race in America than any other single book since *Uncle Tom's Cabin.*" Anderson, p. 51.

9. Franklin, p. 253.

10. These figures are derived from Aptheker, 1977, pp. 610–14. His documentary excerpt is taken from the appendix of Walter White's 1929 study *Rope and Faggot: A Biography of Judge Lynch.* White combined all previous studies from 1882 through 1927. Lynchings were not considered important enough to record until 1882, when the *Chicago Tribune* included them in its annual summary of crimes and disasters.

11. From Dickerson's files.

12. Interview with Mrs. Lovelyn Evans, December 12, 1983.

13. "They were known in the black community as 'sundown' doctors and lawyers. They were nationwide. They carried on their professions after hours, lived off their professional services, not as charity, but because African Americans could not pay more. Their services were dedicated, always filled a need that would otherwise not be met, and often of high professional standards." Ruth Weyand, commenting on a draft manuscript of this chapter, October 20, 1984.

14. "Several news-gathering agencies were established, the most important of which was Claude Barnett's Associated Negro Press. The editors organized the Negro Newspaper Publishers' Association (later changed to the National Newspaper Publishers' Association), and together they sought to establish uniform policies and views with regard to the important issues affecting Negroes." Franklin, p. 415. For a lively sketch of Barnett's life and work, see Evans, 1983.

15. "Remarks on the Occasion of the First Annual Earl B. Dickerson Achievement Award presented by the University of Illinois (Champaign/Urbana) Black Alumni Association," March 13, 1982. From Dickerson's files.

16. Peters, Wilson, and Crump, pp. 1–24. The fraternity's name was formally changed from Kappa Alpha Nu to Kappa Alpha Psi on April 15, 1915. The probable reason was that one evening when Diggs was watching a fraternity brother run the hurdles, he overheard a white student remark, "He is a member of Kappa Alpha Nig." Ibid., pp. 23–24.

Chapter Two

1. The personal information in this chapter is based on nine interviews with Dickerson: on July 18, August 10, September 14, September 28, and November 11, 1983; and on September 25, October 6, October 12, and October 14, 1985.

2. For his private showing of the pro-KKK *The Birth of a Nation* to the chief justice of the U.S. Supreme Court, see Aptheker, 1977, p. 87. For his executive order establishing for the first time racially segregated dining and restroom facilities for federal employees, see Franklin, p. 324.

3. Elkins, p. 13.

4. In mid-1918 the NAACP issued a four-page leaflet titled "What the NAACP Has Done for the Colored Soldiers," including the following item: "*May 1917:* After repeated unsuccessful efforts, the Association works for a separate training camp and secures one at Des Moines, IA." Aptheker, 1977, p. 207. The issue was hotly debated within the NAACP, whose fundamental principle was racial integration. This issue was one of many in which the half loaf argued against the whole loaf and the short term against the long term.

5. Barbeau and Henri, p. 58.

6. The punishments were severe. Eventually nineteen of the black soldiers were hanged, and ninety-nine were sentenced to prison with terms ranging from a few years to life. The last prisoners were pardoned in 1939.

7. Barbeau and Henri, p. 57.

8. Franklin, p. 327.

9. Henri, p. 384, n. 94.

10. Barbeau and Henri, p. 81.

11. Henri, pp. 294–95. The then young disciplines of the social sciences, psychology, and statistics, particularly intelligence testing, were applied enthusiastically and often recklessly to justify convictions that African Americans and new foreign immigrants were genetically inferior to native-born white Americans. Because most of the blacks inducted were intended for labor battalions, lower standards of induction were used for them than for whites. For example, about 22 percent of all draftees in World War I were black, although they made up only 10.5 percent of the

total population. Psychologists, notably Robert M. Yerkes and Carl C. Brigham, made "scientific" assertions that Negroes' low ratings on IQ tests were the result of heredity, not environment. Facing the facts that army tests showed African American draftees from Ohio, Illinois, Indiana, and New York scoring significantly higher than white draftees from Mississippi, Louisiana, and Arkansas, these psychologists had an ingenious explanation: they asserted that these facts did not indicate the higher-ranking northern blacks had benefited by being better educated than the southern whites but, rather, that migration was "selective," with better-class blacks going north and with the northern blacks having more "white blood" than the southern Negroes. For a discussion of these points, with reference to sources, see Henri, pp. 146, 210, 295, and 325–31.

12. General Ballou achieved national notoriety because of his Bulletin 35, rebuking a black sergeant for insisting, after having been refused, on his right, guaranteed by Kansas state law, to admission to the white section of a movie house in Manhattan. The bulletin acknowledged that the sergeant was *legally* right and the movie house manager *legally* wrong, but, it continued, "the Sergeant is guilty of the *greater* wrong in doing anything, no matter how *legally* correct, that will provoke racial animosity. . . . The success of the Division, with all that that success implies, is dependent upon the good will of the public. That public is nine-tenths white. White men made the Division, and they can break it just as easily if it becomes a trouble maker." Henri, p. 292.

This bulletin came to the attention of the NAACP, which wrote an open letter to the War Department protesting it and secured publicity throughout the country. Aptheker, 1977, p. 208. However, Bulletin 35 was mild compared to some documents that are in the army archives but were not publicized. For example, see N.A., R-G, 165, Document 8142–150, printed in full in Barbeau and Henri, pp. 191–201.

13. In a document "Secret Instructions Concerning Black American Troops," Colonel Linard of the U.S. Army appealed to the French authorities not to permit familiar relations with the African Americans, which would offend the American view that they were inferior and must be kept in their place. The outraged French Assembly declared that anyone on French soil would be obliged to respect French law, which proclaimed

equality of all men without distinction of origin or color. Henri, p. 386, n. 117, with source from the Assemblée Nationale *Annales*.

14. Henri, p. 387, n. 140, gives direct quotations and sources of the full texts.

15. According to Henri, pp. 253–54, Patterson had a previous history that involved President Wilson himself. In May 1913, Oswald Garrison Villard, secretary of the NAACP, had urged Wilson to create an all-black section in the Treasury Department and appoint Adam E. Patterson its head. Wilson did name Patterson to be registrar of the Treasury, but southern senators raised such a furor that it was clear Patterson's appointment would not be approved, so Patterson withdrew his name.

16. Henri, p. 300.

17. Theodore Roosevelt Sr. died unexpectedly on January 6, 1919. By that time radio transmission of speech and music was well advanced. For example, on January 8, 1918, President Wilson had transmitted his Fourteen Points to the German people by what was then called "radio telephony."

18. Peters, Wilson, and Crump, p. 37.

19. Aptheker, 1977, pp. 293–98.

20. Franklin, pp. 336–37.

21. Barbeau and Henri, p. 175.

22. Wharton, pp. 189–90.

23. DuBois supported the war. In the July 1918 *Crisis* he wrote: "Let us, while this war lasts, forget our special grievances and close our ranks shoulder to shoulder with our white citizens and the allied nations that are fighting for democracy." But by 1919 the war was over and won— overseas.

24. Spear, pp. 7–8.

25. The following account is based on the Chicago Commission on Race Relations, pp. 1–52, unless otherwise specified.

26. Spear, pp. 213–14.

27. For a summary of the events of the riot, see Spear, pp. 214–18.

28. Occasional attempts that had been made in the 1870s to get black troops accepted as part of the Illinois militia succeeded in 1895 when Governor John Peter Altgeld recognized the Ninth Battalion, a black unit or-

ganized in 1890. In 1898 that battalion became the Eighth Regiment of Illinois Volunteers in the Spanish-American War. The unit became known as the Eighth Illinois Infantry in 1900. Colonel Franklin A. Dennison, who became its commander in 1915, led it in the Mexican expedition of 1916 and in France as the 370th Infantry Regiment of the 93rd Division during 1918. Gosnell, 1968, pp. 111–13; Drake and Cayton, p. 345.

29. Later, the members of the Eighth Illinois agitated for some official recognition of Giles. Edward H. Wright, Louis B. Anderson, and others persuaded the city council to change the name of Forest Avenue to Giles Avenue. Interview with Dickerson.

Still later, Wright pressured the South Park Board to permit the placing of a statue in honor of the Eighth Regiment on Grand Boulevard. Gosnell, 1968, p. 159.

The statue of a black doughboy stands on a pedestal on the corner of Thirty-fifth Street and what is now called Dr. Martin Luther King Jr. Drive. It's named *Victory,* and Leonard Crunell, an early student of Lorado Taft, created it. The headquarters building of Supreme Life Insurance Company was directly east of the statue.

30. Letter from Ruth Weyand, January 22, 1984.

31. Preface, Chicago Commission on Race Relations, p. xix.

Chapter Three

1. The personal information in this chapter is based on twelve interviews with Dickerson: on August 10, August 24, September 14, September 28, October 5, October 21, November 4, November 11, November 18, and December 15, 1983; on August 18, 1984; and on November 12, 1985; on Dickerson's record books (numbers 1, 4, 6, and 7); and on financial records supplied by the secretary of the Supreme Life Insurance Company.

2. In 1942, Green became an associate circuit court judge and, in 1952, a full circuit court judge. Cook County Bar Association, "Centennial Anniversary," p. 2.

3. However, Dickerson did get considerable experience in criminal cases. The professors at the University of Chicago Law School recommended him to several judges who assigned him as defense counsel in indigent cases.

4. These figures are derived from Goldman, p. 10, table 1, and Spear, p. 12, table 1. Goldman's table, based on the twelfth through the eighteenth U.S. censuses, is as follows:

Number and Percentage
of Black Attorneys in Chicago, 1900–1960

YEAR	NO. OF ATTORNEYS	NO. OF BLACK ATTORNEYS	PERCENTAGE OF BLACKS
1900	4,241	46	1.58
1910	3,866	44	1.14
1920	4,553	95	2.09
1930	6,576	175	2.66
1940	7,286	137	1.88
1950	10,006	231	2.31
1960	20,741	237	2.25

5. Interview with Mrs. Lovelyn Evans, December 12, 1983.

6. Wilson was an outstanding figure in Kappa Alpha Psi's history. *The Story of Kappa Alpha Psi* was authorized under his administration as grand polemarch in 1955. J. Jerome Peters, C. Rodger Wilson, and William L. Crump are credited as the authors of the official volume published by the fraternity in 1967.

7. "Two attempts at providing model housing within the Black Ghetto have been realized: a privately financed project for higher income groups —the Michigan Garden Boulevard Apartments ('The Rosenwald Apartments'), built in 1927; and a Federally-financed low-cost housing project completed in 1938. For seventeen years the former has been a symbol of good living on a relatively high income level; its waiting list is very long." Drake and Cayton, p. 660.

The date given above for the completion of the "Federally-financed low-cost housing project" is in error. Its construction was stalled for two years by court injunction until August 1939 when Dickerson as alderman and agitator got the injunction dissolved. "The Project," known as the Ida B. Wells Homes, was not open for occupancy until late 1943, delayed by wartime scarcities. See Strickland, p. 126, for the start of construction and the next chapter of this biography for Dickerson's role.

8. Diane was born on a Sunday. On the following Tuesday or Wednesday, Dickerson met Colonel Albert A. Sprague on the street. "Earl, how are you doing?" "Fine. My wife just gave birth to a daughter." "What day?" "May thirteenth." "That's my birthday, too, and also the birthday of one of my sons."

Dickerson said, "When I was assistant corporation counsel, Mayor Dever had appointed Sprague commissioner of Public Works. He worked with me to break down discrimination in the plumbers union. He made contributions to my political campaigns and also got contributions from his cousin Marshall Field III and others. Sprague was one of the finest men I have ever known."

9. Morris had served in the Illinois House for two terms (1890–94). In 1917 he, with Clarence Darrow, had successfully defended Alderman Oscar De Priest against charges of graft and bribery. He had been a member of the Illinois Constitutional Convention of 1920. See Spear, pp. 61 and 189; Gosnell, 1968, pp. 66, 73, 168, and 173; and Drake and Cayton, p. 345.

10. Gosnell, 1968, p. 66.

11. King, a regular Republican, had been assistant corporation counsel and assistant attorney general. He was state representative 1924–26, 1928–30, and he defeated Adelbert Roberts in the 1935 election for state senator. See Gosnell, 1968, pp. 71n, 103, 109, and 190.

12. An incidental detail of this period is that Dickerson met briefly with John R. Lynch, who during the Reconstruction period had served three terms in Congress as representative from Mississippi and who later wrote two books on the Reconstruction. He came to Chicago and practiced law from 1935 to 1939, when he died at the age of ninety-three. Dickerson went one day to his office to transact a real estate deal. They talked about Mississippi. Lynch had known some of Dickerson's relatives.

13. Dedmon, p. 295.

14. See Ralph Bunche, "The Thompson-Negro Alliance," in Aptheker, 1977, pp. 618–24.

15. Strickland, p. 34.

16. B. Joyce Ross, p. 24.

17. Interview with Elmer Gertz, November 22, 1983.

18. At the beginning of 1925 no neighborhood improvement associa-

tions in Chicago had racially restrictive covenants; by 1930, 40 percent of them had; by 1935, about 53 percent; by 1940, about 78 percent; and by 1945, 100 percent. Long and Johnson, p. 43, figure 8.

19. Strickland, pp. 130–31.

20. "Race" capitalized was the *Chicago Defender*'s style, not Dickerson's.

21. Earl Dickerson quoted in the *Chicago Defender,* October 2, 1937.

22. *The Chicago Defender,* November 16, 1940.

23. Crowe gave black lawyers the highest recognition they had received up to that time. There were at least ten black assistant state's attorneys and about six clerks and investigators. Gosnell, 1968, pp. 207–8.

24. The *Chicago Defender* commented: "The Giles post, which began with only a handful of men, now has 500 members."

25. Peters, Wilson, and Crump, pp. 82–83.

26. Dwight D. Eisenhower appointed Wilkins assistant secretary of labor in 1953. Franklin, p. 453. He was the first African American to receive a presidential appointment to a subcabinet post. Cook County Bar Association, "Centennial Anniversary," p. 3.

27. He was the first African American federal judge to receive a lifelong appointment in the continental United States. Toles manuscript.

28. In 1937, President Roosevelt appointed Hastie as the federal judge in the Virgin Islands. In 1946, President Truman appointed him governor of those islands. In 1949, Hastie became a judge of the Third Circuit Court of Appeals. Franklin, pp. 305 and 455.

29. Interview with Judge James B. Parsons, January 17, 1984.

30. Aptheker, 1977, p. 464.

31. Interview with Elmer Gertz, November 23, 1983.

32. For the rise and fall of Wright—the fall occurring in 1927—see Gosnell, 1968, pp. 153–62.

33. Aptheker, 1977, p. 627, with source.

34. Gosnell, 1968, pp. 90–91.

35. The phrase describes restrictions on the disposition of properties that carry over to subsequent owners though they are not party to them and might not even be aware of their existence.

Chapter Four

1. The personal information in this chapter is based on ten interviews with Dickerson: July 18, August 4, August 24, August 31, December 2, December 7, December 15, December 22, 1983; January 4, 1984; and October 28, 1985; on his record books (numbers 1, 2, 3, and 5); and on his files.

2. Gosnell, 1968, p. 30.

3. Ibid., p. 40.

4. Ibid., p. 30.

5. Gosnell, 1935, p. 110.

6. Ibid., p. 188.

7. The term of alderman was extended from two years to four in 1935. Gosnell, 1968, p. 28, n. 3.

8. The new Third Ward was carved out of the old Third, Fourth, and Fifth Wards in 1935. The Second Ward had a larger and more concentrated Negro population than the Third Ward (in 1931, 78,628, or 95.9 percent, as compared with 52,596, or 69.9 percent). Gosnell, 1968, p. 77. See table 6 and n. 33.

9. Interview with Dickerson.

10. Waskow, pp. 97–104.

11. Interview with John H. Johnson, January 17, 1984.

12. Interview with Mrs. Lovelyn Evans, December 12, 1983.

13. From Dickerson's files.

14. These approximate figures are derived from Gosnell, 1968, p. 77, table 6, and Drake and Cayton, p. 9, table 2.

15. Drake and Cayton, p. 8.

16. Long and Johnson, p. 43, figure 8.

17. Chicago Commission on Race Relations, p. 242.

18. Gosnell, 1968, p. 280.

19. This estimate assumes that between 1930 and 1940 the Negro school population increased by the same percentage, 18.8, that the total Negro population did during that period. Drake and Cayton, p. 8.

20. Ibid., p. 202, n. 3.

21. Gosnell, 1968, p. 281, n. 5.

22. Bousfield had been one of the incorporators of the Liberty Life

Insurance Company and its medical director since 1921. He was president of Liberty for five years after the death of Frank Gillespie in 1925. He was closely affiliated with the philanthropist Julius Rosenwald and was influential in the Rosenwald Fund, which in 1928 was given control of all the Rosenwald philanthropic giving.

23. Drake and Cayton, p. 201.

24. This expectation was before Pearl Harbor; the project did not open until late 1943.

25. Dickerson judged Paul Douglas to be an unsatisfactory member of the subcommittee. His judgment was documented by a story in the *Chicago Daily News* of June 6, 1941, reporting that for the third time the subcommittee had failed to get a quorum "because of the absence of Douglas." The report was read into the minutes anyway.

Throughout the study Dickerson pushed the subcommittee into positions of influence. The *Chicago Daily News* of July 21, 1939, reported: "Alderman Earl B. Dickerson won a promise from Miss Elizabeth Wood, chairman of the Chicago Housing Authority, at the weekly session of Dickerson's subcommittee of the city's housing committee that the subcommittee will be represented at the next meeting of the housing authority when rules for eligibility of tenant families in the subsidized housing project are to be fixed."

26. From Dickerson's files.

27. The results of the official census of 1940 were not yet available. That census counted the Negro population of Chicago at 277,731, making up 8.2 percent of the city's population. Drake and Cayton, pp. 8–9.

28. Dickerson wanted the subcommittee to recommend that the city council petition the General Assembly to declare race restrictive housing covenants against public policy, but his two colleagues would not do so.

29. Strickland, pp. 126–27.

30. Ibid., p. 126.

31. Interview with Dickerson.

32. Interview with Elmer Henderson, January 18, 1984.

33. The preliminary report was published in the Illinois Senate *Journal* of February 25, 1941, pp. 2–8.

34. Interview with Elmer Henderson, January 18, 1984.

35. Interview with Dickerson.

36. In Dickerson's record book (number 3).

37. Interview with John H. Johnson, January 17, 1984.

38. Interview with Elmer Gertz, November 2, 1983.

39. Interview with Weathers Y. Sykes, October 20, 1983.

Chapter Five

1. The personal information in this chapter is based on six interviews with Dickerson: July 18, September 7, September 14, September 22, October 28, 1983, and October 31, 1985; on his record books (numbers 1 and 2); and on his files.

2. There are two types of restrictive covenants: (1) the neighborhood type, in small, compact areas in which all parcels of land are embraced by a single covenant signed by all parties to the agreement, and (2) the community type, in larger, less compact areas in which a certain proportion of the total land area (from 75 to 95 percent of the frontage) is represented in the number of property owners as signatories to the pact. Long and Johnson, pp. 19–20. The covenants used in Chicago are almost all of the community type.

Although the covenants are used mainly against African Americans, the instrument was first invented on the West Coast against Orientals. "We are informed that such agreements have been directed against Indians, Jews, Chinese, Mexicans, Hawaiians, Puerto Ricans, and Filipinos, among others." *Shelley v. Kraemer,* 334 U.S. 1 (1942), n. 26. Some covenants exclude "all races except Caucasians."

3. Meyer, pp. 23–27.

4. *Buchanan v. Warley,* 245 U.S. 60 (1917).

5. *Corrigan v. Buckley,* 271 U.S. 323 (1926).

6. This property is south of Washington Park, which is between Fifty-first and Sixtieth Streets, and between South Parkway (now King Drive)—400 block east of State Street—and Cottage Grove Avenue—800 block east of State Street.

7. *Burke v. Kleiman,* 277 Ill. App. 519 (1934).

8. This was the language of the chancellor, Judge George Bristow, when he later examined the suit in the *Hansberry* case. The U.S. Supreme Court,

in ironic understatement, wrote that in *Burke v. Kleiman*, referring to the attorneys of Kleiman, "It does not appear that their interest in defeating the contract outweighed their interest in establishing its validity" (*Helvering v. Northwest Steel Rolling Mills*, 311 U.S. 46 [1940]).

9. Nothing in Lorraine Hansberry's *A Raisin in the Sun* is more sardonic than this "choice" the court gave Hansberry. What "consideration" would any white give to a black in such a bind?

10. The order of the names in a case changes according to the various stages of the process, depending on which party is taking the initiative at the particular stage.

11. Letter from Ruth Weyand, January 22, 1984. Weyand continued: "Persons whom I remember present at one or more of these moot court sessions (and at the moment I cannot separate the sessions before the *Hansberry* case from later ones) included now Justice Thurgood Marshall, the late Judge William Hastie of the U.S. Court of Appeals, Third Circuit, Judge Spottswood Robinson of the U.S. Court of Appeals, District of Columbia, the late Judge Joseph Waddy of the U.S. District Court, District of Columbia, Judge Robert Carter of the U.S. District Court, Southern District, New York, and Judge Constance Baker Motley of the U.S. District Court, Southern District, New York."

12. The record reads: "Mr. Earl B. Dickerson, with whom Messrs. Truman K. Gibson, Jr., C. Francis Stradford, Loring B. Moore, and Irwin C. Mollison were on the brief for petitioners."

13. The record states, "Mr. McKenzie Shannon, with whom Messrs. Angus Roy Shannon, William C. Graves, and Preston B. Kavanaugh were on the brief for the respondent."

14. No. 29, Supreme Court of the United States, October term, 1940. "Summary of the Argument," pp. 21–25. From Dickerson's files.

15. Nagareda, p. 11.

16. Kamp, p. 493.

17. "The class suit was an invention of equity to enable it to proceed to a decree in suits where the number of those interested in the subject of the litigation is so great that their rejoinder as parties in conformity to the usual rules of procedure is impracticable. . . . In such cases where the interests of those not joined are of the same class as the interests of those

who are, and where it is considered that the latter fairly represent the former in the prosecution of the litigation of the issues in which all have a common interest, the court will proceed to a decree." *Hansberry v. Lee,* 311 U.S. 41–42 (1940). (Class suits are sometimes called "representative suits.")

18. "By 1945 there were practically no white families left in the area." Drake and Cayton, p. 187.

19. Terkel, pp. 8–14.

20. McKissack and McKissack, p. 82.

21. Carter, pp. 21–22.

22. Ibid., p. 65. "Hansberry did not treat racial content and universality as though they were mutually exclusive. Instead, she implied that the underlying assumption that only the lives of whites have universal significance is another of the many racial misconceptions based on the inability of a large number of whites to view blacks directly."

23. Hansberry, 1970, p. xix.

24. McKissack and McKissack, p. 116.

25. Long and Johnson.

26. Ibid., p. 48.

27. Ibid., p. 49.

28. Ibid., pp. 73–74.

29. Interview with Judge William Sylvester White, January 31, 1984.

30. Long and Johnson, p. 90.

31. *Shelley v. Kraemer,* 334 U.S. 1 (1948).

32. Duncan and Duncan, p. 106, n. 9. For a description of what some of these other devices are, see Nesbitt, pp. 275–81.

Chapter Six

1. Drake and Cayton, pp. 214 and 215, figure 10.

2. Myrdal, vol. 1, pp. 409, 412.

3. Granger, p. 75.

4. Ibid., p. 76.

5. Ibid., p. 75.

6. Ibid., p. 76.

7. Ruchames, pp. 14–15.

8. Ibid., p. viii. This volume has many references that led me to other important sources.

9. The personal information in this chapter is based on seven interviews with Dickerson: on August 8, October 5, November 4, November 11, November 18, and December 12, 1983; and November 5, 1985; on his record books (numbers 2 and 3); and on his files.

10. Garfinkel, pp. 34–35.

11. See particularly Anderson, pp. 241–61; Bennett, 1979, pp. 217–34; and Garfinkel.

12. White, p. 192. For a long reconstruction by Randolph of this session with Roosevelt, see Anderson, pp. 256–58.

13. For an instructive contrast to similar events, compare the outcomes of the meeting on June 18, 1941, with one in the White House on November 12, 1914. In 1913, the Committee Protesting Segregation of Race Employees in the Federal Service had presented to President Woodrow Wilson a petition signed by African Americans from thirty-eight states. The president said he would investigate. After a year, during which segregation in federal service had spread, the committee, with William Monroe Trotter, editor of the *Boston Guardian,* as spokesman, met with Wilson. When Trotter said, "Only a year ago you were heralded as the second Lincoln," the president tried to interrupt, saying that personalities should be left out of the discussion. Trotter continued to speak, and the president ended the meeting by telling Trotter that if the organization he represented wished to approach the White House again, it must choose another spokesman. Aptheker, 1977, pp. 70–78. "Trotter later reported that 'the President declared in favor of race segregation as beneficial to both whites and the Negroes.'" Ruchames, p. 7.

14. *Chicago Defender,* June 28, 1941.

15. Ruchames, p. 22, citing FEPC *First Report,* Washington, 1945, pp. 104–5.

16. Dickerson to the National Lawyers Guild, August 19, 1983; from Dickerson's files.

17. There were two reasons for this tactic. One was that Randolph be-

lieved blacks had to champion their cause by themselves because most white liberals had become preoccupied by defense preparations. The other reason is that Randolph wanted to keep most Communists out of the march. Randolph had been a founder and the first president of the National Negro Congress in 1936. During that period of the "Popular Front" American Communists joined many liberal organizations to help stop the menace of Nazi Germany to the Soviet Union. However, they switched lines soon after August 23, 1939, when the Soviet-German pact was signed, which ended the Popular Front. The communist line then changed to oppose America's efforts to arm itself and to aid the allies because, the line went, the war was between "two imperialist powers." On April 28, 1941, Randolph resigned as president and as a member of the National Negro Congress, charging that it was dominated by Communists. The Communists would have been disruptive of the march, and most American Communists were white. The Communists did not switch their line again until Germany attacked the Soviet Union on June 22, 1941, four days after President Roosevelt met with Randolph, White, and other black leaders. Anderson, pp. 231–40 and 253–54.

18. Anderson, pp. 262–63.

19. The NAACP was holding its annual national convention from June 24 to 29, 1941, in Houston, Texas, and it passed a restrained resolution applauding Roosevelt's Executive Order 8802 as a "step in the right direction." It was at this meeting that Dickerson first heard he was being considered for appointment to the FEPC.

20. Ruchames, pp. 25–26.

21. This sum was later increased from the president's discretionary emergency funds; the committee spent $147,619 during fiscal year ending June 30, 1942. Kesselman, p. 18.

22. Interview with Elmer Henderson, January 18, 1984. Henderson remained on the staff of the FEPC, both the first and second committee, until Congress ended it in 1945.

23. Ruchames, p. 28.

24. Ibid., pp. 33–34.

25. Ibid., p. 34.

26. Kesselman, p. 16.

27. Interview with Clementine Skinner, January 18, 1984.

28. Ruchames, pp. 35–36.

29. Ibid., p. 31.

30. Note that Fenton did not concur. He was director of organization at the AFL. During the Chicago hearings he said that members of minority groups should not be accepted into industrial training classes until jobs were available. During the hearings in New York City, he had assured the committee that the Chemical and Oil Workers Union, Local 22206, affiliated with the AFL, would be asked to change its policy of discrimination against African Americans and that if it refused, its charter would be taken away. However, that union was a small one. During the Birmingham hearings, Fenton defended the discriminatory policies of the AFL's most powerful affiliates (Ruchames, p. 38). Fenton resigned from the FEPC in December 1942 and was succeeded by Boris Shishkin.

31. Edward Doty, a plumber, was a leader in the American Consolidated Trades Council, made up of black skilled tradesmen.

32. Interview with Mrs. Lovelyn Evans, December 12, 1983.

33. A Birmingham reporter tagged Dickerson as "the brown baby from Chicago" and Webster as "the black baby from Chicago."

34. Dickerson did not know how this was arranged. He assumed that the executive secretary of the committee had called the office of the attorney general. The marshal met Dickerson when the plane arrived and accompanied him to the plane when he departed. Dickerson stayed at the home of an African American employee of a railroad. The marshal accompanied him home at night, met him there in the morning, and was present both during the pretrial questioning of witnesses and throughout the hearings.

35. Ruchames, p. 220, n. 14.

36. FEPC, p. 33.

37. Ruchames, p. 41.

38. Neither of the executive orders establishing the two FEPCs mentioned "segregation"; both limited the committee's jurisdiction to specific acts of "discrimination." The executive orders were war measures,

like the Emancipation Proclamation. Yet, just as Lincoln's war measure had long-term consequences, so did Roosevelt's FEPC war orders because in social reality the reduction of discrimination entails the reduction of segregation. The experience of the two FEPCs seems to indicate that the acceptance of segregation was necessary as a way of reducing discrimination in the short run, but the recognition of segregation as inherently discriminatory is necessary for the long run. "It cannot be too strongly emphasized . . . that in the long run, segregation must be banished from the American scene if the elimination of discrimination is to be assured." Ibid., p. 98.

39. Ibid., p. 46. One writer suggested that "back of the transfer, as everyone knew, was reactionary Southern pressure. Also involved were top government officials who had been annoyed by the FEPC insistence that they put an end to discrimination in their own departments and agencies." Beecher, p. 250.

40. Ruchames, p. 47.

41. Ibid., p. 48.

42. Ibid., pp. 48–49.

43. Ibid., pp. 49–50. Rankin marked the 152nd anniversary of the Bill of Rights in December 1942 by asserting, "Slavery was the greatest blessing that the Negro ever had. If the FEPC will leave him alone, he will make his own living." Ibid., p. 73.

44. The example most pertinent to the period of his struggle with McNutt is given in the *Pittsburgh Courier* of October 22, 1942. It carried a New York story of the Associated Negro Press headlined "Hints Paul McNutt Is Not Helping to Enforce Fair Employment Order" and stating: "Acting Chairman Earl B. Dickerson said, 'We who have been optimistic that the committee's findings might develop the basis for enforcement legislation have been somewhat disheartened about the transfer to the War Manpower Commission because the effect is to limit the activities of the committee.'"

Some other examples from the preceding period in headlines are "Determined to Get Results, Dickerson, Cramer Promise" (*Pittsburgh Courier*, September 12, 1941); "Dickerson Urges FEPC to End Ban in Hurry" (*Chicago Defender*, November 22, 1941); and "FEPC in Need of

More Power, Earl Dickerson Tells Atlantans" (*Atlanta Daily World*, April 15, 1942).

45. Ruchames, pp. 49 and 226–27, n. 44.

46. Ibid., p. 50.

47. Ibid., p. 52.

48. Ibid., p. 57.

49. Ibid., pp. 53–54.

50. Ibid., pp. 55–56.

51. See Ruchames, p. 57, for a membership list of the second FEPC.

52. Ibid., pp. 57–58.

53. Besides the latter chapters of Ruchames, see Kesselman and M. Ross.

54. This complicated case involved politics in the city government, in the company, and in the union, in addition to racial bias. See Ruchames, pp. 100–20, and Weckler.

55. *Congressional Record*, 79th Cong., 1st sess., 1945, 91, pt. 5:5796.

56. Ibid., pp. 121–36.

57. Ibid., p. 160.

58. Weaver, pp. 79 and 81.

59. Sarnoff's home was on East Fifty-seventh Street. According to Dickerson, it was "a wonderful dinner. We usually met someplace once a month."

60. Dickerson said there were citizens' FEPC committees in Los Angeles, Chicago, and New York. "The people in New York had been fighting a long time for a state FEPC. It was one of the first states to pass one."

61. Dr. Clarence Payne was a socially concerned physician. He had interrupted his training at the University of Chicago Medical School to enlist in the Colored Officers Training School at Fort Des Moines, Iowa. He was commissioned a lieutenant and served in the Ninety-second Division in France in World War I.

62. Mrs. Irene McCoy Goins had been one of the founding members of the Chicago Urban League in 1916. In 1941 she was president of the Chicago Federation of Colored Women's League.

63. E. Franklin Frazier, a sociologist, author of *The Negro Family in Chicago*, University of Chicago Press, 1932, and other research books. In

1941 he was on the faculty of Fisk University but retained a connection with the Chicago Urban League, where he had been in charge of research.

64. Robert R. Taylor, the son of an architect, had been a close friend of Booker T. Washington. Julius Rosenwald gave money for a YMCA at Tuskegee Institute, one of the early YMCAs for African Americans, and he gave money also for the Wabash YMCA in Chicago. When Rosenwald went to Tuskegee, through Washington, he met Taylor. When Rosenwald built the Michigan Boulevard Garden Apartments, "the Rosenwald Building," on the corner of Forty-seventh Street and Michigan Avenue in Chicago, Taylor helped with the design and was appointed manager. He later became the first black chairman of the Chicago Housing Authority. The Robert Taylor Homes are named after him.

65. Interview with Mrs. Lovelyn Evans, December 12, 1983.

Chapter Seven

1. The ANP dateline was five days before the second FEPC replaced the first.

2. From Dickerson's files.

3. In Dickerson's files is a letter dated February 12, 1952, from DuBois to Dickerson urging him to accept the nomination by the Progressive Party as its vice presidential candidate in the coming campaign. DuBois hoped that the slate would be "Halliman and Dickerson."

4. From Dickerson's files.

5. There was publicity. Irv Kupcinet, in his column in the *Chicago Daily Times* of May 16, 1943, wrote: "There'll be a Jim Crow showdown in the Chicago Bar Association shortly. A number of Negro attorneys will apply for membership in the association, which only recently refused to adopt an amendment to its by-laws calling for equal rights for Negroes. If the applications are turned down, many of the city's outstanding attorneys have signified they will resign. Among the Negro attorneys who will seek membership, according to Charles Liebman, secretary of the association's civil rights committee, are Earl B. Dickerson, Archibald J. Carey, Jr., Euclid Taylor, and Sylvester White."

6. Kogan, p. 204.

7. For his valuable services in revising the state election laws he had

been admitted to the Illinois bar. He rose to be assistant attorney for the commission. Gosnell, 1968, pp. 205–6.

8. Dickerson's recollection of his statement is from an interview in 1983.

9. Cook County Bar Association, "Centennial Anniversary," p. 2.

10. From Dickerson's files.

11. Dickerson had engaged in many liberal activities as a private citizen also. For example, the national press on February 1, 1950, reported that fifteen prominent Americans had protested U.S. Judge Medina's threat to sentence for contempt of court and to recommend for disbarment the lawyers defending the "Communist Eleven" then on trial (and later convicted under the Smith Act). Among the fifteen were Thomas Mann, Linus Pauling, Earl Dickerson, and Albert Einstein. Dickerson had gone with a group to Princeton to persuade Einstein to sign the protest. Dickerson said, "His eyes were as though he was looking into infinity. I could understand how he conceived of his ideas of relativity."

12. *New York Times*, August 28, 1953.

13. National Lawyers Guild, "An Appeal to Reason," pp. 4 and 11–13.

14. See Ambrose, pp. 189–92, 303–7, 327–28 on Brown; pp. 55–56, 82, 136, 162–68, 186–89, 219–220 on McCarthy; and p. 620 summative on both.

15. Speech to New York chapter of the National Lawyers Guild, May 4, 1954. From Dickerson's files.

16. This notice was exactly one month after he had told the American Bar Association that he had already made up his mind to do so, without having held any hearings. It was eleven days after he had made substantially the same speech to the American Veterans of World War II (AMVETS) in Indianapolis, on September 5. From Dickerson's files. After that second speech he said to the press, "We're going to take them to the woodshed."

17. Letter from Dickerson's files.

18. His role in the Chicago Urban League from 1939 to 1943 has been described in chapter 5.

19. For example, deep respect for him was expressed at the June 1945 annual league dinner. He was honored for his twenty-five years as a mem-

ber of the league, for his twenty years as a member of the board, and for his six years as president. At that dinner a script of his life, titled "Portrait of a Man," was dramatized.

20. See Strickland, pp. 243–54, for details on this complicated and acrimonious dissension.

21. Ibid., pp. 155–84.

22. Ibid., pp. 179–80.

23. Ibid., p. 160.

24. Interview with Sidney Williams, August 27, 1984.

25. *Chicago Lawyers Guild Monthly*, January 1950.

26. Strickland, p. 161.

27. Text in Dickerson's files. It should be remembered that this was about nine months after Joseph McCarthy had begun his demagogic career in a speech at Wheeling, West Virginia.

28. Strickland, pp. 168–69.

29. Ibid., pp. 183–84.

30. Ibid., pp. 185–86.

31. Ibid., p. 264.

32. Davis, p. 149. The university's white treasurer judged that DuBois's radicalism was damaging the support to the university from white philanthropists.

33. Ibid., p. 142.

34. See DuBois's letter, July 1, 1948, in Aptheker, 1978, pp. 188–89.

35. *New York Times*, October 30, 1947.

36. President Coolidge appointed Cobb, a graduate of Howard Law School, to the municipal court bench in Washington, D.C. He served there until 1935 and then returned to private practice. His firm, Cobb, Howard, and Hayes, was a part of the team of lawyers that in 1950 successfully defended W. E. B. DuBois in his trial for refusing to register as a foreign agent.

37. Interview with Etta Moten Barnett, September 25, 1984.

38. The main source for the information in this paragraph and the preceding one is Aptheker, 1978.

39. In 1958 the U.S. Supreme Court, in *Aptheker v. Rusk*, ruled that the

denial of a passport on the basis of political opinions was unconstitutional. After securing his passport that year, Robeson left the United States to live in England, until he returned to the United States in 1963.

40. "By 1950, it was no longer safe for him to venture beyond the black community." Stuckey, 1983, p. 6. "During the Cold War, Rutgers removed Paul's name from its football teams of 1917 and 1918—those were his All-American years—resulting in the only ten-man football team in history." Ibid.

41. Interview with Dickerson, September 14, 1984.

42. Stuckey, 1983, p. 6.

43. The source of the information in this paragraph is Aptheker, 1978.

44. Interview with Mrs. Diane Dickerson Montgomery, August 23, 1984.

45. The clipping is in one of Dickerson's record books, but the date was not recorded.

46. "The Original Forty Club of Chicago: Fiftieth Anniversary Record," 1970.

47. Interview with Dr. Edwin C. Berry, April 22, 1984.

Chapter Eight

1. Spear, pp. 116 and 182.

2. Spear, p. 183, and Puth, p. 4.

3. Stuart, pp. 81–82. Bousfield had a career distinguished in other ways. In 1929 he became the associate director of medical research with the Julius Rosenwald Fund. In October 1939 he became the first black appointed to the Chicago Board of Education. Ibid., p. 81. He was the first black president of the Chicago Urban League, preceding Dickerson, who was elected in 1939. Bousfield's wife, Maudell, became the first black principal of a Chicago public school. Gosnell, 1968, pp. 294–95.

4. This practice was not unusual. Most of the larger African American churches advertised, or permitted the advertisement of, Negro businesses "to advance the Race." Drake and Cayton, p. 428.

5. Interview with Dickerson, 1983.

6. It added industrial policies about 1927, because few African

Americans had enough money for ordinary life; by the end of 1928 it had $10,401,000 of ordinary insurance in force and $1,964,000 of industrial. Ibid., pp. 6 and 8.

7. This objective was aimed particularly at the young black men and women who were being graduated from high schools in the North and at young black professionals who were being graduated from universities and colleges, both groups in ever-increasing numbers.

8. Puth, pp. 4–5.

9. Ibid., p. 7.

10. "Binga didn't like my father and ignored him." Interview with Edward Gillespie, December 15, 1983.

11. Spear, p. 184.

12. Drake and Cayton, p. 84.

13. Puth, p. 8.

14. Puth, p. 8, table 1.

15. Interview with John H. Johnson, January 17, 1984.

16. Puth, p. 10, gives details.

17. Ibid., p. 11.

18. Ibid.

19. In law a lien is the right to take and hold or sell the property of a debtor as security or payment of a debt. Actually, the policyholders' cash values on their policies were debts owed by the company to them, but the holders had the legal right to assign these cash values to the company to be calculated as assets rather than debts.

20. See Puth, p. 11, for a text of the policy lien.

21. Ibid., p. 12.

22. Interview with John H. Johnson, January 17, 1984.

23. Ibid.

24. See Puth, pp. 13–14.

25. Duncan and Duncan, p. 85, table 26.

26. African Americans made up 96.5 percent of Chicago's nonwhite population in 1950.

27. Puth, pp. 13–15.

28. In 1907 when Dickerson was a student at the University of Chicago

Laboratory Schools, he went a few evenings to White City Amusement Park. The first time he rode the chute-the-chute, it seemed to him that the car was going into a pool of water. Frightened, he jumped out, landed in the water, and had to be fished out.

29. Interview with Dickerson, 1983.

30. *Pittsburgh Courier,* June 28, 1946.

31. Puth, p. 14.

32. Ibid., pp. 14–15.

33. "The Guardian," summer 1956, p. 1. Throughout his presidency Dickerson sought guidance from expert management firms. For example, in 1963 he contracted with Booz Allen Hamilton, a nationally known management firm, which produced a "massive manual." "The Guardian," fall 1963, p. 1.

34. Interview with Edward S. Gillespie, December 15, 1983.

35. Information from the Complimentary Calendar of Supreme Life Insurance Company, 1963.

36. *Ebony,* December 1961, p. 150 (no byline).

37. "The Guardian," fall 1964, pp. 6 and 7–8.

38. Ibid., p. 3.

39. Interview with Alvin Boutté, November 22, 1983.

40. Interview with Edward S. Gillespie, December 15, 1983.

41. Interview with Dickerson.

42. Interview with Edward S. Gillespie, December 15, 1983.

43. Interview with Dickerson, 1983.

44. Ibid.

45. Interview with Alvin Boutté, November 22, 1983.

46. From Dickerson's files.

47. All figures are from the company's statements. Some are rounded off. What the 1955 statement called "insurance in force" was called "business in force" in 1971. The capital and surplus of a company at a particular time is dependent in part on how much money is then committed for various purposes; a lower figure in itself does not signify a decline.

Chapter Nine

1. The sources of the personal information in this chapter are eight interviews with Dickerson: on July 18, August 24, August 31, October 5, December 2, and December 15, 1983; on January 4, 1984, and November 13, 1985; on his record books (numbers 2, 3, 5, and 7); and on his files.

2. Ruchames, p. 179.

3. Strickland, p. 157.

4. All the Chicago daily newspapers gave such extensive coverage to the Illinois Senate's action on these nominations that only citations for key events, issues, or quotations are given as sources.

5. Percy had been head of President Eisenhower's Committee on Program and Progress in 1959: it was his "surprise" appearance to testify in favor of the FEP bill that was credited with the Senate's approval in 1961. Strickland, p. 224.

6. Korshak revealed that the person whom he called and who called the senators was not Kerner but Mayor Richard J. Daley. Conversation with Korshak, February 1, 1984.

7. Interview with Ralph Helstein, February 15, 1984.

8. On King and Highlander, see Kohl, 1984, and Oates, pp. 360–61.

9. Interview with Ralph Helstein, February 15, 1984.

10. Interview with Elmer Gertz, November 22, 1983. The commission's annual budget was one hundred thousand dollars, including the chairman's pay of twelve thousand dollars.

11. Interview with Dickerson, December 15, 1983.

12. Interview with Judge William Sylvester White, January 31, 1984.

13. Drake and Cayton, p. 731.

14. Duncan and Duncan, p. 11.

15. Drake and Cayton, p. liv.

16. The committee was formed in 1950, after Lawrence Kimpton succeeded Robert M. Hutchins as president of the University of Chicago. Dickerson retains no correspondence of this informal committee, and secretaries of the institutions involved could not easily find copies. Dr. Quentin Young remembered hearing about the committee when in 1951

he was in the student health service of George Williams College. Interview with Quentin Young, January 13, 1984.

17. For details see Abrahamson. Julia Abrahamson was the first director of the Hyde Park–Kenwood Community Conference.

18. See Rossi.

19. Interview with Paul Berger, November 19, 1983.

20. Ibid. Paul Berger was one of the founders of the Hyde Park Savings and Loan Association.

21. That morning news came from Accra that W. E. B. DuBois had died the day before at the age of ninety-six. "On the very day DuBois died in Ghana, Dr. King, speaking on the grounds of the Washington Monument and the Lincoln Memorial, said that Dr. DuBois had inspired his own battle for civil liberties." Davis, p. 13.

22. Letter from Ruth Weyand dated January 22, 1984.

23. Ibid.

24. Oates, pp. 367–68.

25. Interview with Lerone Bennett Jr., September 25, 1984.

26. Ibid.

27. Interview with Edwin C. Berry, September 5, 1984.

28. Interview with Judge James B. Parsons, January 17, 1984.

29. Interview with Elmer Gertz, November 22, 1983.

30. Interview with Edwin C. Berry, September 5, 1984.

31. "The Guardian," fall 1964, p. 8.

32. Letter from U.S. District Judge Jack Tanner dated December 8, 1983.

33. Trinidad and Tobago, Jamaica, and Barbados were the principal islands in the federation, but it included most of the British Leeward and Windward Islands also. The federation did not survive; it was dissolved in 1962.

34. Under Nkrumah's leadership the Gold Coast received its independence on March 6, 1957, and in 1960 it became the Republic of Ghana. He was the republic's first prime minister, and in 1961 he was proclaimed "president for life." He was overthrown by a military police coup in 1966.

35. The source of this information on DuBois is Aptheker, 1978.

36. Interview with Sterling Stuckey, September 14, 1984.

37. *Ebony,* December 1984, p. 118. The November 1985 *Ebony,* its fortieth-anniversary issue, had a feature "Forty Who Made a Difference," including Dickerson in company with Marian Anderson, Mary McLeod Bethune, W. E. B. DuBois, Lyndon Johnson, Martin Luther King Jr., Thurgood Marshall, Paul Robeson, Eleanor Roosevelt, Earl Warren, and Walter White, pp. 60–76.

Chapter Ten

1. Interview with Paul Berger, November 19, 1983.
2. From Dickerson's files.
3. From Dickerson's files.
4. Letter from Jonathan A. Rothstein dated January 17, 1984.
5. *Chicago Defender,* September 23, 1939.
6. Interview with Edwin C. Berry, September 5, 1984.
7. Interview with Tom Lewis, December 8, 1983.
8. Interview with Weathers Y. Sykes, October 20, 1983.
9. Interview with Elmer Henderson, January 18, 1984.
10. Interview with Judge Odas Nicholson, January 8, 1984.
11. Interview with Dr. Quentin Young, January 13, 1984.
12. Interview with Edwin C. Berry, September 5, 1984.
13. Interview with Sterling Stuckey, September 14, 1984.
14. Interview with the Reverend Kenneth Smith, December 6, 1983.
15. Interview with Alvin Boutté, November 22, 1983.
16. Interview with Judge William Sylvester White, January 31, 1984.
17. Interview with Lerone Bennett Jr., September 25, 1984.
18. Interview with Dr. Kenneth Smith, December 6, 1983.
19. Interview with Sterling Stuckey, September 14, 1984.
20. Peters, Wilson, and Crump, p. 137.
21. From Dickerson's files.
22. Interview with Sterling Stuckey, September 14, 1984.
23. Interview with Mrs. Etta Moten Barnett, September 25, 1984.
24. Interview with Judge Odas Nicholson, January 8, 1984.
25. Interview with Robert McDougal, November 21, 1983.

BIBLIOGRAPHY

Abrahamson, Julia. *A Neighborhood Finds Itself*. New York: Harper, 1959.

Abram, Morris B. *The Day Is Short*. New York: Harcourt Brace Jovanovich, 1982.

Ambrose, Stephen E. *The President*, vol. 2 of *Eisenhower*. New York: Simon and Schuster, 1984.

Anderson, Jervis. *A. Philip Randolph: A Biographical Portrait*. New York: Harvest Book, Harcourt Brace Jovanovich, 1973.

Aptheker, Herbert, ed. *A Documentary History of the Negro People in the United States*, vol. 3, 1910–1932. New York: Citadel Press, 1977.

———. *The Correspondence of W. E. B. DuBois*, vol. 3, *Selection 1944–1963*. Boston: University of Massachusetts Press, 1978.

Barbeau, Arthur E., and Florette Henri. *The Unknown Soldiers: Black American Troops in World War I*. Philadelphia: Temple University Press, 1974.

Beecher, John. "8802 Blues." *New Republic*, February 22, 1943.

Bennett, Lerone, Jr. *Confrontation: Black and White*. Chicago: Johnson Publishing, 1965.

———. "The Last Half-Hour: Earl Dickerson, Gadfly of the Black Establishment, Makes His Final Stand." *Ebony*, April 1976.

———. *Wade in the Water: Great Moments in Black History*. Chicago: Johnson Publishing, 1979.

Branham, Charles. "A History of Black Politics." *Chicago Journal*, January 26, 1983.

Brook, William R. *Conflict and Transformation: The United States, 1844–1877*. New York: Penguin Books, 1973.

Buckmaster, Henrietta. *Freedom Bound: A Study of the Reconstruction, 1868 to 1875.* New York: Collier Books, 1967.

Carter, Steven. *Hansberry's Drama: Commitment Amidst Complexity.* New York: Penguin Books, 1993.

Chicago Commission on Human Relations. *The People of Chicago: Five-Year Report, 1947–1951.* Chicago, 1952.

Chicago Commission on Race Relations. *The Negro in Chicago: A Study of Race Relations and a Race Riot.* Chicago: University of Chicago, 1922.

Chicago Lawyers Guild. *Lawyers Guild Monthly,* January 1950.

Clayton, Edward T. *The Negro Politician: His Successes and Failures.* Chicago: Johnson Publishing, 1964.

Compton, James W. "Compton Report." Address at Annual Report Luncheon, Chicago Urban League, February 3, 1984.

Conyers, James E., and Walter L. Wallace. *Black Elected Officials: A Study of Black Americans Holding Governmental Office.* New York: Russell Sage Foundation, 1976.

Cook County Bar Association. "Centennial Anniversary of the Admission of the First Black Lawyer to the Illinois Bar, April 20, 1869," 1969.

Cook County Bar Association News, August 9, 1961.

Davis, Allison. *Leadership, Love, and Aggression: Frederick Douglass, W. E. B. DuBois, Richard Wright, Martin Luther King, Jr.* New York: Harcourt Brace Jovanovich, 1983.

Dedmon, Emmett. *Fabulous Chicago.* New York: Random House, 1953.

Dickerson, Earl B. "Negro Rights and the Supreme Court." *The Nation,* July 12, 1952.

Drake, St. Clair, and Horace R. Cayton. *Black Metropolis: A Study of Negro Life in a Northern City,* 2 vols. New York: Harper and Row, 1962.

DuBois, W. E. B. *The Souls of Black Folk.* In *Three Negro Classics.* New York: Avon Books, 1965.

———, ed. *An Appeal to the World!* New York: NAACP, 1947.

Duncan, Otis D., and Beverly Duncan. *The Negro Population of Chicago: A Study of Residential Succession.* Chicago: University of Chicago Press, 1957.

Ebony. "Earl B. Dickerson: Warrior," December 1961.

———. "Active Oldsters," December 1984.

Elkins, Stanley M. *Slavery: A Problem in American Institutional and Intellectual Life.* New York: Grosset and Dunlap, 1963.

Evans, Linda J. "Claude A. Barnett and the Associated Negro Press." *Chicago History* (the magazine of the Chicago Historical Society), spring 1983, pp. 44–56.

Evanston Academy. *The Bear,* vol. 3: *Class of 1909.* Chicago: Campbell Company, 1909.

FEPC. *Press Clipping Digest,* no. 4, July 6, 1942.

Final Report: U.S. President's Fair Employment Practices Committee. Washington, D.C.: U.S. Government Printing Office, 1947.

First Report: U.S. President's Fair Employment Practices Committee. Washington, D.C.: U.S. Government Printing Office, 1945.

Fish, John Hall. *Black Power/White Control: The Struggle of the Woodlawn Organization in Chicago.* Princeton, N.J.: Princeton University Press, 1973.

Franklin, John Hope. *From Slavery to Freedom: A History of Negro Americans,* 5th ed. New York: Alfred A. Knopf, 1980.

Frazier, E. Franklin. *The Negro in the United States,* rev. ed. New York: Macmillan, 1957.

———. *Negro Church in America.* New York: Schocken Books, 1963.

Garfinkel, Herbert. *When Negroes March.* New York: Atheneum, 1969.

Goldman, Marion S. *A Portrait of the Black Attorney in Chicago.* Chicago: American Bar Foundation, Path Publishing, 1972.

Gosnell, Harold F. *Negro Politicians: The Rise of Negro Politics in Chicago.* Chicago: University of Chicago Press, 1935.

———. *Machine Politics, Chicago Model,* 2nd ed. Chicago: University of Chicago Press, 1968.

Granger, Leslie B. "Barriers to Negro War Employment." *Annals of the American Academy of Political and Social Science,* September 1942.

Gray, Peggy. "Earl B. Dickerson: The Effect of His Leadership on the Growth and Development of Supreme Life." Typewritten ms., University of Illinois, spring 1977.

"Guardian, The." Supreme Liberty Life Insurance Company (Supreme Life Insurance Company after 1960), monthly publication. Chicago.

Gutman, Herbert G. *The Black Family in Slavery and Freedom, 1750–1925.* New York: Vintage Books/Random House, 1976.

Handlin, Oscar. *Fire-Bell in the Night: The Crisis in Civil Rights.* Boston: Little, Brown, 1964.

Hansberry, Lorraine. *A Raisin in the Sun.* New York: Signet Books, 1958.

———. *To Be Young, Gifted, and Black: Lorraine Hansberry in Her Own Words.* New York: New American Library, 1970.

Haynes, George E. "Negroes Move North." *Survey,* May 4, 1918, and January 4, 1919.

Henri, Florette. *Black Migration: Movement North, 1900–1920.* Garden City, N.Y.: Anchor Press/Doubleday, 1975.

Journal. Official Organ of Kappa Alpha Psi Fraternity. Philadelphia, October 1985.

Kamp, Allen R. "The History Behind *Hansberry v. Lee.*" *University of California–Davis Law Review,* vol. 20 (1987), pp. 481–99.

Kellogg, Charles Flint. *NAACP: A History of the National Association for the Advancement of Colored People.* Baltimore, Md.: Johns Hopkins University Press, 1967.

Kesselman, Louis. *The Social Politics of FEPC.* Chapel Hill: University of North Carolina Press, 1948.

Kitagawa, Evelyn M., and Karl E. Tauber, eds. *Local Community Fact Book Chicago Metropolitan Area 1960.* Chicago Community Inventory, University of Chicago, 1963.

Kluger, Richard. *Simple Justice: The History of Brown v. Board of Education and Black America's Struggle for Equality.* New York: Alfred A. Knopf, 1976.

Kogan, Herman. *The First Century: The Chicago Bar Association, 1874–1974.* Chicago: Rand McNally, 1974.

Kohl, Herbert. "Letter to the Editors." *New York Review of Books.* January 19, 1984, pp. 51–52.

Logan, Raymond W., and Michael A. Winston, eds. *Dictionary of American Negro Biography.* New York: W. W. Norton, 1982.

Long, Berman H., and Charles S. Johnson. *People vs. Property: Race Restrictive Covenants in Housing.* Nashville, Tenn.: Fisk University Press, 1947.

Lynch, John R. *The Facts of Reconstruction.* New York: Neale Publishing, 1913.

———. *Some Historical Errors of James Ford Rhodes.* Boston: Cornhill Publishing, 1923.

Mangum, Charles S., Jr. *Legal Status of the Negro.* Chapel Hill: University of North Carolina Press, 1940.

Marshall, Marilyn. "Forty Who Made a Difference." *Ebony,* November 1985.

Mayer, Harold M., and Richard C. Wade. *Chicago: Growth of a Metropolis.* Chicago: University of Chicago Press, 1969.

McFeely, William S. *Grant: A Biography.* New York: W. W. Norton, 1981.

McKissack, Patricia, and Frederick McKissack. *Young, Black, and Determined.* New York: Holiday House, 1998.

McNeil, Glenna Rae. *Groundwork: Charles Houston and the Struggle for Civil Rights.* Philadelphia: University of Pennsylvania Press, 1984.

Meier, August. *Negro Thought in America, 1880–1915.* Ann Arbor: University of Michigan Press, 1963.

Melton, J. Gordon, ed. *The Encyclopedia of American Religions.* Wilmington, N.C.: McGrath Publishing, 1978.

Merriam, Charles E. *Chicago: A More Intimate View of Chicago Politics.* New York: Macmillan, 1929.

Meyer, Stephan Grant. *As Long as They Don't Move Next Door.* Lanham, Md.: Rowman and Littlefield, 2001.

Mezerik, A. G. "Negroes at the U.N.'s Door." *The Nation,* December 13, 1947.

Mowry, George E. *The Era of Theodore Roosevelt and the Birth of Modern America, 1900–1912.* New York: Harper Torchbooks, 1962.

Murray, Charles. *Losing Ground: American Social Policy, 1950–1980.* New York: Basic Books, 1984.

Myrdal, Gunnar. *An American Dilemma: The Negro Problem and American Democracy*, 2 vols. New York: Harper, 1944.

Nagareda, Richard A. "Administering Class Adequacy in Class Representation." Revised draft manuscript, August 19, 2003.

National Lawyers Guild. "An Appeal to Reason." New York, 1953 (mimeograph copy).

———. *Resolution on Threat to Independence of the Bar.* Chicago: 1954 Convention, November 19–21, 1954.

Nesbitt, George B. "Relocating Negroes from Urban Slum Clearance Sites." *Land Economics* 25 (August 1949).

Oates, Stephen B. *Let the Trumpet Sound: The Life of Martin Luther King, Jr.* New York: Harper and Row, 1982.

Original Forty Club. "Fiftieth Anniversary Record." Chicago: Original Forty Club, 1970.

Peters, J. Jerome, C. Rodger Wilson, and William L. Crump. *The Story of Kappa Alpha Psi: A History of the Beginning and Development of a College Greek Letter Organization, 1911–1961.* Philadelphia: Kappa Alpha Psi, 1967.

Ploski, Harry S., and James Williams, eds. *The Negro Almanac: A Reference Work on the Afro-Americans,* 4th ed. New York: John Wiley, 1983.

Plotkin, Wendy. "Deed of Mistrust: Race, Housing, and Restrictive Covenants in Chicago, 1900–1953." Ph.D. dissertation, University of Illinois at Chicago, 1999.

President's Committee on Civil Rights. *To Serve These Rights: The Report of the President's Committee on Civil Rights.* Washington, D.C.: October 1947.

Puth, Robert C. "Supreme Life: The History of a Negro Life Insurance Company, 1919–1962." *Business History Review,* spring 1969.

Rhodes, James Ford. *History of the United States from the Compromise of 1950 to the Final Restoration of Home Rule in 1877.* New York: Macmillan, 1893.

Ross, B. Joyce. *J. E. Spingarn and the Rise of the NAACP.* New York: Atheneum, 1972.

Ross, Malcolm. *All Manner of Men.* New York: Reynal and Hitchcock, 1948.

Rossi, Peter. *The Politics of Urban Renewal.* Glencoe, Ill.: Free Press, 1961.

Ruchames, Louis. *Race, Jobs and Politics: The Story of FEPC.* New York: Columbia University Press, 1953.

Schlesinger, Arthur M., Jr. *The Age of Roosevelt: The Coming of the New Deal.* Boston: Houghton Mifflin, 1959.

Scott, Emmett J. *Negro Migration During the War.* New York: Arno Press, 1969 (first published 1920).

Singleton, George A. *The Romance of African Methodism.* New York: Exposition Press, 1952.

Sittler, Joseph. "Aging: An Awkward Problem." *Health and Medicine,* summer/fall 1984.

Spear, Allan H. *Black Chicago: The Making of a Negro Ghetto, 1890–1920.* Chicago: University of Chicago Press, 1967.

Strickland, Arvarh E. *History of the Chicago Urban League.* Urbana: University of Illinois Press, 1966.

Stuart, M. S. *An Economic Detour: A History of Insurance in the Lives of American Negroes.* New York: Wendell Malliet, 1940.

Stuckey, Sterling. "Paul Robeson and the Ends of Nationalist Theory and Practice." *Massachusetts Review.* Amherst, Mass.: Amherst, Hampshire, Mount Holyoke, and Smith Colleges and the University of Massachusetts, spring 1976.

———. "My Father's Son: Paul Robeson's Early Years." *Arts and Sciences* (magazine of the College of Arts and Sciences), Northwestern University, fall 1983.

Supreme Life Insurance Company. "Centennial Emancipation Proclamation Calendar 1963" (with highlights of the company's history).

Terkel, Studs. "An Interview with Lorraine Hansberry." WFMT *Program Guide,* April 1961.

Toles, Edward B. "The Cook County Bar Association and Black Lawyers in Chicago, Illinois." Manuscript, October 13, 1984.

Travis, Dempsey J. *An Autobiography of Black Chicago.* Chicago: Urban Research Institute, 1983.

Waskow, Arthur I. *From Race Riot to Sit-In: 1919 and the 1960s.* New York: Doubleday, 1966.

Weaver, Robert C. *Negro Labor.* New York: Harcourt, Brace, 1946.

Weckler, Joseph. "Prejudice Is Not the Whole Story." *Public Opinion Quarterly* 9 (1945), pp. 126–39.

Weiss, Nancy. *The National Urban League, 1910–1948.* Baltimore, Md.: Johns Hopkins University Press, 1967.

Wharton, Vernon L. *The Negro in Mississippi: 1865–1900.* Chapel Hill: University of North Carolina Press, 1947.

White, Walter. *A Man Called White.* New York: Viking, 1948.

Wilson, James O. *Negro Politics: The Search for Leadership.* Glencoe, Ill.: Free Press, 1960.

Wilson, William Julius. "Cycles of Deprivation and the Underclass Debate," Ninth Annual Social Service Review Lecture at the Social Service Administration, University of Chicago, May 21, 1985.

INDEX

marriages, 22, 45
Original Forty Club, 165
as teacher, 20, 24, 217
travels of, 203–6
Dickerson, Earl B., activism of
and African American skilled
tradesmen, 136–40
assessment of, 209–22
call for fair employment, 114–15
CCCO, 200
Chicago Urban League, 53–54,
152–57
and Civil Rights Act of 1964, 199
in civil rights movement, 103–4,
189–206
FEPC, 113, 117–18, 119–24, 126–
32, 132, 159
and Illinois FEP Act of 1961, 189–
206
NAACP, 51–53, 157–60, 202–3
Dickerson, Earl B., business activities
of
assessment, 207–8
business acumen of, 176
on importance of economic power,
202
Liberty Life Insurance Company,
42–43, 169–70
Supreme Liberty general counsel,
86, 167, 171–73
Supreme Liberty president, xviii,
179–88, 207–8
Dickerson, Earl B., law career
assessment of, 209
assistant attorney general, 49
assistant corporation counsel for
Chicago, 47–48
and bar associations, 50–51, 109,
143–47, 148–52
Burr Oak Cemetery Association,
54–56
criminal practice, 228n3
early law practice, 40–41, 43, 45–
46
Hansberry v. Lee, 96–98
Dickerson, Earl B., military service of
and American Legion, 56–58

effect of military service on, 35–36
at officers' training school, 26–29
service in WWI, xvii, 29–34
Dickerson, Earl B., political activities
of, 61–65
action for schools, 73–75
as alderman, xviii, 66–84, 89–92,
211–12
challenge of Coalition of Judges,
147–48
congressional runs, 86–89, 141–43
and Dawson, 67–70
and Democratic Party, 49, 60
early WWII years, 84–86
fair employment in public transportation, 80–82, 133
health and welfare issues, 82–84
housing, 75–76, 197
runs for alderman as independent,
46–47, 62
Dickerson, Edward (father), xvi, 3, 5
Dickerson, Emma Garrett Fielding
(mother), 3, 5–7, 21–22, 23, 40,
44
Dickerson, Gertrude (half sister), 6, 7
Dickerson, Henrietta (half sister), 10
Dickerson, Inez Moss (wife), 22, 24,
43–44
Dickerson, Kathryn Kennedy (wife)
background, 44–45
and Chicago Urban League, 153
entertained Paul Robeson, 160,
161
final illness and burial, 56, 205
move into Drexel Boulevard home,
108, 163
Dickerson, Robert (half brother), 44
Dies, Martin, 128
Diggs, Watson, 20–21, 24, 32
Dogan, Mrs. (church organist), 7
Domestic Life Insurance Company,
182
Doty, Edward, 123–24, 136
"double victory," 86, 113
Douglas, Paul, 76
Douglas, William O., 98
Drake, Robert T., 143

Drake, St. Clair, 85, 194
Drexel Boulevard Block Organization, 197
Drexel Boulevard home, 108, 205
DuBois, Shirley Graham, 163, 204
DuBois, W. E. B.
  campaign for Negro democratic rights, 1948, 142
  failure to register as foreign agent, 162–63, 244n36
  friendship with EBD, xix, 160–65, 204
  "Gentlemen's Agreement," 61
  influence on EBD, 8, 242n3
  militancy of, 35
  and NAACP, 51, 157–59, 161
Duke, Charley, 135–36, 137–38
Dunbar Life Insurance Company, 182
Dunlap, Mr. (plumbers' union), 123–24

Early, Stephen, 114, 127, 129
economic power, importance of, 180, 201–2, 208
Eighth Illinois Infantry, 39
Einstein, Albert, 243n11
Ellington, Duke, 160–61
eminent domain controversy, 78–79
Epstein, Harry, 130
Ethridge, Mark, 117, 120, 124–27, 130, 214
Evans, Lovelyn, 16–17, 44, 69, 123–24, 135–40
Evanston Academy, 15
Executive Order 8802, 116–17, 125, 127, 137, 140
Executive Order 8823, 117
Executive Order 9111, 125
Executive Order 9346, 132
Executive Order 10450, 150

fair employment in public transportation, 80–82, 128, 129, 133
fair employment legislation, 135, 199
Fair Employment Practices Committee (FEPC)
  EBD's service on, xviii, 85, 104

  establishment of, 54, 117–18
  under Executive Order 8802, 118–27
  legacy of EBD's work on, 133–35, 209
  under War Manpower Commission, 127–32
Faulkner, John, 14–15
Federal Life Insurance Company, 182
Federation of Neighborhood Associations, 107
Feinberg, Michael, 96
Fenton, Frank, 117, 122, 239n30
FEPC. See Fair Employment Practices Committee (FEPC)
Fielding, Emma Garrett. See Dickerson, Emma Garrett Fielding (mother)
Fielding, Luella, 5, 7, 10
Florence (cousin of Emma Dickerson), 10–11
Flowers, Alexander, 55, 168–69, 170
Foch, Ferdinand, 57
Foster, Albon L., 115, 153
France and black troops, 30
Frankfurter, Felix, 98
Franklin, John Hope, ix–x
Frazier, E. Franklin, 139
Freund, Ernest, 40
Friendship Mutual Life Insurance Company, 182

Gandhi, Mahatma, 203
Garrett, Benjamin Franklin, Sr. (mother's father), 4–5
Garrett, Benjamin Franklin, Jr., 4, 5, 7
Garrett, Eliza (grandmother), 21
Gary, Hettye Garrett, 206
Gaston, William, 63
Geigel, Robert, 78
Gentzell, Robert, 55
George, Albert B., 147
George Williams College, 196
German propaganda to African American troops, 30–31
Gertz, Elmer, 52, 61, 89, 143, 144, 193, 201

terrorist attacks on black homes, 107–8, 195

Waddy, Joseph, 235n11
Waldorf-Astoria Hotel, 164–65
Wallace, Henry A., 142–43
Wallace, William, 85
War Manpower Commission, 113, 115, 127–28, 130
Warley, William, 94–95
Washburne Trade School, 74
Washington, Booker T., 22–23, 51
Washington, Harold, 213
Washington Park neighborhood, 195
Waskow, Arthur, 69
Weaver, Robert C., 119
Webster, Milton P., 117, 122, 132
Wells-Barnett, Ida, 37
West Indies Federation, 203
Westbrooks, Richard E., 109, 147–48
Weyand, Ruth, 6, 40, 98, 199
White, George H., 63
White, Mother, 45
White, Walter
    and appointment of EBD to FEPC, 117
    criticism of marriage of, xix
    and discrimination in hiring, 112, 113
    dispute within NAACP, 157
    on March on Washington (1941), 115
White, William Sylvester, 108, 144, 146, 194, 215–16

White Circle League, 155
White City Amusement Park, 178–79
White City Homes Project, 178–79
white flight, 94, 195
white reactions to *Hansberry v. Lee,* 106–7
Whiting, Luella Fielding, 5, 7, 10
Whiting, Thomas, 10, 21–22
Whitman, Russell, 144–45
Wilde, Dr. (principal of Evanston Academy), 15
Wilkins, J. Ernest, 60
Wilkins, Roy, 202
Williams, Bennie, 206
Williams, Eugene, 36–37
Williams, Ira, 115
Williams, Sidney, 153–54, 155–56
Willis, Benjamin C., 200
Wilson, C. Rodger, 45, 163
Wilson, Woodrow, 25–26, 33, 227n15, 237n13
Wood, Elizabeth, 155, 233n25
Woodlawn Property Owners Association, 95–96, 97, 107
World War I, 24, 28–29, 34–35
World War II, xvii, 111–13
Wright, Edward H., 59, 62, 228n29

Yancey, John L., 155
Yergan, Max, 161
Young, Charles, 26–27
Young, P. B., 132
Young, Quentin, 213, 248n16
Young, Roy, 17

ABOUT THE AUTHORS

ROBERT J. BLAKELY (1915–94) was a prominent journalist and educator and the author of six books, including *To Serve the Public Interest: Educational Broadcasting in the United States* and *The People's Instrument: A Philosophy of Programming for Public Television.*

MARCUS SHEPARD is a freelance editor and writer.